Praise for *Your Fully Charged Life*

"If you want more energy and focus, read this book now. You'll find simple, science-backed ways to feel better so you can achieve what matters most, while always staying true to who you are."

—MARIE FORLEO, *NEW YORK TIMES* BESTSELLING AUTHOR OF *EVERYTHING IS FIGUREOUTABLE*

"Meaghan feels like the best friend you've always wanted. She's the positive, Energizer Bunny, confident ally pushing you to do better because she knows you can. Her words and this book will inspire you to be the best version of yourself. You will hear her message in your head, pushing you, believing in you until ultimately you're doing it yourself. Magic!"

—KATE T. PARKER, *NEW YORK TIMES* BESTSELLING AUTHOR AND PHOTOGRAPHER

"As someone who's mildly obsessed with energy management, I found this book to be a refreshing and practical blend of fascinating research and inspiring lived experience. If you want to feel more lit up by your life, look no further!"

—KATE NORTHRUP, BESTSELLING AUTHOR OF *DO LESS*

"In these frenzied and frantic times, it's more important than ever to tune in to what matters most. Meaghan Murphy's book will show you how, by empowering you to tap in to your source of strength—whether it's faith, family or simply making the most of every single day. Tune in to her book and discover new ways to get and stay fully charged!"

—PAULA FARIS, JOURNALIST, PODCASTER AND AUTHOR

"Meaghan Murphy's *Your Fully Charged Life* is a welcome guide in trying times. These inspiring ideas are encouraging and enlightening, and Meaghan graciously takes you by the hand to show you that it is never too late to make every day count."

—JOAN LUNDEN, AWARD-WINNING JOURNALIST AND AUTHOR

T0201619

"Meaghan has a wonderful way of writing that is very easy on the eyes. *Your Fully Charged Life* reads like we're having a glass of wine and she's telling me her story. Well done!"

—LAURIE GELMAN, BESTSELLING AUTHOR OF *CLASS MOM* AND *YOU'VE BEEN VOLUNTEERED*

"*Your Fully Charged Life* is a road map to a leveled-up life on all fronts. I love how Meaghan's simple yet effective way of showing how to Live Fully Charged is as tactical as it is entertaining. Her spark for life is contagious and is exactly what is needed right now with so much negativity, stress and anxiety in the world. *YFCL* reminds us to find the YAY in each day. This book is a must-read for anyone looking to level up, live with more joy and create more energy!"

—BRANDON FARBSTEIN, GLOBAL EMPOWERMENT SPEAKER AND GEN Z ACTIVIST

"*Your Fully Charged Life* is exactly what women need in crisis and beyond to untangle the realities of a world where everything collides—personal goals, work, family and more. Meaghan lays out the groundwork for women to recognize and move beyond the day-to-day challenges to finding fulfillment, joy and happiness in a meaningful and exciting way."

—BLESSING ADESIYAN, FOUNDER & CEO OF MOTHER HONESTLY

"I've always said I wish we could bottle Meaghan's positive energy and now we can—*Your Fully Charged Life* is that secret Meaghan sauce in book form. You are in for a treat!"

—KARENA DAWN, COFOUNDER OF TONE IT UP AND BESTSELLING AUTHOR OF *TONE IT UP: BALANCED AND BEAUTIFUL*

Your Fully Charged Life

A Radically **SIMPLE APPROACH** to Having Endless Energy and Filling Every Day with **YAY**

Meaghan B Murphy

with Beth Janes O'Keefe

A TarcherPerigee Book

tarcherperigee

an imprint of Penguin Random House LLC
penguinrandomhouse.com

First trade paperback edition 2022

Copyright © 2021 by Meaghan B Murphy
Penguin supports copyright. Copyright fuels creativity, encourages diverse voices,
promotes free speech, and creates a vibrant culture. Thank you for buying an authorized
edition of this book and for complying with copyright laws by not reproducing, scanning,
or distributing any part of it in any form without permission. You are supporting writers
and allowing Penguin to continue to publish books for every reader.

TarcherPerigee with tp colophon is a registered trademark of
Penguin Random House LLC.

Most TarcherPerigee books are available at special quantity discounts for bulk purchase
for sales promotions, premiums, fund-raising, and educational needs. Special books or
book excerpts also can be created to fit specific needs. For details, write: SpecialMarkets@
penguinrandomhouse.com.

The Library of Congress has catalogued the hardcover edition as follows:

Names: Murphy, Meaghan B, author. | O'Keefe, Beth Janes, author.
Title: Your fully charged life: a radically simple approach to having endless energy and
filling every day with yay / Meaghan B Murphy; with Beth Janes O'Keefe.
Description: New York: TarcherPerigee, 2021.
Identifiers: LCCN 2020024978 (print) | LCCN 2020024979 (ebook) |
ISBN 9780593188576 (hardcover) | ISBN 9780593188583 (ebook)
Subjects: LCSH: Self-actualization (Psychology)
Classification: LCC BF637.S4 M877 2021 (print) |
LCC BF637.S4 (ebook) | DDC 158.1—dc23
LC record available at https://lccn.loc.gov/2020024978
LC ebook record available at https://lccn.loc.gov/2020024979
p.   cm.

ISBN (paperback) 9780593421444

Printed in the United States of America

Book design by Silverglass

Neither the publisher nor the author is engaged in rendering professional advice or
services to the individual reader. The ideas, procedures, and suggestions contained in
this book are not intended as a substitute for consulting with your physician. All matters
regarding your health require medical supervision. Neither the author nor the publisher
shall be liable or responsible for any loss or damage allegedly arising from any
information or suggestion in this book.

For Pop, my cardinal

From a tiny spark may burst a mighty flame.

—Dante Alighieri, *The Divine Comedy: Paradiso*

Contents

Foreword to the Paperback Edition

Do you ever look back and think, *How'd I do that?!* Finishing this book last year was my "how-wow" moment. It was March 2020 and I had just accepted a big new job as editor in chief of *Woman's Day* when the world shut down. Suddenly, I was homeschooling a kindergartner, second grader and fourth grader, while reenergizing a hundred-year-old magazine from my kitchen table *with* a looming deadline—the final draft of *Your Fully Charged Life* was due in three weeks.

Those early days of the pandemic were life-sucking—even if you were lucky enough to still have a job and your health. I will for sure tell my grandkids "back-in-my-day" stories about opening mail with rubber gloves, disinfecting groceries with Lysol wipes, hanging posters and balloons out the car window for drive-by birthday "parties" and getting really excited about a bulk toilet paper score. When they're old enough, I'll also share the fear and uncertainty of these surreal times. My truth is that if I wasn't crying in the shower, I was bawling through a Zoom workout in the basement or hiding in the car for a Mommy Time-out. The universe had a change of plans for me—for all of us—and I had to lean into my Fully Charged tool kit right here on these pages to cope.

I quickly reaffirmed that I could dress up to feel up—pants that buttoned and a swipe of mascara versus sweats altered my outlook. (See "Dress Up to Feel Up" on page 153.) I was reminded of the simple mood magic of fresh-cut flowers when during a lockdown low I shamelessly grabbed a pair of scissors and marched over to Daffodil Hill to pick my own bouquet ("Tap into Flower Power," page 153). I began to really take my own advice and actively put fun back on our now-empty family calendar. Tuesdays became sacred and our taco parties escalated until we were sporting matching taco tees backlit by guacamole string lights with a spinny condiment tower my husband bought me for Valentine's Day ("Holiday Hard," page 151). And through it all, the reframe I told myself on repeat was *safe versus stuck* at home.

Then, just as we all began to collectively recover from this global crisis, my husband, three kids and seventy-one-year-old mother and I were rocked with another change of plans. We got COVID-19 within three weeks of this book launch. Panic set in. I'm an asthmatic who's been on oxygen during a bout with pneumonia. I was depleted, convinced COVID would wreck me and even if I didn't wind up on a respirator HOW was I going to record the audiobook of *Your Fully Charged Life* and go on *Today* and *Live with Kelly and Ryan* to promote it?! Again, I pulled the tools out of this Fully Charged tool kit—including one I had never relied on before—meditation (page 29). I changed my *Why me?* to a *Why not me?* and created momentum one positive action at a time. (P.S. The audiobook was a triumph! I got through it in twenty hours, sucking on cough drops and mainlining ginger tea. YAY!)

No matter what you're going through right now, I know there's one little nugget of advice that will be your spark, your lightning bolt, to create the Fully Charged Life you deserve. Tell me about it on Instagram @meaghanbmurphy or subscribe to my newsletter at MeaghanBMurphy .com so we can stay in touch. YAY!

Lightning Bolts

Stepping onto a brand-new path is difficult, but not more difficult than remaining in a situation which is not nurturing to the whole woman.

—MAYA ANGELOU

Grumpy. That was my nickname as a kid. I earned it by being the type of sulky girl who always expected the worst. I remember thinking my mom would *for sure* be late picking me up. Or that whatever game was starting would *for sure* be boring and I'd lose. In the third grade, when my family started planning a trip to Disney World, I didn't want to go. Really. Why would I? There would inevitably be long lines and it would be hot, and no thank you let's just stay home. In the fifth grade, when my class wrote and performed a play called *The Key to Understanding*, I created a character in my own likeness: Neggy, the embodiment of negativity. At some point after that my parents gave me a necklace with a gold charm of Grumpy, the dwarf from *Snow White*, standing in all his grouchy glory, arms crossed, mouth turned down. I wore it or just a matching sourpuss until my late teens.

Now in my forties, I still have that necklace, but it's as if it belongs to someone else. In a way, it does. Over the last twenty years or so, I've been called a lot of things—never ever grumpy. These days, my friends joke that I fart rainbows. The necklaces I wear have charms of lightning bolts—a symbol of energy I adopted a few years ago as my own personal logo—and say words like *yay*. The rest of my wardrobe is best described as extroverted; I love bright colors and emoji-esque patterns because they make me and others smile and they spark conversations.

When it comes to chitchat, I don't just talk about what I find interesting or cool, I tend to *evangelize*. Once, during a 6:30 a.m. post-gym stop at Dunkin'/Baskin-Robbins, I hyped up a Santa ice cream cake so much that everyone in line bought one, too—and wished each other "Happy holidays!" on their way out. At parties, I'm the first one on the dance floor, throwing mean side legs and aggressive thumbs-ups until I'm the last one fist-pumping at the end of the night. In my bag I carry rocks that my kids and I paint with positive messages to hide around our town of Westfield, New Jersey. The former mayor even appointed me Chief Spirit Officer because of my passionate involvement in and love of our community. And I usually end simple exchanges with my favorite parting: "Have the best day *EVER!*" because I actually believe it could be.

So many people over the years have commented on or asked about my energy. After they get to know me, they sometimes say they're in awe of all I do in a day or wonder how I stay so upbeat. The comments still surprise me; I'm just living in a way that feels good and works for me: waking up at 5 a.m. to sweat with my good-vibe tribe of fitness buddies, hitting the grocery store after (when it's not crowded, no one needs me at home and I can catch up with my favorite checkout clerks), spending QT with my kids Charley, James and Brooks before they go to school and I head to work at *Woman's Day*, where I'm content director.

When in the office, I'm usually cheerleading my team or shimmying down the hallway to a meeting or someone's desk, yelling, "Faster than an email!" Or I'm racing from editing pages to a TV taping or to record a podcast, then back again, all while giving flyby high-fives and taking selfies and Boomerangs, before hopping on the bus home. Most nights I'm back in time to hang with my kids before bed, soak up some cuddles, then get couch time with my husband, Pat.

Yup, so pretty much the opposite of Grumpy. Which is exactly why I've held on to the charm. It reminds me of how far I've come and the choices I've made and continue to make that got me here. It reminds me of the actions I've taken and keep taking and the work I've put in to fundamentally transform not only how I feel but how I interact with the world and who I am as a person. It's proof—I'm proof!—that you can change. Whether you're a Grumpy or more of a Sleepy, or one of their long-lost cousins Angsty, Gloomy or Discontented, you are not stuck in that role. You can learn to approach life in new ways, see things from a different perspective and take action when you might have otherwise done nothing or felt powerless or down. And when you do, an incredible amount of natural and genuine energy, enthusiasm, joy and positivity starts bubbling inside you.

It starts with a few sparks, then builds into a crackling current that surges as naturally, powerfully and clearly as lightning.

YOU'RE IN THE RIGHT PLACE. YES, YOU.

I don't believe most people need to undergo some crazy metamorphosis to feel those lightning bolts of energy or tap into their currents of lightness, hope, fun, happiness and resilience. Sure, there are hardcore Grumpys and Sleepys out there, and if you're one of them, *welcome*! You're in the right place, too. But few of us are so one-dimensional. We're all perfectly imperfect, complex beings shaped by an incredibly complex world—even more so now, in the age of COVID-19 and the most recent Black Lives Matter movement. We have messy, complicated and shifting emotions and unique problems, a range of privileges and backgrounds. And because of those things, we've developed habits and ways of thinking and behaving that have stuck with us. Some we should stick with, but a lot of them are keeping us stuck. My guess is you're here because, while you have good days and good times, you find yourself slipping into bad ones or tired ones or over-it ones or just *meh* ones more often than you like.

Maybe you've been feeling a certain hard-to-pin-down existential angst or exhaustion at everything coming at you—tough or dull projects and personalities at work (or very likely sudden unemployment); never-ending chores at home; a constant stream of negative, scary news; big, complex social and systemic problems; divisive politics; issues with your kids, spouse, family, friends; and countless other stuff. Perhaps the negativity coming at you is actually coming from inside you, from your own internal voice. Or you feel like you're just going through the motions of life or that your usual MO doesn't feel particularly great, helpful or healthy. Possibly that stuff was around prepandemic and before this racial justice movement, and it feels heavier now—or it just hit you recently.

I get it. I started writing this book months before COVID-19 and finished during the first two months of the shutdown here in New Jersey—shortly after starting my new job leading *Woman's Day* and while suddenly homeschooling my kindergarten, second-grade and fourth-grade kids. I talk all about it in the last chapter, The Recharge, because those were some of the hardest, worst weeks of my life. They tested my energy and ability to find Yay—everything I was and am writing about.

Then, days after I submitted my final draft, George Floyd was murdered and protests broke out all over the world. As millions of white people (me included) began to truly (and finally) wake up to the painful realities around not only police brutality but systemic racism and our own biases, things once again felt overwhelming and heavy.

By the time you read this, I hope the virus is under control. I hope real strides are being made to fight for racial justice and that white folks who committed to anti-racism back in June are still doing the work. I hope you're at least getting by or doing fine in spite of whatever is going on now. The thing is, no matter what's happening, it's easy to feel restless, stressed or unbalanced. Even if you're crushing it in your job or some other part of life. Maybe you're in the thick of raising kids and running a household, and even if you wouldn't have it any other way, it's draining you and you feel shorttempered. Quite possibly you're trying to juggle both a family and a career (or job search or pivot). Whatever your circumstances, do you ever see or meet people who just seem to approach life differently—with a seemingly boundless energy, positivity and enthusiasm—and wonder how they manage to live like that? Especially now? Do you ever wonder whether you could, too?

I went from Grumpy to one of those people, and no matter who you are now or what you're dealing with, the answer is a big, fat, sunshiny *YES*. My approach, which I've been honing and practicing for nearly two decades, involves deliberately following a lot of really simple tips, strategies and habits that power what I think of as this intangible energy and unique vitality. Part physical, part mental and emotional, it's a contagious zest for life that comes from feeling open and game, healthy and capable, motivated, optimistic and a bubbly punch of other positive emotions. And it's all based on one principle:

> **Every day, every hour, sometimes moment to moment, you consciously choose to act in a positive way or look for the positive in situations.**

Making that choice then gives you the energy to make more positive and energizing choices, fueling a cycle that keeps your batteries charged. For the last twenty years, this guiding principle, along with all the tips and strategies for living it that I detail in the chapters to follow, have been powering me—and what I now call the Fully Charged Life. They've kept me not only energized in a go-go-go, upbeat way, but also happy, fulfilled and emotionally and physically healthy. They've helped me recognize and find more meaning and purpose in life and achieve success in my relationships, career and other endeavors, and they've provided plenty of backup and ways to deal with life's unexpected turns and fiery crashes. Even a global pandemic. I won't be so bold as to say I found *the* secret to happiness, but it sure feels close. I'm lucky to say it's been the secret to *my* happiness. And *Your Fully Charged Life* will help you tap into more of your own natural lightning bolts of energy and happiness, too.

WHAT DOES IT MEAN TO LIVE FULLY CHARGED?
The Fully Charged Life operates with a full flow of mental and physical energy that lets you experience joy, love, gratitude and other positive emotions deeply and daily, as well as create meaningful, rewarding and uplifting experiences, opportunities and relationships. There's a fancy-brunch-level Yay buffet out there—social distancing has *not* canceled this spread!—and living Fully Charged helps you fill your plate with as much deliciousness as possible. It's about taking advantage of and loading up on all the good stuff life offers and letting those things empower you to take on life's challenges and deal with its struggles, especially now, as we're all forced to adapt to changes in the world and our day-to-day life.

The tips and tools I share in this book, and the energy they generate, psych you up for and help you go after new adventures and achieve new goals, turn your to-dos into *ta-das!* and just have a ton of fun. They help you work through and overcome stress, anxiety, sadness, fatigue, doubt, the slog of the day-to-day and plain old inertia. And they'll help you adapt to loss, pain, disappointment and major emotional upheavals so those things don't crush you. Overall, living Fully Charged means moving through life in a way that feels incredibly full and best to you.

In life, we all have two choices. We can default to autopilot, go through the motions and get trapped by our brain's evolutionary instinct to focus on the negative. Research has proven that the brain is hardwired to pay attention to and remember bad stuff more than good, which can easily leave us feeling apathetic, helpless, drained or just miserable. You can let your brain take you on that ride, or you can go on a different one instead. You can decide to clearly see the situations, circumstances, opportunities and challenges in front of you and intentionally choose a response or action that's energizing, positive and empowering. The Fully Charged Life chooses the latter. Not once, but over and over again.

Looking on the bright side is part of the equation. But I don't even like using that expression; it's an oversimplified cliché. Because you need to see *all* the sides, then choose to *do* what it takes to go bask in the sun or at least feel more of its warmth. That's how you activate the Fully Charged Life: You take actions that generate positive energy and make room for more joy, love, excitement, opportunity, purpose and everything else that makes life wonderful, meaningful and just full.

You can't only think positively, you must *do* positivity.

Over the years, I've developed, adapted or adopted some specific ways to do positivity: actionable tips backed by solid research that, together, touch on every corner of life to deliver the energy that fuels a Fully Charged Life. Each chapter in this book addresses a different type of "charge," and within each are simple strategies to tap into or generate it:

Take Charge: The energy of empowerment. This chapter gives you more background on living Fully Charged, answers inevitable questions, explains some of the underlying science, motivates you to start taking action and sets you up for success.

The Positive Charge: Energy that comes from making room in your brain for positivity and fostering a more positive outlook and mindset.

The Love Charge: Energy sparked from meaningful connections with family, friends, your community and other fellow humans.

The Work Charge: Energy derived from meaningful work and feeling engaged, supported, productive and accomplished in either your career, job or whatever you do, including the unpaid labor of caregiving or keeping a household running.

The Health Charge: The incredible physical energy and mental boost you get from exercise and sleep.

The Extra Charge: Energy produced from all the fun and uplifting "extras" in life, like your home, fashion and beauty.

The Recharge: Specialized jolts that fuel resiliency, helping you manage grief, extreme stress or extraordinarily hard times; it gives you positive energy when you question whether it even exists.

HOW TO USE THIS BOOK

Let me clear up a few things before we go any further. I'm not going to coach you on finding and pursuing your passion, unleashing your "true" self or setting and reaching lofty goals—other than the goal of living Fully Charged, of course. I don't think you need to hustle harder or chase a big dream, nor constantly strive for "growth" or some measure of success to find meaning, value and fulfillment in life. After you finish this book, you may likely feel *fully* motivated and energized to do those big things—and I hope you find the information here and my tools useful in doing so—but they're neither requirements nor the endgame right now.

So relax. Take a deep breath. Give yourself permission to pursue energy, positivity and well-being for the sake of feeling your best, within the context of the life you're already living and the things you're already doing: spending time with family and friends (together or socially distanced), going to work, raising a family, trying to be a good person and live a good, happy life.

The goal is simple: Move your energy needle and get the most out of what life has to offer. I want to open your eyes to new ways of thinking about and doing things and to different ways to approach and see your world and the world at large. No overhauling anything, no fixing necessary, no real "homework" or journaling required. Instead, I offer thought-provoking science and info, easy ideas and simple, positive, powerful actions you can take starting today.

To that end, I hope you read this book cover to cover because all the charges play a role. Some of the strategies in one chapter might also apply to other areas of your life. And the more charges you go after, the more energized you'll feel overall, no matter where you currently sit on the energy spectrum. That said, you can certainly dip in and out or jump directly to the specific charges you need the most. For example, maybe you've been bogged down by negative thinking. Jump over to chapter 2. Need help feeling more energized about work? By all means, head straight to chapter 4. Research suggests that if well-being increases in one area of life, you're likely to see a boost in other areas, too.

It makes sense. As much as we try to compartmentalize, there's spillover when it comes to our emotions and energy; you've probably experienced this firsthand, for better or worse. Like when you get enough sleep or exercise, you feel more patient and engaged with your family. Or you've perhaps seen how supportive, meaningful relationships (inside and outside of work) help you feel more energized and productive on job tasks. Social support has also been shown to impact physical health and your ability to cope with major life stressors.

However you choose to approach this book, you also don't have to follow every single tip to get the charge. I encourage you to try them all if they feel right and you can, but even if you only find a few that you want to start incorporating into your day-to-day, you'll feel a surge of energy. Living Fully Charged is not an exact science, nor is this a one-size-fits-all, step-by-step instruction book. It's a big ol' toolbox. So get familiar with all your tools, and over time you'll find your go-tos and favorites.

WHY ME?

At this point you might be wondering what makes me an expert aside from living my own life as an Energizer Bunny. Well, I don't consider myself an expert, at least not in the traditional sense. I'm not a therapist, life coach, psychologist or doctor. I discovered, developed or adapted all these strategies over the last two decades as an editor, writer and certified personal trainer immersed in health and well-being—physical, emotional, mental and relationship. I've talked to countless actual experts and dug into their research to find out how everyday people can use what they've discovered. For more than half my life, I've been doling out tips on how to live a fuller, healthier and happier life, first as an intern at *YM*, then as an editor and writer at *Teen People*, *Cosmopolitan*, *Self*, *Good Housekeeping* and, now, *Woman's Day*.

What puts me in a unique position—and might give me some actual expertise—is that the target demographics of these magazines have always aligned with my own life stage at the time I worked there. So all along I've thought of myself and approached my work from the perspective of a reader first. In that way, what I've really been over these years—and what I still consider myself to be—is curious and creative, research-oriented and eager to find inspiration and take ideas from a lot of different people and places, and to try *lots* of different things. Throughout my career, my colleagues and I were paid to find and deliver useful information from a range of sources on a variety of topics. The tips and strategies we've shared were solid and surprising and based on scientific research or were contributed by leaders in their field or sometimes by regular people who had already taken the advice for a test drive. And the sole purpose of it all was (and still is!) to help readers feel good and live better lives. But in the course of doing that, I learned to live *my* best life.

I helped curate, write and edit numerous articles while soaking up everything. I tried all the advice. I kept doing what worked, tweaked what didn't, abandoned the duds and used what I learned to come up with my own tricks, habits and ideas. All of it—my overarching philosophy and the tips, strategies, habits and lessons I employ to live Fully Charged—is the spoils of my time working, and also working on myself: constantly learning how to live in a way that feels like I'm wringing all the possible good out of my days.

HEAR ME OUT

I know some people look at me and think, *She's got everything—of course it's easy for her to be so happy and energetic all the time.* And yes, it often feels like

I've won the lottery; I'm surrounded by good people and have a good job, my family is healthy and I've had amazing opportunities and have been given incredible gifts in life. Some of what I have is dumb luck, but a lot of what I have is from taking charge of my energy and my happiness, from being able to take full advantage of every opportunity *and* create opportunities for myself.

I've also got a quirky personality and an enthusiastic, super-positive, out-size approach to life. It can freak people out. Some find me annoyingly up-beat. Many don't think I'm for real. I've even got a few haters. I'm okay with that. I'm not for everyone. I'm willing to take those trade-offs for what I've been lucky enough to gain: a unique blend of unwavering energy and positiv-ity that's true to me (whether you believe it or not), that fuels my days and helps me weather the storms.

A lot of my skeptics and haters eventually come around, though. We never become braid-each-other's-hair, friendship-bracelet BFFs, but over time they realize my way of living looks pretty damn good—or at least it gets sh*t done without making you feel like sh*t in the process. Or they realize I'm not a fake, nor a naive Pollyanna blinded by rose-colored glasses. I'm self-aware and fully get that life is excruciatingly hard and often unfair, that people will hurt us and that sometimes it can all feel like too dang much.

I've also experienced my fair share of crap. It's exactly why I've worked so hard at figuring out how to handle life's complexities and vicissitudes with energy, positivity and grace. Over the last several years, as more people com-mented on my energy and asked for my "secrets" on how I manage to do it all and still find and bring the Yay, I realized I could help others by sharing what I learned and what's gotten me to this place. And now I'm extremely lucky to do that on a larger scale, especially given all we've been through and every-thing that's changed because of the pandemic. This crisis tested me and pushed me to my limits just like it did for everyone else. It also helped me see with fresh eyes how powerful this philosophy and these tips really are.

Bottom line: I'm not trying to make you like me or be exactly like me or do exactly what I do. Nobody wants a bunch of fully charged robots or Meag-han clones, *trust me*. So go ahead, roll your eyes at some of my stories or how I go over the top with the lightning bolts and Yays and other stuff. You can also hate dancing and embrace your introverted tendencies and love wearing all black everything and still get a lot out of this book. I actually *want* you to blow off the tips and advice that don't feel right for you. Because for this to work for you, you must build *your* version of the Fully Charged Life; I'm here to pass along the tool kit and materials: the concept and all the science, tips and ideas and ways to adapt and get them to stick.

I work these tools hard, and they've helped me create a life where I honestly can find the Yay in every day, where I'm grateful and happy and energized to the point of having lightning bolts flash in my eyes. Do I still have bad days and tough times? OMG—YES. There were some days during the lockdown I felt like hiding in my car, curled up in the fetal position in the back seat. But because of the tools I have to deal with bad days (even the worst days) and what I've built up around them, they don't dominate or dictate anything. As weird as it sounds, I think people sometimes forget life can and should feel really good and make you happy most of the time. Yes, even when things get really, really hard or the world around you feels like it's burning. I wrote this book to help you remember that, and to show you not only is it possible, but *you* can make it happen. This book is meant to excite and empower you to feel good and happy—to live your most Yay-filled, energized life.

CHAPTER 1

Take Charge

*You often feel tired not because you've done too much, but because
you've done too little of what sparks a light in you.*
—ALEXANDER DEN HEIJER

You know those people I talked about in the intro who seem to approach
life differently? Who inspire you with their energy or positivity or general
good vibes? Kate, who works at my friend Shawna's local Home Depot, is one
of them. Shawna told me she wanted to put Kate in her cart, scan her and
take her home because she's a kitchen/bath ninja who knows her stuff *and*
because she turns an otherwise big, cold corner of an even bigger, colder store
into a warm, friendly homelike space. She does it with her smile, unwavering
kindness and by painting her apron with the most gorgeous and impressive
naturescapes—a new one for every season.

Simone Gordon, aka @TheBlackFairyGodmotherOfficial, is another Yay
human. A single mom, nursing student and waitress, she uses Instagram to
connect those who need emergency assistance—regular people in surprise
dire financial straits (utilities on the brink of shutoff, out of diapers or meds
before payday) who've been ignored or turned away by bigger nonprofits—
with those willing to offer help by donating small amounts of money or goods
via Venmo or Amazon wish lists. She does this in her "spare time" with the
help of a few others and all without taking a cent.

One more: my buddy Pete, whose son plays basketball with mine. Any
time a new face walks into the gym and heads his way, he not only gives them

a high-five or shakes their hand and introduces himself, he turns to me and says, "Do you know Meag Murph?" You hopefully know how good it feels to be included, and Pete developed this awesome habit that gives that feeling not only to newcomers but to me and whoever else is lucky enough to be sitting near him.

I could go on and on with stories of fully charged, Yay humans. What they and others have in common is that they take action in either big or small ways. They see and seize opportunities to do something positive, and they do it. That's the crux of living Fully Charged. A long time ago, I realized that the times I felt the worst—the most drained, defeated and down—was when I believed or convinced myself I was stuck: no control over anything, nothing I could do, no action I could take to change how I felt or what was happening.

It took me hitting rock bottom and rising again—which I'll talk about later—to see that there's always *something* you can do. Sometimes it's as simple as deciding to grant yourself grace or to be patient with and accept your feelings or a situation. Other times, it's deciding to control your reaction or how you're thinking about all those things you can't control. All the time, it's a simple decision to do something positive.

Every day, often several times a day, I ask myself, *What can I do to make this day or moment more fun or full or feel better?* Sometimes I can't wait to answer. Other times I want to tell myself to STFU because I get worn down, riled up and stressed out like everyone else. And that's when I choose to do something simple, like breathe and think about what made me say Yay that day; I work out or go for a walk; I compliment a stranger or do something kind for them; I drop off a gift for a friend or connect and laugh with a co-worker or my kids; I buy a $5 bouquet at the supermarket; I put on a lightning bolt sweater and bright yellow heels.

I make the positive choice to draw on my big tool kit of tips, strategies and habits that I know deliver charges of positive energy. That's what this first chapter and the Take Charge energy is all about: feeling empowered to do something—to act, to try new things, to step out of your comfort zone and embark on this journey toward living more Fully Charged.

TIRED AND FULFILLED VERSUS EXHAUSTED AND EMPTY

Admittedly, living Fully Charged can be mentally and physically tiring at times. But aren't you tired already? Isn't that why you're here? Fully Charged tired hits differently; you may be spent and ready for bed by the end of the day, but your energy coffers are still full—you'll feel more fulfilled. You know the saying "it takes money to make money"? The same is true of positive energy. Most of the strategies in this book are objectively easy, but they may feel hard or tiring because they use "muscles" you might not be used to using. For example, you have to invest energy in the form of self-awareness to recognize when you're stewing or sliding down the rabbit hole of negativity. It takes energy to realize doing so only saps more energy and makes you feel worse. Then it takes effort to do something about it—to decide to act in a positive way and follow through. The more energy you put in, the more you'll see that the payoff is inherently worth it because of the energy and happiness you get in return. And that energy not only powers you in the moment, but also keeps powering you.

HOW THE FULLY CHARGED LIFE RECHARGES ITSELF

Fully Charged energy is a self-renewable resource. Here's why:

1. It builds positive energy reserves

Every time you act or respond in a positive way, you turn on positive emotions or put yourself in a more positive state, which research shows energizes you in a number of ways. Depending on the situation, you may feel lighter, more motivated, creative and playful, happier, patient and loving, more confident or optimistic or whatever you need in the moment. That makes a deposit in your energy bank. And those reserves are an incredible resource when life tries to bring you down or the news cycle makes you want to rage or cry or you make a big mistake or otherwise feel like crawling under the covers and never coming out. They buffer stress and foster resilience, so dealing with life's ups and downs won't take as much effort or energy and won't drain you as readily. The ability to draw on all that positive energy you've built up also means you've got more energy to *keep* choosing a positive action or response and to continue charging.

I've experienced this phenomenon for years, and when I started digging into the research, I discovered it closely aligns with the early concepts and research of Barbara Fredrickson, PhD, a professor of psychology and neuroscience at the University of North Carolina, whose groundbreaking broaden-and-build theory of positive emotions explains how even fleeting good vibes contribute to everyday resilience and well-being. Here's how:

- *Broaden.* Say you make the choice to tweak your thinking about a tough situation to feel grateful rather than resentful. The positive emotions that follow expand what's called your thought-action repertoire. In other words, when you feel good, you're more receptive and open to everything and are more likely to act. You become a more creative, curious, flexible and attentive thinker and more easily can see different perspectives, all of which motivates you to engage more and keep acting in positive ways.
- *Build.* That broadened thinking then allows you to *build* resources— psychological, physical, social—that help you to better cope with future challenges. For example, feeling emotions like joy and love and gratitude help nurture supportive relationships, which lots of research shows is about as good a resource for happiness, health and dealing with life's hardships as you can get. Likewise, when you're open to new information, you're more likely to learn things that can help you down the road. What's more, things keep getting better and better; the more you experience positive emotions, the more you're able to keep experiencing good vibes, which creates an upward spiral that enhances and increases your well-being and happiness over the long haul.

Fredrickson's research makes a few other key points. First: "A positive emotion may loosen the hold that a negative emotion has gained on a person's body and mind." That means if you do something that helps you feel good—say, feel grateful or do something kind—you recover more quickly from the effects of a stressful or worrisome situation. Researchers even see the effects physically in how readily blood pressure returns to normal.

Second, Fredrickson concluded that positive emotions help you isolate negative experiences in your head. So instead of seeing getting laid off, for example, as this life-altering tsunami that says all these bad things about you as a person, you're more likely to see it for what it is: a blip on the map of an otherwise big and complicated picture. That lessens its potential negative effect on you and even helps you find positive meaning in it later. And meaning is a key component of well-being (more on that coming).

Bottom line: Cultivating positive emotions, which is pretty much what this book and all the tips do in a nutshell, is a key to energy. It's a worthy effort, not only because you'll feel better or good in the moment, but also because it can set you up for continuing to feel good overall in life, no matter what happens.

2. The positive energy boomerang

The second way the Fully Charged Life recharges itself is through your actions and interactions with others. A big part of living Fully Charged involves putting positive energy out into the world, which delivers a sustainable megacharge. Here's how:

- **First,** doing things that build and strengthen relationships or that simply get you interacting with your fellow humans is incredibly energizing and uplifting on its own. Renowned researcher and the father of the positive psychology movement, Martin Seligman, PhD, a professor at the University of Pennsylvania, even made the bold statement that "other people [are] the best antidote to the downs of life and the most reliable up."

- **Second,** positive interactions with others can produce what's called a "helper's high," a term that researcher Allen Luks coined back in the eighties to describe the documented mental and physical boost that comes from altruistic behaviors like being kind or generous or volunteering.

- **Third,** the positive energy you've put out is likely to boomerang back and can charge you up later in a few different ways. For example, when you're kind to a neighbor, he or she is likely to return the favor when you least expect it or, hopefully, when you need it most. Or when you help a coworker, he or she then feels good and is motivated to help out someone else, and soon the whole office feels like a kinder, more supportive and productive place for everyone.

In fact, positive energy and emotions easily and quickly spread. Social scientists sometimes call it emotional contagion: If you're upbeat, enthusiastic and positive in your interactions, for example, it's likely to influence the energy and emotions of those around you and keep the good vibes flowing. (The same is true of negative energy, FYI.) You don't even necessarily need to be face-to-face. In one study involving almost seven hundred thousand Facebook users, researchers reported that when there were fewer negative emotional expressions in one's feed, people tended to produce more positive posts and fewer negative ones (and vice versa).

One of my favorite examples of the boomerang effect has to do with my neighbor Larry. I started a campaign in my hometown of Westfield called Bestfield Rocks, where my kids and I would paint rocks and leave them in fun places for people in our town to find. We started getting the community involved in painting, too, and wanted to recruit Larry. A creative and artistic marketing executive, he had recently lost his dog, was going through a divorce and was generally not in a good place. We hoped that engaging him in our project might help cheer him up. So one day, my kids and I left a pile of rocks by his fence post. A few days later, we found his finished rocks by our gate. He had transformed them into masterpieces! He went on to paint pizza rocks for the town's 5K pizza run, candy corn rocks for Halloween, flags to celebrate Independence Day and punny ones like crocodile rocks.

The rocks became a touching back-and-forth between our family, who'd leave the rocks by the fence, and Larry, who delivered them to the gate when done. As time and rocks passed, it truly seemed like he took increasing levels of energy from the hobby and the excitement of Team Murphy as we'd *ooh* and *ahh* over his art. I was equally struck by how grateful, happy and excited his rocks made me. I was just as amped running over to the fence as my kids. It also made hiding them so much fun, and soon word got out. Who would be lucky enough to find one of Larry's creations?!

3. Practice, practice, practice

The third way the Fully Charged Life recharges itself is through simple habit and routine. The more you do or practice anything, the easier and more ingrained it becomes. It almost becomes a reflex—just a part of who you are and what you do. This is key. Because when the good times are rolling, it's easy to make a Fully Charged choice and take some kind of positive action; it's harder when you're tired or life is punching you in the face. Instead of defaulting to the negative or choosing not to act, however, your practice kicks in. You show up for your workout even when you don't feel like it. You automatically notice and feel a rush of gratitude for an epic latte. You smile and say hello to someone. Or you instinctively do some other positive, energizing thing because it's what you're used to doing and you intuitively know the charge it delivers.

Practice is why, amidst a particularly grueling, stressful week of work, I didn't think twice about making a care package for a friend starting chemo—I just did it. Practice is why my Fully Charged friend Sarah bought new glasses for the janitor at her office, whose old specs she saw were held together with tape. Her action wasn't self-serving; rather, she saw a simple and kind way to help someone else and knew how it would *also* energize her. She didn't even tell anyone; I found out by accident, and I know she does that kind of stuff all the time.

WHAT LIVING FULLY CHARGED IS *NOT*

Understanding what the Fully Charged Life does not involve will help you better understand it and how to get there. Here's what you are not aiming for:

- **Relentless happiness.** Living Fully Charged doesn't mean being in sunny, happy Yay-mood 24/7 or always feeling charged up to 100 percent. If you're dealing with a work crisis, had a fight with your husband or your kid woke you up at midnight . . . and 2 a.m. and 4 a.m., or you just feel *meh,* you can still live Fully Charged. I know because I've got three kids, a dog, a demanding job, multiple side hustles, a crazy commute and the curveballs that come with all of that. In fact, when life is doing its darnedest to drain you, when you're tired, stressed, unmotivated, deflated or just feel low or adrift, that's when living Fully Charged pays off the most. Because if you can choose to do just one good thing or think about what doesn't utterly suck, it will help you better deal with all those things. It won't erase them; it helps soften their edges—and yours.
- **Quick fixes to complex feelings or problems.** I'm not saying you can just—*poof!*—think your way out of a funk or do a good deed and *bam* the clouds clear, the sun shines in your brain and you forget all the bad stuff. I'm saying you can choose to think and do beyond the funk. Things will still weigh on your mind and you might still feel stressed or any number of other negative emotions, but living Fully Charged helps ensure the weight doesn't crush you and the negativity doesn't swallow you up. Negative feelings will always come in, but they also go out, and you can help them along or make sure they aren't allowed to squat and multiply in your psyche unchecked, stinking up the whole place.

Likewise, you can be deeply concerned or bothered by bigger issues, of which there are *so* many today—racism and social injustice, climate change, gun violence, public health concerns, politics, all of it—and still pursue positivity and protect your own happiness. Get angry or frustrated or fed up, and let it fuel you and incite you to action and to fight for what you believe in. But being angry and upset all the time is not a useful action. It's draining and exhausting.

- **Yes-ing yourself to death.** To live Fully Charged, you can't run yourself ragged doing *all* the things and saying yes to *all* the positivity all the time. Pushing yourself in the wrong ways and faking or forcing enthusiasm or optimism doesn't work, except to drive yourself batty and into the dreaded battery red zone. So a key part of the Fully Charged Life is saying no. But my approach is more nuanced than what we've all been told, *repeatedly*, about decluttering schedules, paring down to-do lists and generally doing less.

We all need downtime, of course, but a full plate can actually be incredibly energizing and fulfilling. I know this firsthand, and I see it in all the Fully Charged dynamos I look up to. Take my colleague Liz Plosser, the editor of *Women's Health*. She's busy with a capital B: She's got three kids, a kick-ass career and is one of the most active, fittest women I know. She takes her kids to school, then often runs (as in, across the Brooklyn Bridge) to the office, makes time for friends, date nights and (active) family vacations, and genuinely enjoys life even though it's a lot and things get messy. I've known her since our days as editors at *Self*, and I'm so inspired by how she makes it all happen while authentically living the healthy, high-energy, well-rounded life her magazine promotes.

Liz would probably tell you what I'm about to: The secret is filling your days and spending your energy only on those things that truly matter to you and that give you energy back. It's not about saying *no* and doing *less,* nor saying yes a lot; it's saying yes to more of what charges you. If you choose wisely—meaning you're truthful with yourself about what really matters and what gives you energy—you can reap the benefits of being active and busy without also feeling overwhelmed or drained or burned out by it all. Do I or Liz or anyone else always get it right? Not even close. But what's important is that you're aware of how you decide to spend and direct your energy, and that you try.

I saw a quote recently from Dr. Caroline Leaf, a neuroscientist, mental health expert and author, that perfectly sums up this idea: "True mental self-care is not chocolate cake and spa days. It's making choices each day that create a life you don't need to regularly escape from." Hits home, right? I'm all for spa days and (gluten-free!) chocolate cake, but if you feel like you crave these somewhat superficial forms of self-care to balance or offset the rest of your life, you're likely not spending your energy in the right places or directing your brain to focus on the right things. The take-home message: Say no a lot, but say yes almost as much. Because it's all those yeses that pave the way to a Fully Charged life.

NOT-SO-WEIRD SCIENCE

I know my approach works, and not only because I live this way and because all the positive, energetic people I look up to are action-oriented. There's real science behind my philosophy and strategies. Much of it, including Fredrickson's broaden-and-build theory, comes from the field of positive psychology, which really only became a thing in the late nineties when Martin Seligman became president of the American Psychological Association. He pushed forth the notion that most psychology research up to that time was only "half-baked"—half-baked because it tended to focus mainly on mental illness and what goes wrong with human emotions and functioning, as well as how to relieve the resulting suffering. Research had largely ignored the other, super-important part of being human: What's *right* about the way we function and what makes us happy in the big-picture sense—what makes life worth living. In other words: how do we not only survive, how do we thrive and flourish?

No Tricks, Just Traits

Seligman and other positive psychology pioneers, including Nansook Park and the late Christopher Peterson, both professors at the University of Michigan, began studying and writing about human strengths: positive character traits that come across in the way we think, how we feel and our behavior. They eventually identified twenty-four different "families" of strengths—traits like bravery, gratitude, kindness, leadership and persistence—and eventually tested thousands of people to determine which ones were most closely linked to or best predicted subjective well-being and life satisfaction.

They then wanted to find out which traits the happiest people among us had in common. Turns out, the two that consistently floated to the top are the two main themes of this book: hope (aka optimism, positivity) and zest (energy, vitality, enthusiasm). Other big themes, including gratitude, love (i.e., close relationships with others) and curiosity (interest, openness to experience), were close behind.

Becoming PERMA-Charged

Seligman later took things further, developing what he called the PERMA theory of well-being. It goes beyond what strengths are important for happiness or other positive outcomes and lays out in detail exactly what it takes for humans to flourish. Deploying individual strengths like hope, zest and gratitude are only part of it. According to Seligman, the character strengths serve as the foundation or underpinnings of and the way to achieve PERMA, which is the acronym for the five elements or cornerstones that his research revealed enabled true flourishing in life:

Positive emotions: Feeling good about the present, past or future, which happens through zest, optimism, gratitude, love and other strengths.

Engagement: Feeling fully engrossed and engaged in activities, be it work, in conversations, with a hobby or a sport, even reading.

Relationships: Connecting with others through love, humor, kindness, social intelligence and more.

Meaning: A sense of purpose—the idea that your life and what you do matters. You can derive meaning from a number of different things like family, work and your community.

Accomplishment: A sense that you've achieved success or competence in some area, whether at home or at work, in sports, a hobby, relationships or otherwise.

In one way or another, these five elements and the feelings of well-being and life satisfaction they elicit are the ultimate outcomes of living Fully Charged.

Prioritizing Positivity

Living Fully Charged is related to another concept known as prioritizing positivity, which was defined by Fredrickson and her colleagues a few years ago. It came about to address research that concluded that explicitly *trying* to be happy can backfire—that it could actually make you *less* happy. They proposed and studied a potentially more effective and authentic route to increased happiness, positivity and well-being: organizing your life in a way that maximizes or increases your opportunities to *naturally* feel more joy and other positive emotions—aka prioritizing positivity.

In other words, when choosing how you spend your time, you prioritize the activities that most reliably lead to positive emotions and happiness. It sounds simple, even obvious, but not everybody does it. Instead, many spend their time with people they don't like, doing things they feel obligated to do or that feel meaningless or that are easy but rarely rewarding. Fredrickson's research, however, shows that people who prioritize positivity show all sorts of markers of greater well-being and happiness.

Prioritizing positivity is exactly what this book aims to help you do. It gives you tips and ways to direct your energy and spend more of your time doing things that science suggests triggers and increases happiness, gratitude, love, joy and lots of other good feelings. I didn't put it all together until later, though. While familiar with positive psychology and some of the research, I hadn't heard of PERMA or the idea of prioritizing positivity until relatively recently. They weren't concepts I deliberately modeled my life after. However, when I dug into the science, it was like, *Yes! It all makes so much sense now.* It felt like I was unknowingly running an experiment on myself, testing these theories in real life. The science felt like proof beyond my own experiences and those of people I knew that I was truly onto something.

So while you may have picked up this book to find ways to feel more energized, it's also about flourishing and thriving, feeling happy and content, healthy and well, in both body and mind. Because that's what ultimately energizes you. Studies actually show feeling good prompts people to feel noticeably more energetic and to engage more and to be more productive. Lots of research likewise shows a direct link between psychological well-being and happiness (as well as specific positive traits like optimism) and outcomes that hint at increased energy, including higher quality of life, better health and greater success at work and in relationships.

For example, happier, more optimistic people tend to have healthier heart function and are less at risk for heart disease. They're more resistant to catching a cold or the flu. And they tend to live longer. A lot longer. One study found that the most optimistic women were one and a half times as likely to achieve what's known as exceptional longevity—living to or past age eighty-five. It was found that optimistic men were also significantly more likely to live longer.

MY TAKE-CHARGE PATH

It's easy to look at me or any other high-energy, positive person and think, *Well, that's just the way they are.* It's true. We are this way. But not everyone has *always* been this way. Sure, some people pop out of the womb smiling or are raised to be optimistic go-getters. But many, me included, have had to deliberately decide that this is where we wanted to be and then work our asses off to get here. I changed from the grumpy, pessimistic kid, but it was a looooooooong road, and things got way worse before they got better. Neggy/Meaggy did not weather her teenage years well. Puberty and high school sent me on a downward spiral that nearly cost me my life.

High school is a hyperemotional, weird and hard time for most people. My emotions felt utterly out of control. You've probably heard the term "roller coaster of emotions." For me it felt like being hopped up on Fun Dip and trapped in a bounce house with a bunch of unicorns—like life was supposed to be this super-fun and exciting thing, but it had somehow turned the corner and became too much, and I couldn't escape and didn't know how to cope. So, along with my best friend, we avoided the chaos around us and inside us by focusing on something tangible we could control: our bodies. We began eating less and less and got sicker and sicker. During soccer practice my junior year, I collapsed on the field and my parents hospitalized me for anorexia. I went kicking and screaming

My friend's parents soon decided she should join me. Except she never made it. On the way to the treatment center, she jumped out of her family's moving minivan. Her frail, undernourished body couldn't recover, and she died a few days later. I felt a sick responsibility for her death and spent the next year in and out of treatment, circling the drain in a pool of negativity. My friend was gone, and my anorexia got worse. The only thing I'd let myself feel was despair and hopelessness, stemming from what I now know was anger and the blame I put on myself. As time passed, I became numb and felt lost and stuck.

AN ANTI-AHA MOMENT

After a while, I also got frustrated. There wasn't any big epiphany; rather, it was more of a slow burn: I started thinking, *Is this really who I'm going to be? Is this how I want to live my life—being miserable and numb and helpless?* It sunk in that I was wasting my life, and nothing good would ever happen if I didn't do something. So I gradually began doing the hard work in therapy that I'd previously avoided: dealing with my emotions—deep sadness, guilt and helplessness, as well as the feelings that had triggered my anorexia in the first place.

I then developed practical tools I needed to get physically healthy. I learned to approach food as fuel and to see exercise as a type of medicine—a way to manage stress and the intensity of my emotions, especially the negative ones. I started using workouts to both channel my energy and gain it instead of thinking of them as a penance or calorie eraser. Those lessons stuck with me. Even today, I don't care what size I am, and I don't sweat to make up for my love of wine and pizza. Sure, that's a small part of it. But the main thing that gets me up at 5 a.m. and into the gym is the fact that it's something I can do, an action I can take that makes me *feel* stronger, healthier, happier and clearheaded, guaranteed. It charges my batteries both mentally and physically.

As I worked toward getting healthy, I wrote an essay about my experience overcoming adversity. It won me a $10,000 scholarship and was published in *YM*, where I later convinced the editors to let me be an intern. I also told my story on a network news special. I had been through such hell that, in a lot of ways, I became fearless. Here I had been this anxious, grumpy kid, always worrying about stuff that never actually happened. Then terrible things I never imagined or worried about actually *did* happen. Entering that contest, going on TV, boldly asking for an internship seemed like no biggie by comparison.

I also saw that even amidst such pain, good could come from it—but only if I was willing to take charge, to see it was possible and do what I could to make it happen. That's around when I really realized that even though I couldn't control a lot of what happened in life, I could control my actions, my attitude and how I thought about and dealt with my emotions—and that doing so often influenced what came next.

By the end of my freshman year in college, I was doing better but still sort of hanging on by a few threads. That's when my friend's parents served me with court papers for allegedly defaming her in the article. Although they had previously applauded me for my bravery, I think it was too much seeing their pain in print, then national TV. An unauthorized made-for-TV movie came next, sensationalizing the whole story and making things worse. It was all so stressful and surreal.

Instead of these blows weakening those threads I was hanging by, they did the opposite. I took the hits and chose to take charge, again: to remember, once more, that while I could not control what everyone else was doing or feeling or what was happening, I could write my story and my role in it all. Except this time I wasn't Neggy. I became The Optimist. I chose to believe that everything was going to be okay because I was okay and I could handle it. The worst had already happened, and I wasn't going back there.

THE COSMO-IC BANG

The first seedlings of the Fully Charged Life started to take root over those early years; however, it wasn't until later, while working at *Cosmo*, that I started digging more into the idea of happiness and positivity. It's funny to credit a magazine with this, much less *Cosmo*, considering all the therapy hours I logged. But just as Seligman pointed out how psychology had been half-baked, my sessions focused almost entirely on what was wrong with me: my relationship with food, the issues that sparked the eating disorder and my feelings over my friend's death—and very specific ways to cope and recover. Once I was "better," that was that; we never covered how to then become my very best self or ways to flourish.

That said, I am a huge advocate for therapy, especially given how much has changed since the nineties. Also know that this book is by no means meant to replace therapy. If you are depressed, have severe anxiety or difficulty coping, please see a professional. And if you don't, still consider seeing one! Sometimes we all need to vent or talk through things or get advice and guidance from a neutral (and expert) third party. It's also nice to have someone peek under our hood for a tune-up once in a while. Therapy as well as medication can be an amazing tool.

Therapy saved my life, but *Cosmo* somehow helped me really live it. Something clicked when I was assigned an article titled "7 Secrets to Happiness." It might sound trite or naive, but up until that point, I hadn't thought much about big-picture happiness. I knew what made *me* happy and energized, and when I felt it and when I didn't, but it never occurred to me to think about or dig into it in a more meaningful, deeper way. Even during all that therapy, I didn't think about happiness beyond the fleeting good vibes you feel when doing something fun or when good things happen or when everything is more or less humming along. I never considered that there were concrete things I could do to feel happier not only moment to moment, but in life overall. Doing the research and talking to experts was a massive turning point.

Since then, I've learned so much from my work and from plenty of doctors, researchers, industry people, experts and editors who became experts, as well as studies and surveys and regular, everyday people. I internalized nuggets of wisdom and tried all the advice. I came to fully understand that the world will suck the life out of you, but only if you let it. Over time, I figured out tons of ways to not let that happen and, more importantly, how to turn things around and use the good bits to feel even more energized and alive.

3 WAYS TO TAKE CHARGE

Each of the chapters that follow will give you specific tips for various areas of life—your mindset, relationships, work, health, etc. However, there are a few universal tips that will help you get started and set you up for success:

Picture Your Version of Living Fully Charged

Everyone wants more energy and a life that feels full. Go deeper. Spend a few minutes thinking about exactly what more energy and living fully means to you. What do you want *your* Fully Charged Life to look like and feel like? Be specific: What exactly will more energy do for you or allow you to do? How exactly will that positively impact your life? What have you struggled with in the past that you hope to change?

For example, if you want more energy to do fun activities with your kids and to better connect with them, imagine a scenario in your mind of how that plays out. How will you feel? What will it look like and mean to you? Or maybe you want more energy and motivation so tasks at work or at home don't feel like such a slog. Maybe you want more energy to start exercising or eating better. What does *that* look like? What will the outcome be? How will that make you feel?

I've never done a vision board and probably never will—and if that's your thing, now's the time to do it—but at least take time to visualize and internalize the reasons you picked up this book and what specific, concrete outcomes you hope to materialize. Having clear *why*s and *what*s both in your heart and at top of mind make trying, following and keeping up these strategies a lot easier.

Answer the Question "What Really Matters to Me?"

This is a requirement. And living Fully Charged demands an honest answer. Then—this is key—you must pursue those things without guilt. So many of us feel guilty for doing or not doing certain things. Or we do/don't do things out of obligation, because we think we should or because other people expect or want us to. It is not your responsibility to fulfill someone else's expectations of you. Why let them define what matters to you? Their expectations and definitions serve them, not you.

If you live your life based primarily on what others expect, want or believe you should or shouldn't do, it is no longer your life. No wonder you're exhausted. So choose to be a little selfish. Let go of feelings of guilt and obligation; they are weighing you down and wasting your energy. And guess what? No one makes you feel guilty except yourself. No one can make you feel obligated except yourself. People will certainly try. You do not have to take the bait.

Instead, listen to your gut or the universe or whatever you want to call it when faced with choices of where to direct your energy or when trying to figure out if something charges or drains you. I believe we all instinctively know—we just don't always listen. Or we let other people's expectations drown it out. Or we're afraid to acknowledge or give weight to what we really want or need because of the possible fallout. It's scary to face the truth and hard to accept that a habit or person or the way you've been thinking or behaving might be doing more harm than good. Try it anyway and see what happens. See how it feels.

You will make mistakes when choosing where to direct your energy, so don't agonize over your choices. If it turns out you make a mistake, good try, you'll get another chance. You'll actually get a million more chances over the course of your life. The biggest mistake would be to not keep trying. I still make mistakes all the time about where to direct my energy.

When my daughter was in first grade, for example, I volunteered to count box tops for a PTA fundraiser but kept putting it off. The last thing I wanted to do after putting the kids to bed and getting some quiet time with my husband was tally three gazillion tiny pieces of cardboard. Weekends? Nope—those are for extended QT with family and friends. I ended up forgetting about the box tops until an email popped up telling me they were due at noon. I was on my way to work in Manhattan and they were in my mudroom in New Jersey. Uncounted. Oops.

I had put them off and eventually just forgot about them because I wasn't being honest with myself about what matters to me when I agreed to the task. I was, as they say, "should-ing" all over myself. I said yes because I thought I *should* be more involved with the PTA, because I wanted the other moms to see I was helping out. But the thing is, I *am* involved with the school and my kids' classes in other ways that fit my schedule and my life better—and in ways that charge me more. Helping the PTA didn't matter to me when I weighed everything else I had going on. And why did I care what the other moms thought anyway? I felt bad about dropping the ball, but it was a lesson I needed.

Just Do It

Many of my tips are objectively easy—and if those are the only ones you want to take from the book, that's great; you'll still feel energized. Others may be more difficult, either mentally, emotionally or physically. Some will require you to step out of your comfort zone or upend long-set habits and ways of thinking. Try them anyway. Just do it. Yes, it can be that simple.

There's a reason Nike made piles of cash off the slogan. Like so many of the best things in life, it's straightforward. It doesn't waste time arguing over BS excuses or even legitimate ones. It doesn't leave room for overthinking or weighing the pros and cons of whether you should or shouldn't. It doesn't invite in other people's opinions. Best of all, it implies that you *can*. So *do*.

If you don't like the outcome or the tip isn't working or doesn't feel right to you, okay, thanks for playing. Choose not to do it again or try something else or do something differently next time. But if it feels okay or better, and you get that charge, what's cool is that each time after, "just doing it" feels easier. It can eventually become automatic. That's your brain's neural plasticity at work.

Let me explain: Your typical ways of thinking, reacting, feeling and behaving have created well-worn pathways in your brain. Like a super-popular hiking trail, the path is clear and requires little extra effort or thought to traverse. The first time you venture off that path and do something different—like change the way you think to make room for positivity, start a new exercise routine or step out of your comfort zone in some way—it forges a new connection in your brain, as if those neurons were explorers finding their way through the jungle.

It's not easy and there's no full-fledged hiking trail yet. But the next time, those neurons make more of a clearing. Each time after that, the connection in your brain grows stronger just like a trail becomes more and more defined the more you walk it. This is how you rewire your brain for positivity, for energy, for gratitude, for love, for everything. Living Fully Charged gets easier with time until eventually it's just the way you live. So let's get on with it.

The Positive Charge

Your living is determined not so much by what life brings
to you as by the attitude you bring to life; not so much by what happens
to you as by the way your mind looks at what happens.

—KAHLIL GIBRAN

A while back I was on the bus headed into the city for work when it broke down smack in the middle of the New Jersey Turnpike. The driver wasn't telling us anything, and the passengers were stomping angrily up and down the aisle. Soon people started barking into their phones and one-upping each other over their hatred for NJ Transit and what they were late for or would miss. I was frustrated and annoyed, too. I try hard to make Mondays, and especially Monday mornings, run smoothly to set a positive tone for the week, and this felt like the most Monday-est of Monday things—and a huge middle finger to my MO. I also was bummed I'd miss our weekly staff meeting, which I love for connecting with editors, going over deadlines and updates and getting my head back in the work game post-weekend.

But instead of joining the bitchfest or worrying or getting huffy, I thought about what I could and couldn't do and change in the moment. Stuck on the bus, surrounded by traffic, I couldn't get off, couldn't fix the engine and couldn't make my meeting. I *could* laser focus on what didn't utterly suck about this situation: *Hey, I'll be able to finish listening to this awesome podcast. And how lucky I just treated myself to Apple AirPods, which will drown out this sh*t show.*

Boom. Settling in, I could physically feel the positive energy fueling my patience and defusing some frustration. This force field of good vibes then helped me to make another positive choice: When the rescue bus finally pulled up and the driver said we had to scale a guardrail to board it, I was in an okay place, so I didn't freak like some passengers. Full disclosure: I did give an initial "WTF, NJ Transit!?" eye roll, but then I took a breath and thought, *Yassss, I'm wearing sneakers and a warm coat, not heels and a skirt.* Then I thought about this ridiculous story I'd share when I got to work, which, by the way, would only be about an hour and fifteen minutes late. Not bad. When I eventually made it, I even felt extra motivated to turn this turd of a morning around. I checked in with my editors individually—actually a nice change of routine—went gangbusters on my to-do list and had a pretty awesome day.

That's the power of the Positive Charge—the physical and mental energy that comes from fostering a positive outlook and mindset.

I love this bus example because it's the type of situation we've all been in: a relatively minor inconvenience that nonetheless can suck the wind out of your sails or capsize your entire boat, leaving you adrift the rest of the day. But the Positive Charge works even when life dumps a bigger load on you. Like when my newly finished basement flooded shortly after moving to our house in the suburbs and shortly after I'd given birth to our third kid in three years.

At the time, the stress of moving and renovations (and with so many babies!) was still prickly. When I walked down to find a foot of rainwater lapping against the bottom risers, toys floating and the carpet underwater, I burst into tears, then got angry. *How could this happen?* Apparently the contractor forgot to turn the sump pump back on. What a boneheaded mistake! I even blamed my husband—clearly it was *his* fault. I mean, why hadn't *he* checked the pump? Why hadn't *he* gone down there sooner?

The next twelve hours were awful. It was devastating to watch big black garbage bags swallow up so many toys, a brand-new carpet and so much other stuff and to see our new couch on the life support of two industrial fans. The flood produced so much waste, and the cleanup was so physically hard. And there was nothing I could do to change what happened.

I cried a lot that day. I also tried to laugh and register droplets of good amidst all the water. I thought about how it forced me to purge toys and stuffed animals, things this sentimental mama probably couldn't have gotten rid of otherwise. I also thought about how the flood gave me a do-over on carpet color; I didn't love the first one. And later that night, exhausted and overwhelmed, Pat and I sat down for an unexpected Sunday-not-so-funday dinner with my parents, sister, brother-in-law and nephews, all of whom had come to help. I looked around the table and thought about how lucky we were to have our family rally for us.

Those little doses of positivity helped energize me to get through that day and all the work and hassles of the following few weeks. Because that's what the Positive Charge does. As Angela Duckworth, PhD, a professor of psychology and researcher at the University of Pennsylvania, explained in one of her recent newsletters, one of the most profound insights of modern psychology is that situations may be objective, but attention is subjective and shapes our reality. So when it feels like the universe is working against you, when you're overwhelmed or drained, sad, mad or frustrated, think about where and on what you're focusing your attention. Making the choice to shift it in a way that invites in bits of positivity can defuse or buffer the effects of stress and negative emotions.

You're not trying to ignore how you feel or downplay the gravity of your problems. Rather, realize you're not a helpless victim of your circumstances. You can plant seeds of positivity amidst weeds. When you do, positive emotions start to grow and will feed you the mental and physical energy needed to better meet and deal with challenges, to feel more capable and in control and ultimately save you from a downward, energy-draining spiral.

THE GOOD, THE BAD AND THE BORING

You feel the power of the Positive Charge most acutely when faced with something stressful or hard, whether big or small, ordinary or unusual—like my bus and flood escapades. But this charge is more than a salve for when things suck. Think of the everyday stuff we all do—tedious, boring or un-fun tasks like dishes, running errands, logging status reports, grinding through the kids' nighttime routine. The Positive Charge can drum up positive emotions around these times and tasks, and attach positive meaning to them, which makes them feel easier. Sometimes even enjoyable. Yep, yard work and laundry and all the rest of it don't have to be such a drag. *You* get to decide what they feel like. What's more, the Positive Charge can make good times and good things even better by helping you savor and find deeper meaning in them.

What's so cool is that positive emotions and finding greater meaning— the idea that what you do and your life overall are important and have a purpose—have even bigger implications: They're essential ingredients in the secret sauce that flavors a good life overall. As I talked about in the previous chapter, they're two of the five pillars of Martin Seligman's PERMA theory of well-being—the measurable elements that research has determined help us humans flourish. Research from Barbara Fredrickson, meanwhile, suggests that experiencing in-the-moment good vibes may matter more to well-being and happiness than having an overall sunny view of your life, and that pursuing or finding meaning, rather than just doing stuff we enjoy, may actually do more for us in the long run.

And you can get there by tweaking how you think. More specifically, how you think about and approach what happens to you and around you and what you see, hear, feel and experience. There's so much in life we can't control, but there's also so much we *can* control—probably more than you realize.

MOVING EMOTIONAL MOUNTAINS WITH YOUR MIND

In any given situation, there are multiple ways to interpret and react to what's happening. At any given time, there's a smorgasbord of things you can focus on and think about that inform how you feel. We aren't passively taking in information like calculators and spitting out one "right" feeling or reaction. No, we're highly complex supercomputers who take in some facts and bits of info while filtering out others and, in the blink of an eye, process the bejesus out of everything, through past experiences, current feelings and ideas and countless other factors. *That's* what informs how we think, react and feel. In other words, our thoughts are largely determined by how we are and who we are—how our motherboard has been programmed that day and over the course of our life. You probably already had a sense this was happening. But ask yourself: How often do you tinker with the coding?

Happiness researcher Sonja Lyubomirsky, PhD, a professor at the University of California, Riverside, proposed and studied a construal theory of happiness: the idea that our happiness and well-being is less influenced by our lot in life or what happens to us than it is by how we construe or interpret what happens. In other words, you and I could go through the exact same things—good, bad, neutral, whatever—but it's how we think about or interpret those things (and, I'd add, what we *do* based on our interpretations) that ultimately dictates how happy or unhappy we are.

Unsurprisingly, Lyubomirsky's research and that of others find that the happiest people tend to naturally see their experiences, whatever they are, in a more positive light, which helps maintain their general feelings of happiness and well-being no matter what comes their way. Rather than a vicious cycle, it's an auspicious one. On the other hand, less happy people tend to do the opposite, reinforcing their relative unhappiness.

But that's just what people do naturally depending on where they may fall on the happiness spectrum. You do not have to stick with whatever negativity your brain spits out. You can purposefully shift your perspective, reframe what happens in a more positive light and do things that turn the tide of your feelings. Sure, doing so can be harder than just going with whatever feelings or thoughts automatically pop up. Ironically, though, taking that easy road will eventually leave you feeling more drained. I'm not saying you can squeeze positivity or meaning out of every terrible or traumatic experience or control every passing bad emotion—nor should you try—only that you hold a lot of power over how you think and feel.

YOU ARE THE BOSS OF YOUR BRAIN—TIME TO START MICROMANAGING

If the idea of bossing around your brain sounds silly, think about how often you notice or question your first thoughts or knee-jerk reactions. How often do you challenge them and make room for other, more positive ones? How often do you think about what you're, well, thinking about and feeling? Even more importantly, how often do you try to *do* something to change a negative narrative, even a little?

You can deliberately direct your brain to get on the Yay bus or even the it-will-be-okay bus, or you can let it take a back seat on the sad or sorry-for-yourself bus. Or the angry bus, the jealous bus, the worry bus, the stress-ball bus, the autopilot bus. You're going somewhere whether you like it or not. You have to go through what you have to go through. We all have to face and do things we don't want to. Most of us have to run errands and deal with flooded basements and broken-down buses and deadlines and pointless meetings and kid problems and, and, and . . . In many cases, you'll end up at the same place regardless of which bus you board, but you get to choose how the ride feels.

By consciously choosing to shift your perspective and what you focus on, by thinking about situations more mindfully or through a more positive lens, by practicing gratitude, fostering optimism and savoring what's good—that's how you buy an unlimited pass on the Yay bus. And over the long haul of your life, research suggests if you do these things, not only will you enjoy the trips more, you'll eventually start going to better and better places; you'll be healthier, happier, achieve more success and feel more content. Because you'll have more energy to do more of what's meaningful, what brings you joy and what charges you.

Lyubomirsky and her colleagues reviewed more than two hundred studies and concluded that while good things and good times make people happy, of course, happiness and well-being also make for good things and good times: "Positive affect" (research-speak for "feeling good") precedes and predicts positive outcomes. In other words, positive emotions give you the energy to go out and make good things happen. They help you build the resources that bolster resilience and help you better weather stormy times and derive meaning from them.

A positive outlook, optimism and gratitude are also all linked to better physical health and longevity. Research suggests a positive attitude and outlook may cut the risk of heart problems by around a third. They help counter the harmful physical effects of stress, encourage you to stay more active and social and to do a lot of other things that keep you healthy and promote longevity. They're also associated with lower rates of depression and anxiety and more success at work and in your relationships. So many good things.

IT'S OKAY TO FEEL YUCKY ON THE YAY BUS

If you've managed to shift your brain enough to board the Yay bus and only feel marginally better, it doesn't mean you're not "bossing up." Pursuing the Positive Charge does not require you to put on blinders, ignore reality and suppress negative feelings. You need those suckers! They're normal and can be healthy and incredibly useful even. Sometimes they motivate and energize you *more* than positive emotions. Acknowledging what's awful and experiencing hard times help us more fully and deeply appreciate the good. Just know the negativity doesn't have to consume you.

Research shows negative emotions don't necessarily mess with your positive ones. And the presence of negative feelings doesn't make you any less able to be happy or resilient overall. Two opposing thoughts—what's awful *and* what's awesome (or at least what's not awful)—can coexist simultaneously in your brain. You can feel angry or annoyed while also appreciating what's good in a situation. You can feel defeated but also optimistic. You can be sad or stressed and still laugh your butt off. It sounds cheesy, but during these times I feel so fully alive because I'm experiencing the gamut of human emotions.

To me, the positive vibes suck most of the power from the negative ones, then recycle it and use it as energy. The negative emotions might still be there; they just don't have the same muscle. When it comes down to it, getting the Positive Charge is really a matter of learning a few mind games.

THE POSITIVE CHARGE TOOL KIT

Practice Being Present

I studied acting at Rutgers University, and while I knew early on I'd never win an Oscar, or even star in community theater, I got a solid-gold consolation prize: learning the value of being present. I don't mean in a clichéd, rah-rah, "live in the moment!" kind of way. I mean consciously choosing to direct your attention to what's going on around you, thinking about it and considering how you want to react, respond, feel and express yourself.

In my acting classes we used to do this repetition exercise where you'd stand in front of another actor and repeat the same word back and forth, changing your tone, inflection, facial expression and other cues based on how your partner said the word to you. We may have only been saying "hello," but it showed me what can happen when you're fully engaged, mindful in the moment and paying attention. If I were thinking about what I had to do tomorrow or what happened yesterday, I would miss important cues and details, and I wouldn't be able to express myself in the best way or the way I wanted.

Living Fully Charged requires similar awareness. Because in order to consciously choose to look for, make room for and let in positivity, it helps to get in the habit of living more consciously and mindfully. Research links being more mindful to higher levels of life satisfaction, optimism, positive emotions, self-esteem, behavior regulation and vitality (i.e., energy). On the other hand, it's a lot easier for negativity to sneak into your psyche when you're not paying attention.

Meditation is one proven way to boost mindfulness, but it's not the only way—and thank God, because it's not something I've ever been able to do. Instead, I prefer more loosey-goosey strategies, which are similar to what Harvard psychologist Ellen J. Langer, PhD, who's been called the Mother of Mindfulness, advocates for: "The very simple process of noticing new things." In an interview with NPR's Krista Tippett, Langer explained that when you spend more of your day actively noticing new things, it puts you both in the present moment *and* forces you to be more engaged with and more open to different versions and interpretations of what's going on—and that those effects are enlivening.

Langer has said this form of mindfulness also gets you to the same place as more traditional meditation or mindfulness interventions, meaning it likewise can improve well-being, reduce stress and lead to other positive, proven benefits. Except it skips over the, *ahem*, more boring parts and is easier to incorporate in day-to-day life.

I feel this whenever I practice this kind of moving meditation or active mindfulness. I feel calmer, but also more open and energized. Waking up to the world around me—instead of being stuck in my head or in the past or the future—helps me feel more alive and pick up on things I may have otherwise missed. Here are three steps to help you there, too:

• **Catch yourself on autopilot.** It's so easy to go through a day not noticing or thinking much about what we're doing, saying, seeing, hearing, experiencing or feeling—especially when we're busy, stressed or tired. There's value in zoning out or escaping into your phone—it gives your brain a break or can help you work through problems and reflect on things. Just consider whether you let your mind occasionally and briefly wander or turn off, or if you routinely give your consciousness carte blanche for regular and extended trips into the past, future or alternate Instagram universe.

• **Be bored—and curious.** Once you find yourself in autopilot mode, replace it with the sort of active mindfulness Langer described. Rather than trying to make every bit of microdowntime "productive"—at stoplights, while waiting in line, in elevators, in the shower, brushing your teeth—just be. Leave your phone alone. Do not mentally add to your to-do list, and avoid thinking about a problem or that thing you're going to do later or did earlier. Instead, focus on wherever you are and whatever you're doing, notice what's new or different and how you're feeling.

• **Change up your routine.** The other day I walked to the train on the opposite side of the street. It was such a small, simple thing, but I automatically found myself paying more attention and noticing new and different things simply because I had literally changed my perspective. Since we're all creatures of habit, there are lots of ways to try this: Take an alternate route anywhere, whether you walk or drive. Pick a different area of the gym or coffee shop than your usual. Hit up a different bank branch. Sit or stand or park somewhere new.

MEDITATE YOUR WAY

I don't meditate. I just can't (or, okay, don't really want to) sit for a period of time focusing on my breath or quieting my mind. Could I benefit from it? Heck yeah! Meditation is magic. Research shows even brief mindfulness meditation reduces stress and anxiety and can boost energy as much as logging forty-four extra minutes of sleep a night. They're even teaching it at my daughter's school, and I've seen how it helps her focus and quells anxiety.

I became even more pro-meditation after interviewing Dan Harris, author of *10% Happier*. I had fallen into the trap of thinking there was only one way to do it, and that only certain types of people meditated. But here was someone I could relate to: a high-energy go-getter of a TV anchor dude—not a yogi with crystals in his pocket—and he busted my silly stereotypes. His story of stumbling onto meditation, starting with just five minutes a day and customizing his practice, is inspiring—especially in how it helped him beat anxiety, kick a drug habit and feel naturally more energized and happy.

If you're curious, try dipping your toe into meditation. Check out Dan's book or a meditation app and start with just a few minutes a day. Or listen to a podcast like *Meditative Story*, which combines storytelling with meditation cues—a sort of compromise that actually works for my busy, meditation-averse personality.

Go Deeper into the Good

The Christmas before losing my dad to pancreatic cancer, I remember sitting on my parents' green leather couch soaking up as many details of that day as I could. And with all nineteen family members crammed into the house, there were *a lot*. The day was tinged with sadness, knowing it would be our last holiday with Pop, but love, laughter, warmth and joy drowned out most of it. Even today, I can still remember the feel of the leather, parts of it smooth and buttery, other parts rough from where Redbank the cat, who everyone was allergic to but loved anyway, had scratched. I can hear the Christmas album on repeat and smell the burnt mashed potatoes wafting in from the kitchen.

The next time you find yourself in a special moment, stop and actively build these kinds of vivid memories. Consciously log details and imprint moments on your mind as if you were creating a scratch-and-sniff, 3-D photo album. Active memory building is a proven strategy for savoring, a powerful tool known to intensify and prolong positive experiences and emotions, according to the work of Fred Bryant, PhD, a psychologist at Loyola University and expert on the topic. Savoring good times and good feelings not only maximizes their uplifting and energizing effects in the moment, it also has lasting effects on our well-being and happiness. For example, Bryant's research and that of others has linked savoring to higher levels of optimism, resilience, life satisfaction and self-esteem, plus better health and relationships.

Savoring is related to mindfulness in that you've got to be aware of what's going on to savor it. But it goes beyond noticing. It's about recognizing and valuing what's happening or what's happened (like how special it was to have the family together that Christmas) *and* registering and valuing your feelings about it (*all* the love and gratitude and joy in my heart). Think of savoring as adding flavoring to the best parts of life; it makes good times better, joy more joyful, love more powerful, success sweeter and so on. For me, fully absorbing the details of that Christmas and its significance helped me feel, appreciate and experience all that love and goodness more deeply and intensely. It made the day and my place in it that much more meaningful. It was an incredible feeling then and still is now.

Check Yourself Before You Wreck Yourself

On the flip side of savoring lives rumination: when your brain replays that face-palm or cringe-worthy moment, problem, failure, stressful situation, sucky circumstances or other terrible thing. It's normal to latch on to negative things. When people see photos meant to elicit negative, positive or neutral feelings, the negative images trigger more activity in the brain's circuitry. It's just the way we're made.

But if your mind swims in the muck for too long—if your brain's natural negativity bias spirals into stewing, dwelling and obsessing—you'll drown. Studies show that the more you ruminate, the higher your risk for depression and anxiety and feelings of anger and aggression. It can make it harder to actually solve problems. Even worse, rumination not only sets your brain ablaze, it cranks up your body's physiological stress response. All together, it's a mega mental and physical energy suck.

How to Slam the Brakes on Your Runaway Brain

Rumination can feel like being on a speeding train—a thought pops into your head, picks up steam and *bam* you're on the Acela to Sucksville. But you're the boss of your brain, remember?

- **Press pause.** When you start to obsess, take a moment, a breath or whatever to notice. Don't beat yourself up; *do* think about the futility of what's happening. This is similar to a parenting technique experts say helps you keep your cool when kids inch dangerously close to your last nerve. It works amazingly well when your brain tries to lock you in for a marathon viewing of *Everything's Terrible*. Pausing is mindfulness in action, and studies consistently show mindful people stew less and that the simple act of being mindful puts the kibosh on rumination.

- **Don't stew, do.** After pausing, do something. How can you fix the problem or manage it better? Maybe all you can do is put on your big-girl/-boy pants, tell yourself to suck it up and move on. For me at least, I sometimes just need to call myself out on the ridiculousness or pointlessness of whining, stewing or my own BS. Sometimes *doing* means being gentle with yourself—going for a walk, distracting yourself, talking to a friend or otherwise *doing* something (anything!) other than passively letting negative thoughts swallow you whole.

RUMINATION VERSUS REFLECTION

Don't confuse rumination with healthy self-reflection or problem solving. Researchers describe rumination this way: repetitively and *passively* focusing on bad feelings and their (real or imagined) causes and consequences without actively working to solve or change the circumstances at the root of the problem. *Passively* is a key word. In other words, rumination fixates on the problem and feeling bad *only*; there's little, if any, deeper thought about what to do about it or ways to distract yourself or move on.

Reroute Your Brain

Ever heard the phrase "Perception is reality"? It's the truth. Fredrickson and a colleague did a study in which they told two groups of people they had to give a speech. Predictably, everyone got anxious and their heart rates spiked. But the group researchers coached to think of the speech in a positive way— i.e., as a challenge rather than a threat—responded differently. They got an increase in blood flow, which would energize them to meet a task but *without* the blood-vessel-constricting effects that come with *negative* stress. They also bounced back from the effects more quickly than the group primed to think of the speech as a scary thing.

Other research has found that patients told to reinterpret pain as "sensations" took fewer sedatives and left the hospital sooner, and those who believe they are fitter and stronger tend to recover faster and stay healthier. Those are just a few of several studies showing that deliberately changing the way you think, talk about or perceive hard or scary things can lead to real and measurable positive outcomes.

Science suggests there are two main ways to do it. The first is by making over your mindset, or changing your core beliefs about something—usually stress or something else you attach negative connotations to. In one study, for example, workers were shown videos explaining the "enhancing" nature of stress (how worthwhile challenges lead to worthwhile outcomes). Those employees later reported improvements in work performance and general health, effects not seen in colleagues who watched videos about stress's debilitating effects or watched no videos. The second is through a similar strategy called cognitive (aka positive) reappraisal or reframing. It involves either reframing an event or situation in more positive terms (although still realistic ones) or looking for and focusing on what's positive about a crappy situation.

You can apply these techniques to pretty much any situation that's draining or triggering negative feelings, and they can help regulate all sorts of emotions. For example, research shows reappraisal lowers stress *and* contributes to long-term happiness, resilience and better health. Mindset shifting, meanwhile, can boost productivity, energy and happiness, too. Just understand that you're not trying to eliminate negative feelings or stress; you're changing how you think about them or negative situations, rendering them less harmful.

These tactics also help attach positive meaning to stress or negative situations. For example, if I'm going bananas juggling five different big projects at once (true story), and I look at things not in a woe-is-me, ugh-I'm-so-overwhelmed way, and instead recognize I'm gaining valuable experience and reaching important-to-me goals, well, suddenly my struggles have more meaning, and I'm taking them on with more gusto. That's huge, because as I covered earlier, meaning in life is a key predictor of well-being and psychological health.

THE CONTROL-COMPLACENCY CAVEAT

Reappraisal works in a lot of situations, especially those that are out of your control. In ones you do have control over, be a little bit more careful. Here's what I mean: Sometimes you need big, negative emotions to kick you in the rear hard enough that you'll take steps to actually change things. Say you hate your job but tell yourself, "Hey, I'm lucky to even have a job." That's true, and it can help you get through a rough patch—and that's valuable—but over time, that kind of reappraisal may placate you. It can stifle the fire that would otherwise drive you to send out résumés, enroll in classes or look for a better gig—and find truer happiness.

Here, some easy and easy-to-remember ways to put reappraisal and mindset shifting into practice. You can deploy them in any moment, on the fly or in a more reflective way when thinking about a negative situation in the past.

- **Turn a *boo* into a *boo-yah*.** One of my most-used phrases is "Yes, but . . ." because I put a positive spin on almost anything. Out of eggs on pancake Sunday? Yes, but we also need paper towels, so I can pop over to the Stop & Shop quickly and also grab chocolate chips and whipped cream. Even if you're faced with a harsher reality, notice that it's awful, then try to find something that's awesome—or at least alright.

- **Swap *have to* for *get to*.** My friend Jen recently started shifting her mindset around bedtime for her three young girls, going from *Ugh, I have to do the routine* to *I get to put these three strong women-in-the-making to bed.* And it changed everything. Life isn't fun 24/7, but it does not have to suck so hard. This tweak helps you realize that you honestly *don't* have to do much; you *get* to live this life, which, for the most part, you created and create.

- **Rename what's lame.** A writer friend told me she used to dread getting feedback from editors—until she began thinking of notes not as criticism, but rather as lessons and directions for delivering better copy. The language you use, the meaning you attach to things and your own preconceived beliefs all have the power to shape how you think and feel. And the good news is, you can change them! (Although I'm still trying to get my kids on board for a leaf-raking par-tay.)

- **Turn *to-don'ts* into *to-dos*.** Trying to save money at the grocery store? Trade "Don't spend so much!" for "Stick to the list." For years, I've coached my editors to tell readers what to *do*, not what *not* to do. Because how miserable is it to be faced with a bunch of *don't*s and *shouldn't*s? Framing things that way shuts you down. It tells you to not act. Approaching anything from the opposite perspective is inherently energizing because there's a solution baked in—a way forward rather than a stop sign.

- **Go from *Why me?* to *Why not me?*** When Molly Luppino was diagnosed with a brain tumor while in grad school, she didn't feel sorry for herself. Instead, she chose to see that she was the right person to take on the cancer and long recovery: young, strong, no kids, on her parents' excellent health insurance and still living in their house. Her philosophy: There's often no explanation for why sh*tty things happen, but what's important is how you look at your situation and what you do with it.

Make a Daily Yay List

Several years ago I started what's called the Yay List. Almost every day on Instagram Stories, I post things that made me say Yay! that day—an LOL meme, yummy pumpkin waffles, a sweaty workout. The idea was born from grief after my dad was diagnosed with cancer. (I talk more about its predecessor, #operationgoodgrief, in chapter 7.) Now, years later, my Yay List is still a game-changer that helps me and lots of others approach life with lightness and lightning-bolt energy.

All it takes: recognizing what's good in or about your life and why it's happening. That's it. At first I had to work a bit at finding Yays, but over time it got easier. This simple daily habit conditioned me to almost automatically see and register the good in life. It gradually felt as if there were more Yays around, and it cemented a deep and permanent sense of gratitude.

The Yay List works because, at its core, it helps you dwell on the positive *and* maintain an attitude of gratitude. And science has shown over and over that both are magic for your energy and mood: Taking a few minutes to think or write about what's good or what went well makes us more aware of and grateful for it. We then tend to savor those things more and they help give life greater meaning and counter our natural negativity bias. Reflecting on good things also drums up positive emotions in the moment *and* triggers long-term increases in happiness, well-being, contentment and more.

Meanwhile, studies suggest that listing things you're grateful for (compared to focusing on hassles) helps you feel more optimistic and better about life in general, and it can increase ratings of happiness. And gratitude may lead to fewer physical complaints and encourage you to exercise more, eat better, get more sleep and even make more progress toward goals.

The Yay List in Action

The Yay List is similar to a gratitude journal, but writing in a journal felt like homework to me. There was something more energizing and fun about thinking of gratitude and positivity in terms of what makes me say Yay! I put it on Instagram because that's where I was already spending time, plus it let me spread the Yay, spark connections and conversations and provide a small but mighty counterbalance to all the nastiness on social media.

As the Yay List caught on, I loved seeing what made other people Yay. Meta-Yays! I've seen so many over the years—Yays for long jogs or just making it to the gym, for sunshine and cozy rainy days inside, for new shoes and old friends. I even started a stand-alone @theyaylist Instagram account, and during the COVID-19 crisis, especially, I noticed that what people needed and wanted during that time was, well, something Yay-worthy.

I think part of the reason the Yay List resonates so widely—and hopefully why it will work for you—is because it's almost effortless, and it's highly personal. What you list can be major or seemingly insignificant. It can be material or abstract. It doesn't matter what kind of person you are or what you're going through. You don't have to share it or you can shout it from your social media megaphone. Best of all, it doesn't require trying to wrestle yourself away from negativity—it just happens naturally.

THE POWER OF A GRATITUDE ADJUSTMENT

Even if you don't want to do a daily Yay List, try to pursue gratitude in whatever way works for you; it is one of the best gifts you can give yourself. In all sorts of people, from healthcare workers at risk of burnout to recovering alcoholics to everyday people like you and me, gratitude is proven to increase well-being, happiness and other positive emotions.

Emiliana Simon-Thomas, PhD, the science director of the Greater Good Science Center at the University of California at Berkeley who leads its Expanding Gratitude project, explained to me how it works in this way: When you feel grateful for something or maintain an overall attitude of gratitude, the glucose and oxygen in your brain that might have otherwise fueled negative thought patterns instead take a hard right turn toward the pleasure pathways and regions, which helps you feel happier and more alive. Research also shows gratitude has other specific powers, too:

- **It helps us manage stress better and increases self-esteem.** If you recognize and appreciate your "gifts" in life, it sends your inner bully the message that you're worthy.

- **We become kinder and more helpful, generous people.** That sets off a chain reaction that builds relationships and social support. (More on why that's key in chapter 3.)
- **Gratitude shuts down comparison.** If you're grateful for what you have, it creates a force field against energy-draining emotions like jealousy, envy and resentment.

Create Highlight Reels

I'm a photo junkie. I've got thousands of pics organized into folders on my phone. I order Chatbooks (photo books created through an app) every few months and after vacations and special occasions. I even bought one of those spinning postcard stands and stuff the slots with a rotating collection of printed snapshots. I capture major events and milestones, of course, and lots of random, everyday and seemingly unremarkable moments. Because when compiled with snaps from beach vacations, birthdays and big days, they serve as the highlight reels of life. Here's how (and why) you should create yours:

- **You'll want pictures more than you think.** My kids roll their eyes and call me "momarazzi" when I whip out my phone, but sorry, not sorry. Nobody looks back at photos or videos of everyday life and thinks, *I really don't need these.* (Except videos of concerts—does anyone *actually* ever rewatch those?!) Science proves it: In a series of experiments, researchers at Harvard Business School found that people indeed underestimate how much they'll be interested in, value and have fun rediscovering experiences from their past, even the ordinary ones. And that leads them to skip opportunities to document the present. So go ahead, be shameless.

If you're self-conscious about grabbing your phone, explain to your kids or spouse or whomever that you want to cherish and remember the moment. Also realize that taking pictures doesn't mean you're experiencing life through a smartphone screen; simply snap a pic and then reengage. And remember to put yourself in the frame once in a while. Your loved ones will appreciate those snaps later, too.

• **Taking pictures helps you savor, appreciate and squeeze good vibes out of unexceptional moments.** University of California researchers found that taking daily snapshots of things that make you happy boosts levels of happiness and energy. Study participants said it made them more mindful, reflective and appreciative, especially of simple things and family members. If that sounds similar to the Yay List, it sort of is. The difference: Your highlight reels are Yay All-Stars—not only what makes you say Yay one day, but the things and people that make you say Yay every day. They represent who you are, whom you love, where you've been and what you've done.

• **Looking at pictures sends a positive charge through your eyeballs and straight to your heart.** It's about as close to time travel as we can get, because snapshots and videos help you tap into memories. And reminiscing in detail about specific positive memories is a positivity pill; it can reduce stress and stress hormones, increase activity in the part of your brain related to emotion regulation and cognitive control, may help reduce negative thoughts and feelings about yourself and protect against stress-induced depression.

So dust off your digital archives, separate your photos into highlight reel folders or start filing away one-a-days or any photos as you take them. Or try any of the billion or so apps that turn your phone's photos into real photo books. Then, when you need a "pic-me-up," go through them. Life feels even more meaningful when you take the time to look back on where you've been and what you've done. My kids are learning this every time they go to the postcard rack, and whenever I'm down in the dumps—like when Charley, at peak tween-ness, tells me she hates me and I'm the worst mom ever—scrolling through my folders or leafing through a Chatbook feels like I'm mainlining a cocktail of joy, optimism and gratitude cut with love.

Find the Awe in What's Awesome

My friend's pal Rick, normally an energetic, active and upbeat guy, recently posted a picture, taken through his car's rearview mirror, of his kindergartner confidently walking into school by herself. Under the picture he wrote, "Every once in a while I take a momentary pause from being a tired and cranky parent to feel overwhelmed at how far the kids have come and [am] taken aback at how fast time is moving. It happened this morning."

That's awe: a feeling of being in the midst of or noticing something major or more special than you normally experience. It's how you feel during those times something has stopped you in your tracks and made you go, *"Whoa."* When awe grabs your attention like that, it connects you to something bigger and more remarkable than yourself and what you're used to, forcing you to see and think about the world—and your place in it—differently. And in an instant, it can make challenges, stress and bummers feel smaller and less significant.

Big awe energy is a thing, and it's uplifting and enlivening on its own, but research links awe to tons of specific benefits: Studies show awe can make you more humble, generous and helpful. Awe helps you feel more connected to others and less stressed, and helps you think more critically and openly and expand your perception of time. For example, in one study, people who wrote about an awe-inducing experience felt less impatient afterward. Another study found that awe helps life feel more meaningful. All those things help explain why this emotion boosts overall well-being and life satisfaction, and why even a single awe-inspiring moment increases positive emotions.

The world is chock-full of awe-someness, and every day holds opportunities to experience it. Like Rick, sometimes all it takes is slowing down for a second and noticing it. But there are a few other ways:

- **Get out in nature and travel.** Being outdoors or coming face-to-face with something huge, new or mind-blowing naturally inspires awe: Think of the Grand Canyon or even a tall tree or open field.
- **See things through a kid's eyes.** We did a story on awe in *Good Housekeeping*, and this trick stuck with me. So much is new and amazing to kids that they'll help you recognize awe if you let them. I remember one night co-coaching Charley's softball practice, and a huge rainbow appeared. Charley and I ran to the outfield and twirled under it. I don't remember much from that season, but I'll never forget the magic of that moment.
- **Focus on the details.** Awe can spring from simply looking or thinking about regular stuff in a new, more detailed way. So look at the curves of your child's nose and think about how he grew on what seems like a steady diet of only milk, Goldfish crackers and cuddles. Or, next time you watch a game, marvel at humans' potential for speed or coordination.

Set Your Life to a Soundtrack

Long before becoming VP of fitness programming for Peloton, Robin Arzón was a junior associate at a law firm. Before assisting a partner in court, she used to psych herself up by listening to the Wu-Tang Clan and Dolly Parton's "9 to 5." When she told this story, I thought of my own pregaming at a Starbucks before my interview at *Self.* I sat there going over my notes and listening to Eminem's "Lose Yourself" on repeat. I had spent hours preparing and hearing the rapper tell me "*You only get one shot, do not want to miss this chance or blow this opportunity that comes once in a lifetime*" threw gas on the smoldering fire of my confidence and energy.

Music is mood food, plain and simple. Research shows it triggers the release of dopamine, a feel-good chemical and part of the reward center of your brain, and that it has a unique ability to motivate, inspire and physically energize you. For example, during physical tests that require short bursts of energy, people do better if they listen to upbeat music first. Similarly, people don't get exhausted as quickly during a workout when listening to an upbeat, motivational playlist. A study in the *Lancet* even reported that listening to music before, during and after surgery lowered levels of perceived pain and anxiety postprocedure. Other research suggests that if you're trying to feel happier, listening to upbeat tunes can work.

If music can do all that, take better advantage of it. Create a soundtrack or pick a few go-to songs for your day or the challenges you face or when you're dragging, same as you would for a workout, and listen. You know how in movies when there's a montage of the main character transforming or on the cusp of triumph and it's set to an emotional whopper of a song? Like in *Rocky*, when you see him jogging and otherwise being a total badass set to "Gonna Fly Now"? Infuse your mornings or afternoons or whenever with that kind of montage-song energy.

Become an Expert Mistake Maker

I move at 110 mph and have zero filter, so I mess up *a lot*. I've been careless with friends' feelings. I've called people I should know by the wrong names. I got caught in a lie. I've made the wrong choices about how to spend my time and energy. I sent my daughter to school when she had strep throat thinking she was faking it and got shamed by the nurse, and sent my son to his peanut-free school with a PB and J sandwich, forcing him to eat alone in the office.

Yeah, those and my other (many) mistakes make me feel awful. But a screwup does not have to drain or derail you, because *you* get to decide how to handle the aftermath. Beating yourself up, placing (or misplacing) blame and dwelling on mistakes only messes you up and doubles the carnage. A better way: dealing with a mistake, learning from it and then moving the hell on—in your head and in life. Here's a step-by-step process that helps me. (And yes, they all start with an F word because *the* F word is usually what first pops into my head when I mess up.)

Step 1. "F*! I f*-d up." Guess what? You're human! Yay! Everyone fails. Everyone makes mistakes. And it's going to be okay. Sit with it for a minute—but just a minute.

Step 2. Figure it out. Ask yourself WTF happened and answer in as nonemotional, nonjudgmental a way as possible. Because this one thing is not a referendum on who you are or what you're capable of in the future. Then use the information to make your next move.

Step 3. Fix it. Take action. Is there something you can do to correct the situation, lessen the fallout or make sure you don't make the same mistake again? Do it—ASAP. If you're not sure, ask for help. And if there's nothing else you can do, look for the positive(s). It won't change things, but it may help crowd out discouragement, shame or other negative feelings and help you to move on.

Step 4. Flashback. Build yourself back up by revisiting your greatest hits—all those things you've done and do right. Think back to where and when you've succeeded in the past and how your behavior and choices got you there. Give yourself credit for your effort.

Step 5. Forget it. You've done what you can. Now remember the lessons and leave that mistake in your dust. Need help? Go back to page 31 and read the "Check Yourself Before You Wreck Yourself" section.

Be Amazing

What are you good at? How did you shine this week? In what ways did you totally crush today? You are likely doing many, many things every single day that set you apart, that other people admire and that you can be proud of. We're all fighting the good fight and racking up wins, big and small—and it's time to more regularly and intentionally celebrate them.

Unfortunately, we aren't always good at relishing our well-earned accomplishments, our inherent strengths and hard-fought habits—especially women. We take them for granted or are quick to share the spotlight or move on. One study found that it's due to "backlash avoidance." There's a lot to unpack there (for another book), but what I'm suggesting is simply recognizing your triumphs *to yourself.* Because if you can't recognize your victories, no one else will. And when you celebrate and take ownership of your awesomeness, the swell of positivity and confidence energizes you to do even more amazing things.

Research shows that when people focus on what they've done well, or even on small achievements, ratings of well-being and mood go up—they're happier and mentally healthier. And not only in the short-term. One study found that people who journaled about their accomplishments daily for just a week had higher well-being scores even six months later. No wonder: Accomplishment is one of the five cornerstones of Seligman's well-being theory—but recognizing it is key. If you want to fill a journal with all the ways you're killing it, do it. Here are a few other simple ways:

- **Give yourself a pep talk.** My son James will tell you he's the best basketball player on the court, the fastest dude in lacrosse, the best artist in class . . . Kids point out how they shine because recognition and attention feels so good. That doesn't change when we grow up. Take a minute every day to pat yourself on the back (try doing it while brushing your teeth!) with even a fraction of kid-level swagger. Or do it when you feel drained and need extra juju to take on a challenge.
- **Connect the dots.** Achievement hits harder when you link a successful outcome to something you did, your hard work or a decision you made. Like how a friend told me that whenever her boys are being particularly awesome, she thinks about how her parenting efforts, sacrifices and choices helped get them there.
- **See yourself through a friend's eyes.** What do people notice about you? What do they compliment you on? Or if *you* were your BFF, how would

you give you props? Make the voice in your head your best ally and hype person, not an adversary or neutral nobody.

• **Own your piece of the puzzle.** Resist the urge to attribute your achievement to others—whether you're talking to yourself or accepting praise from someone. Yes, it takes a village. (And by *it* I mean everything.) You can still take credit; be humble *and* proud.

• **Accept all the compliments.** I know this woman who bats away compliments like mosquitos. It makes me want to shake the praise into her! While you might think it's cool or funny to be self-deprecating—and sometimes it is—if you can't celebrate even a little when someone points out how much you rock, what's the point?

Be Awful

I'm a terrible cook. Seriously awful. I attempted to get better because I thought I *should*, but I could never seem to rise above below average or get to the point where I enjoyed cooking. Eventually I asked myself: *Did it really matter whether I made dinner or whether Trader Joe's or Ferraro's in Westfield did?* So I gave myself permission to accept that this was not my thing, and I quit.

Giving up didn't make me a quitter; it made me smart. There's incredible freedom in shedding the pressure we put on ourselves to do or achieve certain things. Toiling away without being rewarded with progress, satisfaction, lessons, enjoyment, money or something else you value is the ultimate drain. Consider how energizing and empowering it might feel to walk away.

It took a while for me to get here. I grew up thinking I could do anything if I tried hard enough. I appreciate that the belief probably helped develop confidence, a growth mindset and work ethic. With time and age, I (like most people) realized I couldn't literally do *anything*. No matter how hard I worked, I wouldn't, say, grow to be six feet tall and dunk a basketball in an NBA game. The problem is, I think we sometimes don't take things far enough or consider the nuances of "hard work = success." Instead, a crippling fear of failure or blind confidence or other things keep us from throwing in the towel when all the signs are showing us where to chuck it.

So try to embrace the idea that it's not only okay to quit, it can be incredibly energizing. Here are some ideas to help:

• **Let go of expectations.** I've noticed a pervasive and destructive message swirling around the ether: that if we're not setting and working toward big goals, being "productive" or striving for some type of growth, we just need to put in more time and energy, hustle harder or want it more. That may be true in some cases, but if you've been grinding away, platitudes implying you need to do more or that you're not passionate enough can be demoralizing and harmful. Forget about what you or others think you *should* be doing and think about what you *could* be doing instead if you quit.

• **Pick up on the signs.** Consider that repeatedly failing despite your best efforts—working your ass off, making smart moves, learning from your mistakes, etc.—is the universe trying to lead you somewhere else. The good news: Figuring out what's *not* your thing gets you closer to what is.

• **Do regular gut checks.** To be clear, keep chasing your dreams and important goals, even when you fail. But at points along the way, make sure it's worth your energy. Ask yourself point-blank: *Is this the best way to spend my time and efforts? Am I getting somewhere and something out of this?* If you still feel energized and excited even when things get really stinkin' hard, great! *Stay the course.*

• **Pivot.** I saw a quote once that said, "The pessimist complains about the wind, the optimist expects it to change and the realist adjusts the sails." Living Fully Charged embraces optimistic realism: You adjust the sails *and* believe the wind will pick up. That does not mean endlessly adjusting or maintaining endless optimism about your skill or the wind. Notice if there's a Jet Ski nearby you could jump on instead.

Own Your Decisions

The *Cosmo* article on happiness I talked about in the introduction was full of good advice, but one tip in particular was so simple, surprising and useful that I still think about it: the dangers of "mental browsing," or when you keep thinking about (or obsessing over) all your choices even after you've made a decision. I think of it as second-guessing on steroids or indecision after the fact. Here's an example: When my husband Pat and I were looking for houses in the 'burbs, we found our current house, which hit all our must-haves, and put in an offer. But I kept stalking Zillow, questioning whether we made the right choice.

Mental browsing can occur with decisions big or small. Either way, you doubt a perfectly good decision or fret over whether it's the best or right choice simply because you have other options. And it's pointless. The only thing you accomplish by obsessing over or questioning a decision *you've already made* is filling your brain with doubt and discontent, which leaves you unsettled and anxious. It also robs you of the positive emotions and excitement you could be feeling over what presumably is a good choice. So here's what to do instead:

- **Trust yourself.** When making a decision, tell yourself you've used all the relevant information you have at the time. Realize you're smart enough to weigh pros and cons effectively and are capable of making a good choice. Yes, you.
- **Go all-in.** There's a quote that goes something like "The grass is greenest wherever you water and fertilize it." Water and fertilize your decision by focusing all your brainpower on why it's so great. That's how I eventually broke my Zillow habit—by mentally decorating and daydreaming about backyard hangouts and the walk to the train.
- **Listen to your instincts, not indecision.** If you get a nagging feeling you made a mistake, be sure it's not indecision in disguise. If it's indeed instinct, change what you can or look back and learn. But you cannot know for sure until things shake out, so don't waste your energy on regret before then.

BEWARE THE ENERGY VAMPIRES
Worry Wormholes

It's human nature to worry. We do it because we're scared or trying to control an uncontrollable situation or prepare for a worst-case scenario. If you dwell on the worst of the what-ifs, however, you usually only end up feeling the worst.

Anxiety is debilitating, and if you struggle with severe or clinical forms, please see a professional. For the rest of us who occasionally fall down a run-of-the-mill worry wormhole, realize that worry is rumination's close cousin—negative thinking about the future versus the past. And, like dealing with rumination, if you can be mindful of where your brain tries to take you, you can grab the wheel and steer it in another direction instead.

Try this simple mantra: "Stay in your day," which I borrowed from my friend Amy Jo Martin's mom. Meaning, look at what's happening *right now*. Realize things are probably okay *today*. That's what I told myself during a health scare involving my son James and countless times since, especially during the COVID-19 crisis. Because, as Corrie ten Boom once said, "Worry does not empty tomorrow of its sorrow. It empties today of its strength." Even if the worst does come true, how will it feel to look back and realize you wasted perfectly good, even beautiful days suffering? Try not to let worrying about *what-ifs* keep you from enjoying *what is*.

Certainly acknowledge the possibility of a bad outcome. Even try it on in your brain in case there's a way to ward against it. If there's not, shift gears. Remind yourself that most of what we worry about never happens—91 percent of it to be exact, according to one study. Those are good odds. Jess Ekstrom, author of *Chasing the Bright Side*, sums things up this way: "Optimism and anxiety require us to imagine something that hasn't happened yet. If we have the ability to worry about the future, it also means we have the ability to imagine a better one." I'd rather expect the best and risk being disappointed than expect the worst and be right.

Toxic Positivity

"Stay positive!" "Whether you have a good day or bad day is up to you!" "Never give up!" These are classic examples of toxic positivity—unrealistic and overly simplistic messages around positive thinking that end up doing the opposite of what they intend and what you may need. Because the truth is, while we *do* have a lot of control over our energy and emotions, it's not absolute.

Unfortunately, that gets lost in translation. And so toxic positivity messages suggest, whether overtly or not, that if you're stressed, grumpy, anxious, overwhelmed or feeling anything other than "good vibes only!" you're not trying hard enough. And they can make you feel worse by piling on a side helping of blame, shame and guilt when you can't simply make things "all good!" It might also cause you to sweep under the rug some emotions and behaviors that you'd be better off dealing with.

Instead, resist buying into those platitudes. More than anything, the COVID-19 lockdown reminded me that it's okay to feel however you feel. Don't blame yourself for it or run from painful emotions; sit with them for a minute. Human emotions are complex and valuable, even when they're messy. And while there are always actions to take that can help you feel better, if you can't or don't want to do anything, it's okay; try again later. Because the best life, a Fully Charged Life, above all is an emotionally full and honest one.

MURPHY'S LAWS

Frontload your Yays
Start your day with *all* the really good stuff. For me, that means an endorphin-filled workout with my friends, yummy breakfasts, QT with my kids (before we're all worn down from a long day) and listening to podcasts on my way to work.

Erase *hate* from your vocabulary
Language has power, and *hate* is one of the most powerfully negative words in existence. Yes, truly evil things and people exist and deserve hate. But never giving myself the option to say the word ultimately does me more good than expressing my hate ever could. I tell my kids on repeat: *There's no room for hate in our hearts.* And if you believe it, there won't be.

Straighten up
How you carry yourself affects how you feel. Researchers call it "embodied cognition," finding that slouching can activate a negative

mood and make it harder to bounce back when you're down. Sitting or standing up straight, on the other hand, helps maintain self-esteem and boost mood and the ability to think positively.

Crack a smile

Nobody likes hearing "Give me a smile!" But if you're down, frustrated or angry and you are ready to feel better, smiling or laughing might be the nudge you need, even if it feels forced at first. Facial feedback research suggests there's indeed a two-way street between facial expressions and emotions.

Talk to yourself like a friend

Positive or motivational self-talk can physically energize you, according to research, so be sure the voice in your head treats you accordingly. A trick that might help: Use you or the third person for self-talk, rather than I. As in, "C'mon, [insert your name here], you got this" or "You tried your best." Doing so creates psychological distance—you think of yourself more as someone else—and it helps you better regulate emotions and be kinder.

Move "onward!" from disappointment

A while back, I was up for a big job and felt crushed when I didn't get it. As I left her office, Joanna Coles, the hiring director, said, "Onward!" It didn't erase my hurt exactly, but it struck me as productive and helpful. While "Forward!" and "Move on!" come off dismissive or not applicable (we often can't move past mega letdowns right away), you can always move . . . onward!

CHAPTER 3

The Love Charge

Where there is love, there is life.
—MAHATMA GANDHI

"No, no hyphen—M-U-R-P-H-Y," I said excruciatingly slowly into the phone. I was about eight minutes into what should have been a five-minute phone call (*tops*) to renew my kids' prescriptions. As I spelled and respelled each name and overexplained what I needed, it was clear the clerk was getting overwhelmed and I was getting annoyed. When it finally came time to give my credit card number around the sixteen-minute mark, I needed a chill pill more than my kids needed those damn vitamins. And I wanted to tell this dude as much.

I didn't, however, want this interaction to get the best of me. We've all lost our cool in situations like this (if you haven't, high five!), and it feels gross. This man didn't really deserve the lava of rage that was bubbling under my surface. At the same time, if I didn't do something about it, chances were good it would erupt on the next poor soul who walked into my office and dared to be anything but a fluffy therapy dog. So I said something.

"You know, you have a really cool voice." Because even as he struggled with names and numbers, it was as rich and smooth as cough syrup. "You could have been a radio DJ. What's your name?"

He was quiet, but I swear I heard relief tinged with surprise. Or maybe it was me—the sound of my psyche downshifting. Either way, I found out

Dave *had* in fact been a radio weather announcer back in the day, and although retired, he took a job at the pharmacy to stay busy. We chatted for only a few extra minutes, and after hanging up, I felt like myself again, not the tantrum I almost became.

Yes, that call lasted way (*way!*) too long. That part sucked. But thanks to those final minutes, I made a new friend I'd see in person at the store later. And while it wasn't easy in the moment, deciding to see and connect with this human instead of focusing only on my business, my time and my inner mean-girl monologue made all the difference.

Before the coronavirus upended life, most of us interacted with all sorts of people every single day. And while right now no one knows what the future will look like, I'm guessing (hoping!) we'll share space with people again—total strangers, our loved ones and countless others who occupy the space in between. Sometimes these encounters are frustrating, upsetting or make us want to lose our cool, like how the call with Dave started. Sometimes they feel special, like how it ended. More often than not, the interactions seem routine, mundane or tedious. We go through the motions preoccupied or distracted, even with those we're closest to and love the most. Sometimes *especially* with those we love most.

Each of those moments and every interaction we have is actually an opportunity. They're chances to form a connection or strengthen a bond, to see and be seen, to share your humanity with another and register theirs.

When we seize those opportunities to go above and beyond the bare minimum of what's required, what's expected or what we usually do—even just once in a while and even just a little bit—something special happens.

Those everyday interactions take on more meaning and unleash a current of positive energy. It gives those we interact with a charge *and* it has a profoundly uplifting effect on our own energy and lives. *We* come away feeling happier, stronger, more energized, motivated, hopeful, calm and loved. That's the Love Charge—the energy you get from meaningful interactions, connections and relationships.

WE NEED OTHER PEOPLE

It's that simple. The Love Charge works because we all have an innate and fundamental drive to connect with fellow humans—to be seen, to form relationships, to feel a sense of belonging. In terms of survival, health and well-being, that need pretty much falls in line with food, water, shelter and safety. And research shows that if it isn't met, the effects can be devastating—as dangerous to your health and mortality as a fifteen-cigarette-a-day habit.

People who feel disconnected or alone are at higher risk for depression, anxiety, poor sleep, fatigue, and they may have trouble concentrating. Loneliness is linked to high blood pressure, inflammation, obesity and other problems. You're more likely to catch a cold or get sick if you feel socially isolated. The irony isn't lost that while we're all self-quarantining to *stay* healthy, doing so may bring its own set of health risks, especially for those who live alone.

The need to connect is so important that the hurt we feel over social rejection—when someone is cruel or breaks your heart—shares the same neural pathways as physical pain. Scientists think it's evolution's way of encouraging social bonding, love and kindness precisely because they're so essential for our survival and ability to thrive.

Indeed, study after study shows that positive interactions and relationships—both the big-love kind and the casual, low-stakes sort (even with those we don't know)—keep us physically, mentally and emotionally healthy and happy:

- They reduce the risk of chronic and other health conditions, and have been shown to cut the risk of early death by half.
- Social bonds and positive interactions slay stress and generate positive emotions, which boost mood and unlock energy.
- Friends make us feel stronger and the hard stuff in life more doable. One study showed people perceive a hill as less steep when standing next to or even just thinking about a supportive friend.
- Overall, relationships of all kinds offer a smorgasbord of support, resources, opportunities, sources of motivation and other good things that positively impact what we do, how we feel, our resilience and much more, all of which can lead to greater happiness and well-being.

To be clear, other people aren't responsible for your health and happiness. It's the connection. It's that they provide means or motivation to do things that make you happy and feel more energized. It's worth saying that people can sometimes be the worst. I've never met anyone whose family or friends or strangers don't occasionally drive them batty or cause more stress and strain. There are times when sharing space with anyone (hello, quarantine!) makes solitary confinement sound lovely. Nurturing and maintaining good relationships is really freakin' hard. Relationships aren't perfect. People aren't perfect. They often don't act how you want or need them to. *We* don't always act the way we want or need to.

Still, in spite of that, people and relationships are the most amazing, wonderful, best things in the world, and they're worth every ounce of effort, struggle and heartache. When asked to briefly explain positive psychology—which, if you recall, is the study of what's right and good about us humans—the late Christopher Peterson, one of the field's pioneers and a professor at the University of Michigan, responded simply, "Other people matter. Period." Because they make our life rich and worthwhile in so many ways. They offer so many opportunities for happiness, love, fun, humor and lots of other things that feed you the healthy emotional diet needed for an energized, Yay-filled life.

THE POWER OF WEAK TIES

It's easy to see the value of close relationships—and I get into it more later—but science shows connecting with those outside our circles, including all those casual interactions with strangers plus low-stakes friendships (called "weak ties"), does wonders for our happiness and energy, too. One study showed that when people at a coffee shop made eye contact, smiled or had a quick chat with their barista, they felt happier and experienced a greater sense of belonging than those who focused only on the business of getting coffee. Other research finds that meaningful daily interactions with acquaintances or strangers—like a barista or the plumber or a security guard—were better at predicting lower levels of loneliness than relationship status or having close friends.

That's incredibly heartening. As adults, we spend so much of our days alone or away from those we love and who love us—at least, that was the case pre-pandemic. What's more, after age twenty-five, social circles naturally start to shrink, according to research. Even though you know you're loved and supported, it's easy to also feel alone. Interacting daily and in positive, meaningful ways with weak ties and strangers is an antidote; it makes the world feel kinder and less lonely.

These interactions help us in other ways, too. For one, they can make us more empathetic. Talking to and getting to know people outside our usual circles, who do different jobs, lead different lives, come from different backgrounds and have different lived experiences, can blow open our worldview. We are then able to understand what others go through and connect. The conversations also exercise our brains; even simple chats can be mentally stimulating, often more so than when we talk to friends and family, with whom conversations can become routine and easy. That familiarity and ease is comforting, but talking with a stranger or acquaintance forces neurons to work in new or different ways, and it feels good, even invigorating.

> **Interactions with weak ties are like snacks; they keep your energy up throughout the day.**

Just like we have to eat, drink and sleep every day—i.e., meet our basic human needs—we need regular human connection. And the more interactions you have, and the more meaningful and high quality they are, the better they nourish and energize you. The throwaway, all-business, transactional interactions that are all too common—the "Gimme an oat milk latte to go" while staring at your phone—are empty-calorie junk food.

Making eye contact, giving a kind word or smile, waving to a car ahead of you—these microinteractions charge you with little hits of emotional sustenance so you're less likely to come home to your family or roommate emotionally hangry, drained or pissed off. Instead, you're better equipped and have more energy to pour into the important relationships that sustain you in a bigger way.

LOVE WINS

If meaningful connections with weak ties are snacks, meaningful interactions with loved ones fill you up and energize you like Sunday supper.

Relationships are, of course, one of the five pillars of Seligman's PERMA theory of well-being and arguably the most important. In one study, when people were asked what most gave their life meaning (the *M* in PERMA), the top answer was "feeling connected to others and cared about." Similarly, twice as many Americans said family gave their life meaning than said their career did. And in the longest-running happiness study to date—in which a group of men were followed for decades—Harvard scientists found that one of the strongest links to health and happiness throughout life was close relationships.

Relationships can be the source of experiences that enrich our lives and boost well-being, *and* they make all the other good stuff about life better.

That's a large part of why relationships are so vital. In a past newsletter, to drive home the centrality of relationships, Seligman asked readers to think about some of the best moments of their lives. Think about yours now, or even the best moments of last year—the times you felt joyful, energized, happy, fulfilled or truly alive. Other people were probably involved, right? Even if they weren't—say you experienced or accomplished something incredible on your own—consider how it felt to tell someone or talk about it with those who felt as thrilled or proud or excited as you or even more so. (Moms, I'm looking at you.) Consider how much more fun it is to do anything with someone you care about and love being with and how those people make great times amazing and make boring or annoying tasks more tolerable or even fun.

Unfortunately, it's easy to take close relationships for granted. We feel like we don't have to try as hard to connect or create meaningful interactions because we see those people all the time or know they'll always be there. So we get lazy or prioritize other things, people or demands on our energy, even if it means there's little left for the ones who matter most. Don't feel bad—it's normal. I'm as guilty as anyone. I hit the jackpot when I married Pat. He's also the one who gets the short end of my energy stick, and I'm not always good at showing him what he means to me.

Life will inevitably create tiny cracks in the foundations of your most important relationships. If you ignore them and keep on keepin' on, more and deeper fissures develop, and those relationships can start to drain you more than they energize you. Luckily, though, it doesn't take much to patch the cracks when they're small. And it's easy to add reinforcements that make your relationships as strong and resistant to damage as possible.

KINDNESS IS MAGIC

This chapter aims to give you the tools and tips to sustain and strengthen your closest relationships, as well as build new ones and forge other meaningful connections. At the center of nearly every tip lives kindness. That sounds trite, I know, but it really can be that simple. Henry James summed it up when he said: "Three things in human life are important. The first is to be kind. The second is to be kind. The third is to be kind."

If you can be mindful of how you treat others and be kind—friendly, patient, helpful, curious, compassionate, generous (even with just time or attention)—you will connect in more meaningful ways, and it will profoundly improve your own energy and happiness.

The research is overwhelming: Acting kindly is one of the most reliable ways to spark and grow happiness. Acts of kindness trigger the release of feel-good chemicals in our brain and protect us from and lower stress. Nine in ten people even say they get an emotional boost from doing something kind for others, which is similar to the "helper's high" I talked about in chapter 1. And a review of more than two dozen studies concluded that helping others improves overall well-being.

What's cool is that the kinder you are, the more likely *you* see yourself as a good person, which increases self-esteem. Studies also show kindness and compassion build trust and closeness with others, strengthening our relationships. And when we feel all these warm fuzzies, we're more likely to engage in even *more* of what researchers call "prosocial behavior"—we continue being kind, helpful, decent humans. And this cycle of good deeds and good vibes will energize us for life.

Every day holds endless, easy opportunities for kindness and connection—each one a lightning bolt of energy and Yay. You just have to act. Don't wait around for someone else to do the right thing or be kind to or connect with you. Make the first move. Reach out. The good things you create will only lead to more good things. Here's how to set it all in motion.

THE LOVE CHARGE TOOL KIT
Turn on Your Cab Light

People are like taxis. We all have a version of the light on the roof that signals we're ready to let people in or they shouldn't even bother trying. We flip it on or keep it dark in different ways—body language, eye contact (or lack of), facial expressions, what we say and how we say it, and the general vibe we project.

In a way, the light—this air of approachability and openness—is an expression of optimism. It says, *I believe there are good things and good people out there, so go ahead and flag me down.* That's the vibe I want to give off: I want to let people in, make a connection and take the ride with you because I'm hopeful it will lead somewhere awesome, whether you're a stranger or my kid.

So, the first and easiest step to making more and more meaningful connections is sending the signal that you're open to them. What would you think of you if you saw yourself in the wild or had to talk to yourself, the stranger, on the phone? Be honest about the energy you give off and consciously try to be more aware of it and open. You don't have to make a big show; it's as simple as head up, eyes open, noticing versus filtering, listening versus hearing. It's a softness, presence and consideration of others. It's being more aware of the people you share space with and making room for a small, shared moment—for kindness, empathy, curiosity, patience or compassion.

If you're not used to moving through the world this way, it can feel uncomfortable at first. That means you're doing it right. Also, not everyone will want a ride and you won't always feel like giving one. That's okay. But when you're drained or on edge and your instinct is to shut down, allow for the possibility that connection may be exactly what you need. By giving yourself the chance to be flagged down, you might just find yourself on an exhilarating trip.

Talk to Strangers

My friend's husband, John, was coming home from a business trip a while back when an older woman plopped into the seat next to him and let out a big sigh. He usually wears headphones, in part to avoid these moments, but he decided to ask if she was okay. As it turned out, she and several girlfriends from around the country were going to visit a dying friend. She told a tragic but beautiful story, which led to an inspiring, beautiful and refreshing conversation—and to John feeling grateful he hadn't ignored her.

Not every story about a chatty seatmate ends this well, of course. And yes, zoning out sometimes also feels beautiful. But isn't it funny how there's all this research proving social interaction makes us happier and healthier, yet so few people seem to actually *want* to talk to others? That's a question researchers have recently tried to solve, and what they uncovered is enlightening:

- **You'll like talking to strangers more than you think.** In a series of experiments with commuters, most started out believing they'd prefer solitude, yet those who talked to other passengers actually reported feeling *more* positive about their commute. Another study showed that when people talked to one stranger a day for five days, 99 percent had at least one pleasantly surprising chat, and around 40 percent made inroads toward an actual friendship.
- **Strangers will like talking to you, too.** Both those who initiate a conversation *and* those on the receiving end report equally positive experiences, according to research from Gillian Sandstrom, PhD, from the University of Essex. She and her colleagues coined the term "the liking gap" to describe this tendency we have to underestimate how much new people like us and enjoy interacting.

I'm not suggesting you spend every commute or errand making BFFs. Just once in a while, consider getting out of your own world and briefly into someone else's. A simple and quick chat may energize you in a way that whatever you're thinking about or listening to or reading can't. Connect for a sec, *then* you can always put your AirPods back in.

HOW TO CHAT UP A STRANGER WITHOUT FEELING LIKE A CREEPER

All you need is an opening—not even a window of opportunity, just a peephole. As someone who talks to strangers like it's her job (which it kind of is), try one of these:

- **Give a compliment.** So easy. Who doesn't like hearing something nice about themselves, especially from an objective stranger? Be sure it's sincere; false flattery does more harm than good.
- **Ask a question.** Research shows questions cause people to like you even more— they appreciate the interest. They also usually feel compelled to answer, so you're almost guaranteed more than a grunt. One day at the Stop & Shop, for example, I asked the cashier Ed about his name. Finding that it's short for Edison felt like we were bonding over a "secret." Now we're buddies.
- **Lean into name tags.** I love conferences (ahh, remember those?!) because everyone wears name tags and you can walk up and say, "Hi, Meaghan! I'm [so-and-so]." Aside from offering an easy opening, even just working someone's name into an otherwise standard interaction automatically makes it feel more intimate and friendly. As in, "Hey, Mike! Can I have an iced coffee, please?"
- **Look for a convo starter—or wear your own.** I love wearing clothes and accessories that invite comments and questions, and this tip works especially well for my less extroverted husband. If Pat sees someone in Rutgers gear (his alumni team), he'll say something like, "How 'bout that game!?" Or you can look around for something to talk about or gush over: "Hey, did you see the sign for this year's 5K pizza run? Are you going? It's a blast!"
- **Make small talk bigger.** "What do you love about what you do?" That's what Supreme Court Justice Sonia Sotomayor asked Brad Montague, author of the book *Becoming Better Grownups*, at an

awards reception. She told Brad she prefers that question more than the usual "What do you do?" because it gives people more meaningful topics to talk about. Also, this: "When you know what somebody loves, you know who they really are." Other areas to mine: favorite books, movies, TV shows, vacations, neighborhoods, whatever. Most people will be thrilled to talk about what they love, and you'll probably be more interested, too.

Create Your Version of the *Cheers* Bar

Walking into Baron's Drug Store in Westfield is like walking into a hug. I get a "Meaghan! Hi!" from Moira and Zoe, the beauty department ladies, who want to chat makeup. Teresa, the manager, waves hello or we talk. When I head to the pharmacy, Dave, the radio-announcer-turned-clerk collects my prescriptions before I get to the counter and we catch up about what's up in town.

This is the "Cheers effect"—everyone knows my name and I know theirs, plus we know all about each other's families and lives and dogs—and it instantly makes this big, often harsh world feel smaller and kinder. Building these sorts of casual relationships at go-to spots creates charging stations all over town. If it's a basic need to feel like we belong and meaningful interactions are paramount to happiness, the more you meet that need, the better.

I've become the Norm to all of Westfield's Cheers, but you should try starting with only one or two spots. Most of us are creatures of habit in terms of where we go and when, whether it's the grocery store, pharmacy, dry cleaner, gym, gas station, coffee shop, barber shop, even school drop-off and pickup. Choose your place and notice who's there. Who has their cab light on or recognizes you? Introduce yourself. Use a name tag. File away personal details and share your own.

My neighbors Mr. and Mrs. Mancini are good examples. They walk the same loop around Elm Street a few times a day, and there's not a homeowner, delivery person, service worker or dog they don't know by name. They're the IRL version of the NextDoor social networking app. It's amazing how quickly weak ties form when you put in a teensy bit of effort like they do—and how strong those ties can become and how powerful an effect they can have.

Cheerlead for Your Community

A few years ago I was legit appointed Chief Spirit Officer of my town. The whole thing started when I convinced my friend, the designer Vern Yip, to fly in to do a book signing in Westfield for his new book. The then-mayor showed up, and Vern joked that he had never met anyone with more town spirit or passion about where they live than me, and that I should be the town's CSO. The next day, the mayor called, we had a meeting, I shared some ideas and soon after I was cheerleading for Westfield in an official (volunteer) capacity.

I wanted the gig for the same reasons I had gushed all over Vern about "Bestfield": because I felt extremely lucky we landed there. I craved a strong sense of community and selfishly wanted to see our town thrive. "Home" holds such meaningful connotations, and if you call somewhere "home," why not go all in and #lovewhereyoulive, take pride in it and do what you can to make it worthy of the word—the best, happiest, healthiest place it can be?

Even if your 'hood isn't great or wasn't your choice, you still have a choice: Complain about the problems and harp on what you hate, or find what's good and contribute to and build on those things. Embracing your neighborhood, warts and all, gives you the energy to fight because it gives you something worth fighting for. You may not be able to solve all the problems—maybe you can't solve any or don't want to try, which is okay!—but you can still do simple things to make it a place that charges you with love and a sense of belonging.

At the very least, get to know your neighbors and support local businesses and organizations. As much as possible, be aware of and involved in what's happening. One review reported that good neighbor relationships specifically, as well as an attachment to and sense of community, increase feelings of safety and security, well-being and satisfaction with where you live, plus community identity and engagement. Volunteering with community groups, meanwhile, predicts better mental and physical health, higher ratings of life satisfaction, self-esteem and happiness and lower risk of depression and psychological distress. Easy ways to get involved are:

- **Show up.** At a neighbor's to say hello, on a community Facebook page, at the block party or neighborhood event. Community cheerleading doesn't mean being captain of the squad; it's okay to turn up in the stands with your pom-poms only on game days.
- **Think small.** Feel like an insignificant fish in a big-city pond? Jump over to a smaller pond. Or a puddle. Find *your* people or *your* niche. Maybe it's your block or neighborhood, maybe it's single parents, an LGBTQ+ group or fellow fitness fanatics. These days, there's a Facebook group for everything, and if you can't find what you're looking for, start one.
- **Schedule it.** If you can volunteer with a community organization, look for one that asks for a commitment and counts on you to show up. Otherwise, you're likely to find reasons to blow it off. A friend used to volunteer at her town's emergency homeless shelter once a week. When her 6 a.m. slot rolled around, she was never psyched to get up and go, but she always came home psyched that she had.
- **Add friends.** It can be intimidating to turn up at a community meeting, event or volunteer opportunity on your own. If a friend is already involved, ask to tag along. If not, recruit one and go together.

Find Your Kind-spiration

It's human nature to want to help others—a drive ingrained because of the deep emotional and other benefits it unlocks. And there are a gazillion ways to go about it. Some you (hopefully) already do, like holding open a door and saying please and thank you. To realize the biggest happiness gains from kindness, you gotta do a little more. But not much more. While lots of Yay humans are naturally good at spotting and seizing kindness opportunities, some of us need a little help or some ideas:

- **Pay attention.** Sometimes all it takes is opening your eyes to see a need you can fulfill or that someone is struggling. I remember a viral post about a grandma who noticed a young man on the subway platform struggling to tie his tie, and she elbowed her hubby who then helped him. Or take ER nurse Martha Phillips, who bought $150 worth of undergarments for rape survivors when she realized most left the hospital with none. She ended up posting a call for donations and they poured in, as did a commitment from the hospital to purchase more.

- **Borrow the best ideas.** Remember a few years back around the holidays when someone posted online about leaving out a basket of snacks for hardworking delivery drivers? The post went viral and soon goodies and thank-you notes popped up on lots of porches. Some even resurrected the idea during the COVID-19 shutdown. There's no copyright on acts of kindness, so let others inspire you. Keep an eye on social media or the news. And Instagram accounts like @goodnews_movement, @tanksgoodnews and @upworthy will restore your faith in humanity *and* can give you a blueprint for showing yours.

- **Do what *you* can.** Thank goodness for the magical unicorns out there starting nonprofits, mobilizing groups of people or otherwise devoting their lives to doing big kindness. And if you want to go big, *please* do. The reality is, most of us can't or won't, and that's fine. Don't feel guilty. Do feel inspired by the unicorns to try your own pared-down version.

Here's a great example: My friend started the organization A Birthday Wish after finding out kids in foster care often don't get presents. We wrote about it in *Good Housekeeping*, and the story touched my boss, Jane, so much that every year on her birthday, she donates a cartload of gifts instead of splurging on herself.

#KINDNESSGOALS

You're more likely to follow through with any new behavior if you're specific in your goals and plan and write them down. Try it: Write a note challenging yourself to do one super-kind or extra-helpful thing a day or decide to designate one day a week and go kindness crazy, then tack it on the fridge as a reminder.

Surround Yourself with Sunshine

Think about the people in your life who feel like a sunny day. They wrap you in warmth, you look forward to spending time with them and being together feels easy and good. Maybe you're extra inspired or more grateful or calmer with them. Or you laugh so hard your face hurts. However your time together goes, coming home feels like the end of an epic summer day; you feel lighter and happier and problems seem less dire.

Prioritize time with these people! Whom we choose to be around influences our energy, happiness, mood, behavior, motivation—everything. The phenomenon is sometimes called emotional or social contagion because we can literally "catch" emotions or traits like a cold. Research shows we pick them up from things like facial expressions, speech patterns and body language. Research also shows a zest for life and passion (the energy with which you talk about something and the motivation you show) especially transfers to others. And if your friends are physically active, you're more likely to be, too.

Researchers Nicholas Christakis, MD, PhD, a sociologist and physician at Yale, and James H. Fowler, PhD, a political science professor at UC San Diego, have studied social contagion and, specifically, what's called the "dynamic spread of happiness"—that happiness actively rubs off on others; it's not only a matter of happy people finding each other. They even quantified it: You're 34 percent more likely to be happy if your neighbor is happy and 25 percent more likely if you have a happy friend living within a mile. And for every happy friend in your circle, you're 9 percent more likely to be happy yourself. Unhappy friends, meanwhile, cut the likelihood by 7 percent. And, as it turns out, happiness spreads up to three degrees: If your friends are happy, you're likely to be happier (first degree), plus your other friends (second) and their friends (third), too.

The Friendship Audit

The problem is that many of us perpetuate friendships we shouldn't, with people who drain us rather than fuel our energy and happiness. For that reason, Terri Cole, a relationship expert who was on our *Off the Gram* podcast, suggested that once a year or so, we audit our friendships. It involves thinking about the people you spend the most time with and asking yourself:

- How do you feel when you think about hanging out with them?
- How do you feel when you're together?
- How do you feel afterward?

They're simple questions, but try it. Life is too short and your energy too precious to waste on people who feel like a rainy day or worse. If you answer anything other than some version of *good* or *great*—excited, happy, supported, inspired, loved, enlivened, uplifted—consider cutting or loosening ties. I don't mean ditch a friend going through a hard time, of course; realize the difference between truly stormy people and the sunny ones caught behind cloud cover. Then, after your audit, build and invest in your sunshine committee—a term coined by my sunny friend Maria Menounos. Here's how:

- **Be intentional.** Some people thrive with lots of different friend groups. Others prefer the intimacy of one tight-knit crew. The size or number of your sunshine committee(s) is irrelevant. What matters: that you deliberately make time for people who make you feel the best. Invite them out. Ask if they want to join your workout or if you can join theirs. Suggest an outing with kids. Yes, it can feel a little awkward if you're not pals yet, but how else do you get there? Besides, just as we underestimate how much strangers will like talking to us, the same goes for making friends.
- **Be flexible.** My daughter, Charley, constantly tries to define her friendships and mine. Kids want to figure out their place in the world and where everyone fits. We adults don't always outgrow this, and it's one reason we either cling to friendships we shouldn't or don't nurture the ones we should. Instead, accept that friendships are fluid; they can come and go, run hot then cool off. After all, people are fluid. We change, as do our needs and personalities. Our situations, schedules and locations change. Ride those relationship waves. Don't let history be the only criteria for giving someone space in your present or future.
- **Be inclusive.** Try this: You may naturally gravitate to people who are like you, which is fine, but also be open to or deliberately seek out relationships with those who are nothing like you or with whom you only share one or two things in common. These types of friends open

our eyes to new perspectives and deliver wisdom others can't. Because of that, the relationships can be incredibly enlivening, inspiring and fun. Think about the unlikely friendship between Martha Stewart and Snoop Dogg. Or read the hilarious memoir *Early Bird* by Rodney Rothman, who moved to a Florida retirement community at age twenty-eight. Or consider my pal Jason Wimberly, a gym owner who wears high-heel boots and makeup to the club and posts racy snaps on Insta. I'm a suburban mom from Jersey. On the surface we're nothing alike, but we bond over fitness. He's unapologetically living his Fully Charged Life and I'm here for it—and better for it.

Add Gravy to Your Gratitude

If you take only one thing from this book, I hope it's the amazing, energizing power of gratitude—feeling it, as I talk about in chapter 2, *and* expressing it. It's the secret sauce for making every relationship healthier and more energizing. A sampling of all the good stuff research shows:

- Expressing gratitude strengthens relationships more than simply feeling grateful or having a positive interaction. It also helps you feel more comfortable talking about your relationship; you're less likely to sweep issues under the rug, where they can cause bigger problems later.
- Gratitude for others encourages you to be kinder, more helpful and cooperative, and this type of "prosocial behavior" ultimately boosts your own feelings of happiness.
- People who feel more appreciated by their partner tend to reciprocate— they appreciate *you* more—which creates a feel-good feedback loop. They're also more responsive to your needs and more committed over time. In fact, openly expressing gratitude to each other predicts relationship quality six months down the road.
- Expressing gratitude even once for something small your partner does increases feelings of connectedness and relationship satisfaction that extend into the next day.

Even with all that proof, research still finds we tend to underestimate how happy and surprised people are to get our gratitude. Give yours more credit!

How do *you* feel when you get a heart-swelling thank-you note? I got one from a former intern that made mine explode. She'd heard me on a podcast and said I inspired her, that she got lots of Yay from my Instagram posts, and called me a role model. Who doesn't want to hear stuff like that?! If you're grateful for someone, treat them to the gift of knowing and knowing why— it's one of the most generous gifts you can give.

That includes people you're closest to. Most of us probably say thank you regularly to our spouses, family and friends—we're not monsters!—but it's easy to be mindless about it. We mutter a quick, throwaway "thanks" or even forget to say anything. I'm guilty for sure. I'll sometimes come home and inhale whatever (amazing) dinner Pat's whipped up without so much as glancing in his direction. I'm working on giving more and better props to my peeps, and you can, too:

Step 1: Recognize the small stuff. The small stuff can be a big deal. As often as possible, think about the everyday but great things people do for you. Look them in the eye and sincerely tell them, "thank you." Send a text or leave a note. Even (especially!) if it's their "job" in your house or it's something they always do or do for themselves, too.
Step 2: Add the gravy. Tell the person *why* you're grateful or how the person's actions made you feel or helped you. Here's what I told Pat recently: "I was so hungry and tired, and it was so *nice* to just come home and eat." Details hit gratitude receptors harder—yours and theirs—and turn an otherwise forgettable *thanks* into a meaningful morsel.

If You Have Something Nice to Say, Say It!

I'll never forget the woman who came up to me in the parking lot after an Orangetheory class and said: "It really seemed like you were having fun and living your best life in there—so awesome." How amazing is that? I smiled the whole drive home.

No one ever gets sick of hearing nice things about themselves, and re-search shows giving compliments is a win-win-win—for you, the other person *and* the relationship. First, compliments—especially about someone's personality or their actions—make the receiver happy. (A *Vice* article likened receiving compliments to a mini-orgasm for the brain because it stimulates reward centers in a similar way.) Second, the person then attaches those good vibes to both you and the relationship. Third, complimenting someone gives *you* a direct boost because it's rooted in gratitude (it shows you appreciate something about that person) and is an act of kindness, both of which unleash positive energy.

So starting now, dole out compliments like candy on Halloween. Point out how amazing your loved ones are whenever the thought pops into your head, or make a point to intentionally notice and tell them. Social distancing? Send a text that says *I'm missing your hugs!* Email or snail mail or drive-by works, too. Try something like: *It's so funny/clever/creative/inspiring how you . . .* or *I love when you . . .* or *You're a great friend/partner/kid/mom because . . .*

The only rules: Make your compliment honest and meaningful. Compliments focused on a person's personality or character, their work or something they've done are more powerful than appearance-based praise. Not that you can't tell someone they're h-o-t; just spread the love to other things, too. Also recognize effort: It feels extra good to get noticed for our successes *and* the hard work we put into them.

Own Your Apologies

Most of us try to be good people and good friends, spouses, children, siblings, coworkers. It's in our nature. So is making mistakes that can damage our relationships or hurt those we care about. The most powerful tool for repairing the relationship *and* helping both the other person and yourself feel better: a solid apology.

However, we humans tend to suck at saying sorry. That's actually in our nature, too. But you can get better, and knowing what to say is half the battle. Research has pinpointed six key points to focus on when apologizing:

- **Regret.** Your remorse shows the person you understand what went wrong *and* that their emotions matter and their reaction was valid.
- **Reasons.** Most people want some kind of explanation. This is not the same as trying to justify what happened. So avoid placing blame or defending yourself, and instead use "*I*" type phrases: "*I* misunderstood" or "*I* was thinking about . . ."

- **Responsibility.** It's your fault. Full stop. Whatever happened, whatever went wrong, whatever the person is feeling, own your role in it.
- **Repentance.** You'll try to do better.
- **Repair.** Is there something specific you can do to right the wrong?
- **Request forgiveness.** Straight up ask for it.

The point likeliest to yield forgiveness and resolution, according to research: responsibility. So even if your apology can't hit all six, target that one. Easier said than done, of course. People are self-preservationists by nature, and accepting fault threatens our self-image and chips away at our confidence—exactly why good apologies are so hard! But if we try to avoid those feelings and half-ass it, we compound the mistake by messing up our chance to earn forgiveness and fix the relationship.

I've certainly messed up apologies by backhandedly trying to defend or protect myself. I've said things like "I'm sorry *you* felt that way, but . . ." What to strive for instead is along the lines of: "I'm sorry *I made* you feel that way." Even if you didn't intend to. Even if the other person messed up, too.

Here's a cool trick that research shows might help: Before apologizing, give yourself a little self-affirming pep talk; think about what you value and your positive characteristics and strengths. Doing so reminds us we're good people, reducing the threat and fear of admitting our mistakes, which makes it less painful to offer an effective apology. You'll probably still feel vulnerable, but that can be a good thing; vulnerability invites empathy, encourages forgiveness, and builds a bridge to deeper connection.

WHAT IF YOU DON'T GET TO APOLOGIZE?

I recently acted like a truly crappy human. I was careless with my words and hurt someone badly. I tried calling to apologize, my cheeks flushed with fear, regret and embarrassment, but she didn't pick up. I sent a text that read, *I owe you an apology.* I don't expect to ever get the chance to earn her forgiveness or get closure. It stinks, and I have to live with it.

Apologies can be at least partially selfish; we want absolution to help us feel better, too. However if you never get the chance to say sorry, give up; don't keep chasing closure if the other person isn't ready to give it. Accept your mistake, forgive yourself and do better next time.

Listen for Likes, Collect Clues

A friend once sent me a text that read, *I BELIEVE IN YOU.* It arrived a few minutes after I told her I was struggling with a work challenge and doubting myself. It touched me so deeply because the week before I had mentioned that one major thing I missed about my dad was that he always believed in me no matter what. I teared up knowing she had remembered.

I'm lucky to have friends who do this kind of stuff all the time. Another buddy picked up a lightning bolt sweater for me at Nordstrom Rack just because, and during quarantine, a rainbow balloon arch magically appeared on my lawn. Being on the receiving end of thoughtful gestures feels like a giant lightning bolt wrapped in a hug. And, as with gratitude, the giving end feels just as good. Science suggests that generosity—even small, no-cost and low-cost acts—extends its own benefits on happiness, well-being and even physical health. Even *thinking* about being generous can give you a boost.

So try to read between the lines of what your loved ones say in order to get at what they need, love or would appreciate, then surprise them with it; show them you're listening, that you remember. Maybe it's a text and picture that says, *Saw this and thought of you!* Or add an item they need to your next Amazon order. Listen to what frustrates them and do something that might help. Or what big thing is coming up for which you could send a "You're going to kill it!" voicemail?

These actions send the message that what's important and meaningful to them means something to you. They're also all perfect ways to connect when you can't be together—whether because you're social distancing or actually physically distant. It shows you're listening when you talk or are together and think of them when you're not. And if actions speak louder than words, this shows the person they matter to you. Isn't that what we all want and need from our friends?

Practice Radical, Compassionate Honesty

Over the years, I've gone to football games, concerts, dinner parties, game nights and all sorts of other places and events I didn't want to, and did things I knew would drain my energy. I did it because I wanted to spend time with someone or show them I care. I've also lied to get out of stuff in an effort to protect both my energy and time and others' feelings. Once a friend asked if I could watch her son, but we already had extra kids at my house, and frankly I couldn't deal with another one. So I lied about why I couldn't. It felt extra icky because I got caught in the lie, and especially because I could have just told the truth.

Ugh! Why do we do this to ourselves? Why should spending time with people we like or showing them we care come at the expense of our own energy, happiness, honesty or sanity? Answer: It doesn't have to!

When I added more to my work plate, I had even less energy to spread around willy-nilly. And the lies, even little white ones, felt increasingly slimy and like playing with friendship napalm. So I started practicing radical, compassionate honesty: a double shot of the truth followed by a compassionate-caveat chaser. I tried it first on my mom when she asked me to go with her to a hyper local community theater production, which I'm slightly allergic to as a former thespian. In the past I would have sucked it up or lied. This time I said: "That doesn't really sound fun to me, but I want to spend time with you. If it's important to you, I'll gladly go. But what if we went shopping instead?" It seemed so simple and felt so empowering and freeing. Why hadn't I ever tried this before?! As for my mom, she was glad I told her the truth, touched I would have gone *and* agreed to shopping instead.

Bottom line: If you're going to call someone a friend or if they're family, trust that person with your truth—as long as you're kind—and believe they'll understand and love you anyway. If they don't and won't, well, maybe it's a sign that person shouldn't play a starring role in your life.

Bring the Hype

My friend Francene is the most amazing hype woman. Although we've never actually met—we're virtual friends who connected on Instagram—she reads or listens to all my media interviews, watches my TV segments and high-fives all my other wins and the everyday good stuff I share. It feels incredible, and I cherish this unlikely, special friendship.

We all deserve a Francene, and we all should try to *be* a Francene for at least one other person. The thing is, most of us are better at showing up for friends in bad times—with a listening ear and hug, bottomless glass of Malbec or freezer casserole. Aim to offer that same level of urgency, enthusiasm and support when things go right.

Think about it: Hearing "I had a great day!" from your spouse might elicit a "that's awesome, honey," but it probably doesn't stop you in our tracks like "*Ugh*, I had a crap day." We take the good for granted, thinking, *Oh, whew, everything's okay, you don't really need me.* However, we're missing a huge opportunity to capitalize on that person's good vibes.

In one study, researchers watched couples discussing both positive and negative happenings, then asked how understood, validated and cared for they felt, and followed up on their relationship later. Turns out, responding actively and enthusiastically to the *good* stuff your partner shares best predicts relationship well-being, even more than responding supportively to bad stuff.

So pull out a few more stops when someone shares good news, whatever it is. Get excited, ask questions, compliment, congratulate, talk about it. Being an "active and constructive responder" (versus passive and/or destructive) leads to both people feeling closer and more satisfied with the relationship. The science also found that trust swells, conflicts shrink and couples have more fun together. Because no matter how big your confidence or pride, no matter how much you recognize and appreciate when things go well, having someone cheerlead and megaphone your Yays back to you drives those feelings—and, by extension, the relationship—deeper into your heart.

Share the Hype

If you want someone to be your hype man, you gotta give 'em something to hype! Share when good things happen to you—and not only big things but the everyday stuff, too. Text your friend a fresh-from-the-salon pic and share your Yay over finding hair love (at last!). Tell your spouse what awesome thing your boss said about you. Call your mom armed with a parenting win or how you met your workout goal.

When we acknowledge, share and celebrate good things that happen to us, our brain drips out extra dopamine. Research also finds that spilling the good-news tea helps us savor those experiences and value them more, which fills our cup of positive emotions. And, as described above, if the person you tell brings the hype, a stronger relationship is the cherry on top.

When Things Get Rough, Show Up and Shut Up

When my kids were babies and I would freak about something, moms who had been in the trenches before would often throw around the phrase "Little kids, little problems." They were trying to help me chill out about poop everywhere, breastfeeding fiascos, nap drama and countless other "little problems" that felt *enormous* to me.

As my kids got older, I understood what those moms had meant. The baby-stage disasters sound downright pleasant compared to bullying, peer pressure and tween-daughter drama. So when a new-mom friend called in a tizzy about her newborn swallowing soap at bath time, I laughed and said, "He'll fart bubbles. Little kids, little problems."

Later, I felt like the problem.

What I had done in a few words was judge her reaction, compare her experience and diminish her feelings. Thinking back to my own new-mom freak-outs, they aren't necessarily about bubbles and poop, are they? They're often manifestations of self-doubt, guilt, fear, stress, hormone hijacking and all the other mind-f*ckery that babies bring on.

The point of this story is that no matter what a friend or loved one is going through or feeling, whether it seems small or is a certified whopper, there's probably more wrapped up in it and their reaction than you know. I realized too late that what my friend needed—what we all often need when we're struggling—is someone to listen and tell us we'll be okay.

People aren't good at telling you what they need, but it usually isn't to assess, rank or categorize reactions or experiences. They also probably don't need you to try to fix things or give advice unless asked. The urge to do it comes from a good place, like how I wanted to ease my friend's soap-xiety. But I missed an opportunity to be a better friend. What I should have said was: "Isn't this stage *so* hard and confusing? He'll be okay and so will you. How are you managing otherwise?"

Also, leave yourself out of the conversation. Listen, validate feelings, ask questions. Try things like "I can tell this bothers you" or "That sounds so stressful." Or offer only company, a hug, food or a distraction. Usually we just need to be told/reminded we're going to be okay. So resist the urge to offer more or fill the silence. Doing so might feel uncomfortable, but it's okay. You'll be okay, too.

Treat Social Media Like Real Life

People love to hate on social media. And while there's plenty to dislike— cyberbullying, disinformation campaigns, the ease with which I'm influenced to blow my paycheck—the problem isn't usually social media; it's us and how we use it. You don't blame the sun for your sunburn if you didn't wear SPF, right?

There's also a lot of good that can come out of FB and Insta. Research shows social networking can help us feel more connected. It can be a place where we learn new things and find different perspectives on just about everything and can be exposed to a range of different types of people. It also offers easy avenues for getting and giving support. Think about what Simone Gordon does—the @TheBlackFairyGodmotherOfficial I talked about at the beginning of chapter 1. Or what can happen among friends and strangers in comment sections and DMs, in moms groups, on career networking pages and other virtual gathering places. And that's to say nothing of the inspirational quotes or stories, hilarious memes and eye-opening perspectives.

The best way to maximize the good while minimizing the scary, nasty, self-esteem-wrecking parts: Apply the same rules to social media as you do to IRL interactions:

- **Actually talk to people.** You don't go to parties and not speak to anyone, right? That would be a waste of time. And yet, that's what passively scrolling feels like. And people who say time online is a waste report more negative effects from it. On the other hand, those who have positive interactions online say they get a mood boost and feel more support and a greater sense of community. So comment, post and otherwise connect and build real relationships, even if they stay virtual.

- **Choose your friends and follows carefully.** Do not follow people you don't like. Do not follow those who are negative or nasty or who don't make your life better in some way. Do follow people who encourage you, who help you learn and think, who look different from you, who might challenge you in a positive way. Bottom line is that *you* control what you consume, and one mega advantage social media has over real life: easy-out buttons that read "unfollow," "mute" and "hide friend."

- **Set limits.** We don't spend 24/7 with friends, coworkers or strangers IRL, so don't let their online versions invade your life. Even though social media can do good, the research is clear that overuse can leave you lonely and anxious, especially if it replaces in-person connection.

- **Find your niche.** Just like being at a huge party where you don't know anyone, large groups on Facebook can be intimidating and impersonal. Posts and comments also easily go off the rails. Instead, find or create smaller groups where you can better connect and feel more at ease interacting.

- **Don't be a jerk.** It baffles me that people waste their energy being nasty online. While there's always room for discourse and disagreement, check your judginess or tone at the virtual door. If you're offended or want to hate on someone for a post or comment, remember you're essentially a visitor in that person's online house. Would you say that comment to their face? Is it necessary? Is it worth it?

- **Catch yourself comparing.** Much of the research showing negative effects of social media point to comparing as the conduit. So try to be mindful and remind yourself that what you see is *always* filtered in some way. Then consider *why* you're comparing. For example, if you compare yourself to a family who seems to have lots more fun than you, maybe it's a sign to let loose more with your crew. It's not about trying to be perfect or someone else; rather, it's about using your feelings to figure out how to be the best you can be.

High-Five the Haters

Not everyone will like you, and it's not worth trying to make them. Unfortunately, some people you don't jibe with can turn into full-on haters who actively spend their energy talking smack about you—or worse. And the more you put yourself and your energy out in the world, the more likely this will happen.

When I took on the role as Chief Spirit Officer of Westfield, for example, which involved becoming more active in and vocal around and about the town, I suddenly found myself face-to-Facebook-post with a surprising amount of hate. Some called me a political pawn. Others said I was an elitist, spandex-clad snob with ulterior motives. It hurt, especially since I was trying to spread good energy. Yet I realized that what haters need more than anything are high fives. Here's why:

- **Heroes always have villains.** As long as you're not a scummy human, hate directed your way usually signals strength, bravery or fearlessness—you've got enough of those things to put yourself out there or express an unpopular, different or strong idea, opinion or perspective. Just consider my daughter's favorite YouTuber, JoJo Siwa, who has faced hate because she stays true to herself and doesn't fit the mold of what some think pop stars should look like or speak about. So high-five haters for reminding you you're a strong, authentic badass just being your superhero self.

- **Haters need help.** Most people spend very little time thinking about you; we're all too consumed being the star of our own shows. Why, then, do haters care enough to waste energy hating you? Because it's easier than focusing on themselves. That's a bummer—for them, not you. What people hate on is often related to what they're insecure about in their own lives; they're trying to make themselves feel better. And that must *really* hurt. That person must have gone through or is going through awful stuff. Meeting hate with a wee bit of compassion and empathy takes the sting out. Then let it go; you have better things to focus on, too.

- **Haters can help us.** Hate is often baseless and subjective. Ignore that. However, if the hate you hear hits a different nerve or nags at you, explore whether there's a valid point buried in there. Unfortunately, useful criticism, perspective, lessons and questions don't always come wrapped in constructive, kind packages. Sometimes hate is the slap across the face we need that wakes us up. Rethinking what you've put out there doesn't mean you're weak or second-guessing yourself. It can mean you're strong enough to be open to different perspectives and criticism, and that you're honest and humble enough to realize you're not always right.

Take politics for example, where so little discourse is polite or constructive. Maybe a fresh look at your position *and* opposing ones cement your views even more, helping you feel extra confident. In that case, *thanks, haters!* Or maybe a second look opens you to a new perspective and you evolve your position for the better, which also warrants an *Up high, haters!*

Team Up

When my oldest kid was one year old, I started referring to our family as Team Murphy. I've always been a sports-loving jock, so it started out just for fun. As time went on and our family grew, it took on greater meaning. If it is a basic need to feel like we belong, a team dynamic, what a team represents and the word itself aligns closely with what I wanted family life to be—even more than "family."

Let me explain: I want our fam to internalize that we aren't only bound by blood and marriage—that the kids aren't just kids and Pat and I aren't just their parents; rather, we chose to create this family and choose to nurture it every day. I want us all, even the kids, to recognize we have a responsibility to each other *and* our team as a whole. To me, that's true belonging: You as an individual are cared for, and we all look after this bigger thing that protects us and makes us strong.

Treat Your Family Like a Team

If I wanted to cultivate those feelings, I had to do so intentionally. Calling ourselves Team Murphy is a big part of it. When we're out and I yell, "Team Murphy?!" everyone comes together. It's cool. (And it's caught on to friends; I got eight Christmas cards last year from "Team" families.) Even more important is acting like a team. On Team Murphy, we understand our individual jobs, needs, strengths and weaknesses. We celebrate when one member shines extra bright and offer help and support when one struggles. When someone slacks off or makes trouble (me included!), everyone gets a lecture and runs laps. (Kidding—usually just no Friday night movie or no video games.) We also give out awards for MVP and have benchwarmers and walk-ons, too—grandmas, babysitters, cousins. And everyone gets one-on-one coaching.

Even if you don't have kids, you can still field a team. Because at the end of the day, it's about appreciating that you're playing together, no one's out there alone and everyone does their part to make magic happen. A decade in, our team isn't perfect, but none ever is. It still feels like we're winning.

Slip Surprises into the Schedule

I thrive on routine. Without one, my world and psyche would devolve into chaos and collapse. That said, routine has a dark side. Knowing exactly what's going to happen day in and day out sucks the excitement out of life and can make relationships feel robotic. As psychologist Rick Hanson, PhD, author of *Hardwiring Happiness*, explains in his book: The brain tends to filter out what doesn't change (a process called habituation), and it can keep us from experiencing or creating opportunities for joy.

Something new or surprising, on the other hand, releases a rush of dopamine to our feel-good centers and forces us to pay attention. Happy surprises also hit our positive-emotion buttons harder and better than predictable moments of joy. They make us feel cared for and loved. And engaging in novel and exciting activities (versus routine ones) with those we love improves how people view the relationship. Even for yourself, spontaneity is linked to better well-being.

So while the predictability of routine is comfortable and easy, mess with it sometimes. Think of simple ways to shake up the everyday or add a surprise. Like when my friend Lindsey turned the bathtub into a ball pit for her toddler. His expression said it all: "Best day ever!!" Or when I surprised my kids with a mystery bike ride to a rope swing over a pond (followed by crumb cake—breakfast!). Lightning bolts and hearts shot out of their ears. Cake every morning? It would spark only as much excitement as the sugar high delivers. A few additional ideas: Try swapping your go-to date night spots for the new ax-throwing place or try a trivia night. Or do a chore your partner usually does or has been putting off. Routine saves your sanity; surprises add spark.

Get Your Vitamin T(ouch)

The COVID-19 crisis and lockdown shined a light on so much for so many of us. One big takeaway was how much we need physical closeness and touch—and how much we took it for granted. During an Easter (socially distanced) visit, my son, mother-in-law and I all burst into tears when I had to grab him before he instinctively ran over to smother his grandma. And as I write this, it hurts that I can't hug my mom on Mother's Day.

Lots of research over the years has shown that hugging, hand-holding, cuddling and other nonsexual touch can boost mood, energy and even our immunity, plus strengthen relationships, lower stress and negative feelings, promote relaxation and help keep you mentally and physically healthy overall. Part of its power comes from being a physical signal of that social support that's so good for us.

That's why, when the pandemic is under control and we start hugging friends and family again, I really hope we don't abandon other kinds of touch—the high fives, the gentle hand on someone's arm, the pat on the back. That kind of supportive touch is powerful. In one study, the more high fives and hugs NBA athletes gave teammates, the better they and the team played later in the season. Likewise, supportive touch from doctors creates a bond with patients, and from teachers, it can boost student test performance.

Touch also gets superpowers by triggering the release of oxytocin, a hormone that produces feelings of trust, support, bonding and love, as well as helps reduce stress. That's why it's *so* crucial—and so easy to get. Yet before this crisis, many of us rarely slowed down long enough to get our fill. I'm grateful I get hugs from each kid and Pat at least twice a day. And I can feel the difference when I get more cuddles. I feel more emotionally close to them, calmer, more loved—and like I'm loving them more.

Maybe you don't need to hear this, but for those who do: If COVID-19 is no longer a threat by the time you read this, take every opportunity to hug, kiss, cuddle or hold hands, and hold on longer and harder. Double or triple your pre-lockdown dose of vitamin T. If you're coupled up, turn quick kisses into five-second Frenchers. If you're not, slide closer to friends and loved ones. Those extra moments may seem negligible, but they hold a ton of energy, happiness, love and affection.

ALL TOUCHED OUT?

If you have or take care of young kids—especially if you're a breastfeeding mama—chances are the last thing you want after a day of kids clinging, clawing and climbing you like a human jungle gym is more closeness. That's okay. Reclaim your body. Then, when you feel ready, try holding the hand of your partner, your mom, a friend—anyone who isn't screaming for a snack, milk, toys, attention or otherwise wants anything except to support *you*. You might be surprised how good this very different and gentle closeness feels.

BEWARE THE ENERGY VAMPIRES
FOMO

One lazy weekend Pat was scrolling through Instagram and saw that several families we often hang out with were together at a BBQ. Without us. We hadn't been invited. It stung. I realized later that what bothered me most wasn't the being left out. It was that they were doing *something* and we weren't doing anything. It was good old-fashioned FOMO—fear of missing out.

A true energy vampire, FOMO is linked to negative mood, fatigue, stress and less sleep. Another study found that enjoyment of whatever you're doing takes a hit when you come face-to-face with what you're missing. In other words, FOMO can lead to actual MO—missing out on your good times because you're focusing on someone else's. That's what happened to me; I felt great about our quiet afternoon at first.

When FOMO strikes, channel those feelings into positive action, like the power of gratitude. In my case, we were getting much-needed and rare down-time. So I could feel grateful we weren't invited. Or try to energize whatever you're doing. It's not about one-upmanship; rather, ask yourself if there's a way to make whatever you're doing better. I ended up rallying my troops for a trip to the new ice cream place—on a school night! You can also safeguard against future FOMO by making plans yourself. I hate making plans, but FOMO helped me see that if I want to be social on the weekends, it's on me. So I called a friend and scheduled a few double dates.

Poisonous People

No matter how positive a person you are, we're all susceptible to others' negative energy. For example, I've been hanging out with a gossip monger, and after a while, suddenly I realize I'm talking sh*t, too. When I get home, I feel like I need a shower. I'm not blaming this person—I'm responsible for me—but it's easy to accidentally fall in line with whomever you're spending time with, even if things take a hard wrong turn.

We often get caught because we want to connect and find commonality with people. Research even suggests we might bond better over negative feelings and attitudes than positive ones. After talking and listening to a negative person long enough, their energy, language and behavior starts to feel normal and acceptable—you kinda just get worn down.

The solution: Socially distance yourself from toxic people as much as possible. And if you can't, vaccinate: Stay mindful and aware of how you're feeling and acting—simple awareness may be enough to inoculate against someone's negativity. Remind yourself of who you are and who you want to be, and empower yourself to stay above the fray.

SIX TYPES OF TOXIC FRIENDSHIPS

Terri Cole, the relationship expert I mentioned earlier, broke down different types of poisonous pals for our podcast listeners. Here, signs a friendship may be sucking your energy dry:

- Your friend makes you feel guilty—usually about your behavior toward them or the relationship.
- They can't be happy for you when good things happen, or they make you feel bad for your successes.
- They take and take so they end up feeling great, while you're left depleted.
- The person comes on way too strong.
- You're afraid of their disapproval.
- You pity them and remain friends because you feel bad or want to "fix" them.

One-Way Friendships

You probably know what I'm talking about: You do *all* the inviting and planning. Or you're constantly calling, supporting and showing up, but when something's going on with you—crickets. Or your friend makes everything about him or her. Perhaps it's the opposite; your friend does all the work because you're ambivalent. You don't click with this person and haven't disentangled yourself, or you feel obligated to stay pals.

Either way, sorry to tell you, you're complicit in creating and feeding these energy vampires. So here's some tough love: Stop it. Friendships are not always balanced, but if one feels like it's on life support, it's okay to pull the plug. What does that look like? Saying no or nothing. That's it. Every time this friend invites you out or needs something, ditch the qualifiers and reply, "No, sorry, I can't." Don't give an excuse. Don't let awkwardness add a "wish I could" or "but maybe next time." And don't reach out either. In most cases, the friendship will fizzle. You're not abandoning this person or being mean. You are protecting your energy.

MURPHY'S LAWS

Greet your peeps like a puppy
When I come home, my dog is so excited to see me he pees on the floor. It's the worst (from a housekeeping perspective), but also the best (so much love!). Meet your crew with even a fraction of that enthusiasm: with longer, more intense or playful hugs, or say something like "Wow, I am so excited to see you!" or "I *really* missed you today."

Smile at the A-holes
It confuses the heck out of them and can disarm even the biggest bully, transferring their power to you. Yes, your instinct may be fiery anger—totally valid! Take a breath and try to turn your fire into warmth, even if it's fake. Consider the longevity secrets of Chitetsu Watanabe, once the world's oldest man at 112 years young: "Don't get angry" and "Keep a smile on your face."

Silence your inner A-hole
We all deal with stress. We all have *days*. We all reach our breaking point thanks to incompetence, thoughtlessness, ignorance and a million other things. Try to breathe through this fire, too. Releasing your rage on someone is a temporary palliative that ultimately wastes energy and leaves you a lot to clean up later.

Believe in your crew
It's one of the best ways to love someone. Straight up tell your kids, spouse, family and friends that you believe they can do whatever hard or scary thing they're up against. It's as good as tying on their superhero cape because it helps them see they have power and ability. It creates an amazing bond, and most of the time, they'll work to live up to your expectations.

Carve out one-on-one time

As much as I love Team Murphy outings and vacations with family and friends numbering in the double digits, there's nothing like time alone with each kid, with Pat, with my mom or sister or a close friend. Just as we need to belong to something bigger, we also want to know we're the sole star in someone's universe, and that can't happen with the entire night sky present.

Ban the word *maybe*

I used to say *maybe* a lot. As in: Can Charley's friend sleep over this weekend? Maybe. Do I want to go away next month? Maybe. What *maybe* really says: I'm unwilling to invest my energy into fully considering this question. Or it gives false hope. Loved ones deserve better. So now I use "I don't know" when needed, but otherwise don't spend time sitting on the fence; it's a pain in the butt.

Do a double check-in

When you can't see friends or family in person—whether because of social distancing or just plain old distance—text often and ask: "How are you doing today?" Depending on their reply, consider following up with a "How are you *really*?" Sometimes even our close friends need an extra push to open up.

Just say f*!# it!

While there were plenty of takeaways from my time as a sex editor at *Cosmo*, the most useful wasn't about how to please my man or have sex in the shower without cracking open my skull. It was that sex and self-pleasure are important—for your health, energy, relationship and well-being. If anything keeps you from a fulfilling sex life, whatever that means to you, explore it, and talk to your partner, a doctor or a therapist if needed.

CHAPTER 4

The Work Charge

Work is about a search for daily meaning as well as daily bread,
for recognition as well as cash, for astonishment rather than torpor; in short,
for a sort of life, rather than a Monday through Friday sort of dying.
—STUDS TERKEL

The best job I ever had was at The Icing, a clothing store in the Bridgewater mall, when I was fifteen. Every weekend, I'd overaccessorize and head out to help the store's endless stream of Carmela Sopranos shop for bedazzled, body-hugging outfits. I *loved* it. I loved hearing about their upcoming parties, lunch dates, weekend plans and vacations and putting together ensembles for each. I loved convincing them they *had* to splurge on jewelry, handbags and scarves to complete their looks. I loved watching them treat themselves and walk out feeling like a hot cannoli. The best part was connecting with and helping these ladies feel good about themselves.

Yes, they were well-off, glamorous, bling-loving New Jersey housewives. I wasn't feeding the hungry—only my customers' insatiable appetite for sequins—nor otherwise saving humanity. Still, every time I saw a face transform in the mirror because of an outfit I had slipped through the dressing room door, I believed I was making a difference. And that made all the difference in how I felt about my job and in my energy and happiness there. It was why I worked hard and earned fat commission checks.

Today, I think about work in much the same way. At every magazine, with every article, program or project, including this book, my goal has been to connect with and give people the tools to find a spark, improve their health and happiness and feel inspired to live their best lives. That's what makes work feel meaningful, and it's a big part of what motivates and energizes me and why I've loved all my jobs. That's the Work Charge in action.

The Work Charge is the positive energy that comes from finding meaning and purpose in what you do—believing your work is important—plus enjoying yourself and feeling capable and engaged, no matter what your job or day-to-day tasks include.

WORK MATTERS

Ever encounter people who legit seem to love their jobs? Whether they work for a company, themselves or as their family's chief caregiving officer, they don't only work, they *werk*. Like this crossing guard I drive by. She attaches different messages or items to the bottom of her stop sign every day. I've never seen her without a smile; she chats with walkers, waves at cars and genuinely brightens everyone's day. She seems to be having fun, and because of her, drivers are more careful, kids listen and we're all safer and happier. Each time I roll past, I think, *Damn, she's good at her job.*

People like her tend to bring just as much Yay to their off-hours because how we feel about and at work is closely tied to how we feel in life and vice versa. Loads of research shows a two-way street between job satisfaction and life satisfaction, happiness and other markers of well-being. Part of it is due to what researchers call the spillover hypothesis: that experiences in one domain of life (e.g., work) influence experiences in others. One study, for example, shows that zestful people—those who exude upbeat, positive energy and enthusiasm for life—tend to be happier at and more satisfied with their jobs in part because they bring that joie de vivre to work.

This means fostering good vibes with the advice and tips in the other chapters is likely to help you feel more energized at work, too. Still, work itself is a big piece of the Fully Charged puzzle. How could it not be? Most of us spend more hours working than doing just about anything else—especially you stay-at-home parents. If you're bored or unhappy, focus only on being underpaid or overworked or feel that you're toiling away for nothing, it can crush your energy, and that negativity will spill over into other parts of life.

On the flip side, feeling energized and good about what you do leads to all sorts of good things both jobwise—research links it to better creativity, problem solving, productivity, innovation, leadership and more—and for overall well-being. Remember the PERMA theory of well-being from chapter 1 that lays out the five things it takes to flourish in life (positive emotions, engagement, relationships, meaning, accomplishment)? You can hit all of them at work, and hit them hard.

YOUR ACTUAL JOB MIGHT NOT MATTER

The truth is, for many people work often feels more like a drain than the energizing charge it could be—even apart from pandemic-related energy vampires, even if you're supremely grateful to be employed right now or glad to be a stay-at-home parent. The thing is, your job or day-to-day tasks may not be the problem. Salary and job security issues aside, believing everything would be better if you were doing something different or working somewhere else can be a myth that feeds discontent. And it can prevent you from taking steps that can actually help you feel happier and more energized right now, doing whatever you do for work.

Don't get me wrong, there are plenty of circumstances where the job, people or culture are the problem. Sexual harassment, discrimination, corporate malfeasance—all big, fat, toxic-sludge problems to run away from while sounding the alarm. Also, some jobs just aren't a good fit or they're a temporary means to an end. (If the shutdown reaffirmed anything, it's that I am *not* meant to be a homeschool teacher!) Even if your grievances are more minor, you very well might be happier doing something else somewhere else, so it might be worth exploring other options or opportunities.

That said, be careful of a "grass is greener" mentality. Be careful of romanticizing the idea that "following your passion!" or "doing what you love so you'll never have to work a day in your life!" will make everything better. Listen, if you want to pursue your dream job and it feels right, right now, go for it. But those clichés tend to be piles of poop emojis.

Let me explain: For me, I was lucky I could go after jobs that interested me and focused on topics I was passionate about. In that way, I guess I followed my passion. And as anyone who lucked out like I did will tell you, it is still *incredibly* grueling and not-always-fun work that, at times, can make you wish you were doing literally anything else. You might even push yourself harder than is healthy or make poor personal decisions because you're blinded by passion or hyperfocused on a dream. Plenty of people follow their passion all the way to burnout or bankruptcy or worse. Sometimes it's worth keeping your passion a hobby and just having a job.

The point is, any type of work can potentially drain your energy and happiness—whether you're passionate about what you do or you're just working for the weekend, whether you're trying to make ends meet, you're on your way to something better or making meals, changing diapers and running a household. Most jobs involve energy vampires of some sort—tricky coworkers (I see you, toddlers and teens), weird or bad managers, stress, deadlines and bottom lines, tedium, frustration, setbacks and *all the things*. Enduring crappy times and tasks can be the price of doing business, any business.

Here's the good news: If your work or unpaid caregiving and home-caretaking labor doesn't excite or energize you or add much to your life, you can change *that* without changing jobs. Likewise, if you enjoy some aspects of work but struggle with others, there are things you can do to feel better about them and more energized overall, too. The secret:

You must infuse your work with more meaning; focus less on the *what* of your work and more on the *why*, the *who* and the *how*.

PURPOSE IS THE NEW PASSION

We all want to feel happy at work, and it's a worthwhile goal. The Work Charge and feeling Fully Charged go beyond that, beyond enjoying what you do. When it comes to work, research is actually mixed on just how far happiness can take you in terms of feeling and being productive, motivated and successful. Meaningful work seems to be the golden ticket.

Studies show that meaningful work is intimately connected to happiness and increased job satisfaction, as well as better performance, motivation, engagement and productivity. One survey found it's the number-one factor determining a positive employee experience. It may also help buffer stress. People who say work is meaningful tend to have better attitudes and are better coworkers, miss fewer days and earn more money over time. People also seem to value meaningful work more than better pay and working conditions and opportunities for advancement.

Meaningful work can also give life more meaning. It's linked to better mental health, less stress, greater life satisfaction and other positive feelings— even when you're off the clock. It even helps predict longevity, too.

You probably have an idea of what meaningful work is or feels like: a sense that what you do matters and is important in the greater scheme of things. That's not wrong; however, there doesn't seem to be a single, simple definition or explanation experts use. So I like the following from Michael F. Steger, PhD, founder of the Center for Meaning and Purpose and a professor of psychology at Colorado State University. In an article for UC Berkeley's Greater Good Science Center, he wrote, "work becomes meaningful when you are using the best of yourself to strive toward a purpose, which creates both a sense of personal fulfillment and positive outcomes in the world around you."

If that still seems a little vague, there's a reason. Meaningfulness, like beauty, is in the eye of the beholder. *You* decide what personally fulfills you and creates a sense of purpose. Different people can find meaning in and from different things. In one study of doctors, for example, the majority rated patient care as the most meaningful as you might expect, but a full third put other aspects of their job, like research, in the top spot.

THE BIG THREE OF MEANINGFUL WORK

More important than defining meaningful work, of course, is actually finding it or making our work feel more meaningful. Again, the research offers various ideas, theories and studies, models and frameworks, but no simple answers. After digging into the science, however, three main themes seemed to keep coming up:

Purpose Beyond a Paycheck: The *Why* of Work

For the vast majority, the why is helping others in some way. In one study, when researchers asked what made someone's work meaningful, 70 percent said helping others and 16 percent said contributing to a greater good. For some professions (nurses, firefighters, teachers . . .), it's easy to recognize the meaningfulness of work. For the rest of us, it's easy to get caught up in the minutiae or challenges of a job or feel like your day-to-day tasks are so far upstream from any human impact that we question whether we're contributing anything meaningful at all. However, you can say that every job plays a role in making someone's life better in some way. And the more you can see and connect with that, with how your work serves or benefits others—and "others" can be anyone or anything you deem important and worthy—the more meaningful you're likely to find your job.

Positive Work Relationships: The *Who* of Work

In a sense, work is a microcosm of life, and just as positive relationships are a boon for well-being and can give our lives a sense of purpose and meaning, research suggests the same goes at work. We can all help make our workplaces and work culture kinder, gentler and more fun. We can all foster a sense of belonging, community and camaraderie, and give and get support (even if we're working from home more). And when we do that, we leverage all the good things and opportunities relationships bring, and studies show it delivers; it makes work feel more meaningful.

For example, a survey found that strong social support at work coincided with a 47 percent higher rating of meaningfulness. Another showed that helping others was the one behavior most closely tied to feelings of meaningfulness. Work friends also celebrate our achievements, which helps develop a sense of meaning. Beyond meaning, science shows good workplace relationships help us thrive in other ways: We're more motivated, engaged, happier and more satisfied with our jobs. Having good friends at work may increase employee satisfaction by 50 percent and make work more worthwhile and fun.

On her last day, my predecessor at *Woman's Day*, Susan Spencer, wrote the most touching goodbye post on Instagram that sums up the role work relationships play in how we feel about our jobs: "It will take a few days of processing, but I can say this: the people, the crew, my friends—they made this job the best ever. In 10 years I probably won't remember what we made, but I will remember who made it."

Capability and Accomplishment: The *How* of Work

Using your strengths, skills and talents to complete tasks, reach goals, add value or otherwise make a positive impact in any way is closely tied to meaning. Researchers found that meaningfulness often grew from a sense of pride and achievement—the satisfaction of a hard day's work and job well done. Those things breed confidence and self-worth. And other research suggests that confidence in your abilities, feeling capable of doing your job and doing well and having autonomy over how you do it all contribute to a sense of meaningfulness, too.

WORK FOR THE MOMENTS

No job or task feels meaningful 100 percent of the time. In that way, meaningful work is kind of like a great novel. Not every individual word may move you; rather, it's a poignant paragraph, plot twist or character, or how the book makes you feel. You have to take a moment to reflect and think about it. That's what creates a novel's impact. And it's true of work, too.

The researchers concluded that meaningfulness is most often felt or captured in moments, and it's up to us to look for them, recognize them, reflect on them and create them. And that's what the tips in this chapter help you do. They help you make and take moments that hit all three of the categories of meaningful work: Feel that your effort and you as a person have purpose and are helping others in some way; connect with your coworkers and create more fun, supportive, positive and mutually fulfilling interactions; and help you work smarter, not harder, so that you feel more engaged, confident and capable to do your job and succeed. You may only need to focus on one or two of the three, or maybe you need the deluxe package. Either way, the more you can find meaning in your work, the stronger the charge you'll get.

THE WORK CHARGE TOOL KIT

Look for Meaning and You'll Find It

Just as harnessing the power of gratitude requires only that you recognize what you appreciate in life, research suggests the simple act of reflecting on how your work improves someone else's life can flip a switch and help it feel more meaningful. That's it. So if you haven't already or recently, think about who or what your work benefits—whether you think in terms of the big picture or drill down to individuals doesn't matter. What does matter: connecting your role to some greater good for someone else.

During the pandemic, for example, grocery store staff, delivery drivers, janitors and other essential workers suddenly got a lot more of the props they (rightfully) deserved. That's great, but let it be a lesson for you: It shouldn't take a novel virus or anyone else to show you that your work matters and that you make an important impact on others' lives.

Do More of What Matters

Over the last few years, I've shifted how I spend my working hours. I now devote more to panel discussions, podcast interviews, TV appearances and the business side of things and delegate a bigger portion of the traditional pen-to-paper editing tasks. I still find editing meaningful—and still do it—but the shift plays to my extrovert strengths and has energized me in how it lets me connect with and help people more directly and makes me feel like I'm contributing more to the company's success.

The name for what I did/do: job crafting, a concept introduced by Amy Wrzesniewski, PhD, a professor at Yale, and Jane E. Dutton, PhD, a professor at the University of Michigan, that involves molding or reimagining parts of your job or completing tasks in ways that feel more personally engaging and meaningful. It's about subtly changing how you spend time or how you work so your day-to-day work falls more in line with your personality, strengths and values.

Few people are robots at work who—*bleep, blorp*—perform in the same exact ways day in and day out. You probably enjoy at least some leeway over your time. How can you subtly change the way you work or what you work on? Think about the crossing guard, whose basic job description requires only stopping cars and getting kids across the street. All the extras are an example of job crafting, and it's likely a big part of why she loves her work. For me, I thrive in social situations, so creating opportunities to get out from behind my computer has been a win-win for the company and me.

Yes, job crafting requires you to take the initiative and put out some initial energy. That's a good thing: Only you know what's meaningful to you, what lights your fire and what you're best at. Ideally your company or supervisor would help draw this out of you, but if you wait for someone else, you may be forced into their idea of meaningfulness. Or never even get there.

Take Advantage of Your Job

Most companies support charitable initiatives in some way. When I worked at Victoria's Secret, for example, the company encouraged us to read to school kids through a local literacy organization. For those of us who spent our days writing about push-up bras, reading to six-year-olds was the lift and support we all needed.

Research backs up the benefits of what's called corporate or employee volunteering. Along with the usual well-being boost from volunteering, company-sponsored opportunities increase feelings of job meaningfulness and work engagement, especially if the volunteer project is related to your job. Volunteering also improves employee morale and job performance and builds skills.

So find out what kind of good your company is up to, and if it resonates with you, sign up. Or talk to your supervisor about setting up a formal relationship or partnership with an organization that does. Ask to do it during business hours. If you're a stay-at-home parent, find something you can do with the kids. Get a group together and make it a team-building or social event.

Put Your Paycheck to Work

I have a friend who pretty much hates his job. He's in finance, and while it provides flashes of greater-good meaning—he helps clients stay financially secure—work is mostly a paycheck. However, it's not meaningless because he chooses to connect deeply with what that paycheck affords him and his family. That's where *he* derives meaning. And because of that, he's thrown himself into family life more than his career—home every night for dinner, helping with homework, coaching kids' sports teams.

Researchers may disagree, but I believe that if you can't find significant meaning in who you're helping and can't job craft your way to more meaning, take your job for what it is—a paycheck. The catch: Use that paycheck in part to find and bolster meaning in other areas of life. Use the skills you've gained to find purpose elsewhere. Actively choose to see your work as affording you the time, energy, knowledge and funds to make an impact on those you believe *are* worthy: like your family, a Little League team, a neighbor.

Not Working for Something? Work Toward Something.

Like my finance friend, another pal is in a similar boat. She finds work somewhat meaningful; however, it evaporates in the face of toxic management, unrealistic expectations, a near-constant threat of layoffs and a host of other issues. She needs a change, and that's her long-term goal. But she decided to stick it out for a while to set herself up for her next move. And as such, she's hyperfocused on learning new skills and growing her network so that she can better position herself for success. Recognizing that helps give this job more meaning and helps keep her going.

The point is, if you truly need a change but aren't ready or can't right now, find meaning in how your job can propel you. Clichés like "Start before you're ready!" or any other sound bites about not putting your dreams on hold make for good Instagram fodder, but there are times when the best thing you can do is wait. Like a chess player, think about moves you can make at work now to improve your chance of success or set you up to win big in the future. There's meaning to be found in strategically helping yourself get to where you want to be.

Pivot When Purpose Runs Dry

My buddy Jerry used to be a hedge fund partner. Although financially flush, he was emotionally drained. Was his job meaningful? Sort of; he valued his experience and knowledge, as well as what his paycheck afforded him and his family. Over time, though, it felt more like he was only helping the wealthy print money. He was good at his job, but the success didn't matter so much anymore. And he himself had made more money than he needed. So he quit.

For work to be meaningful, it has to align with your own personal values and worldview. When the *why* of your job—the benefit you see your work bringing to others or yourself—diverges from what's important or worthwhile to you, it's probably time to jump ship. Jerry no longer valued helping the rich get richer. It's not that they didn't deserve help or the job wasn't worth doing; it had lost meaning and wasn't worth it *for him*.

So Jerry went out on his own and began investing in people and things that *were* meaningful to him. He partnered on a string of healthy neighborhood restaurants that boosted small-town economies, created community hangouts and provided space for local fundraising. He helped another friend who had endured unthinkable tragedy realize his dream of opening his own gym. Jerry actively focused on some of the same things he did in his old job—investing, making money—but it felt way more meaningful. Even better? Jerry ultimately developed a strong sense of community and close friendships that he says he had never really experienced in his personal or professional life until this point. Winning!

Treat Everyone the Same—with Respect

Obvious, right? Kind of like hearing you should drink more water. And yet, just as tons of people walk around dehydrated and need reminding that coffee and wine don't count, A-holery runs rampant, especially at work. And it can rob you and others of meaningful relationships at work and do a lot of harm overall. Research shows when people don't feel valued, appreciated, respected or listened to, they report a lack of energy and other negative effects both on the job and after quitting time. Being an A-hole can also circle back and negatively impact you, your performance and the culture as a whole.

But here's the rub: We might not always realize when we're being the A-hole. I recently attended an allyship seminar organized by Hearst and had the honor of learning from Chelsea C. Williams, a diversity, equity and inclusion speaker and the founder and CEO of College Code, an organization that helps companies retain diverse talent. Over the Zoom meeting, many of us got a long-overdue and important education in microaggressions. Essentially, we all hold implicit biases and stereotypes about so many things, and especially around race. Microaggressions are often how these biases come out: Our words, attitudes, facial expressions, gestures, body language, tone, behavior and so much more—including our silence—can marginalize and be deeply offensive and damaging to our coworkers, friends, relationships and the workplace as a whole, even if that's not our intention.

It's essential to educate ourselves about biases and microaggressions around race—and to actively recognize, acknowledge and fight against them—but don't stop there. Chelsea shared a very personal story with me on a follow-up call about her time on Wall Street. Every Monday a coworker would blurt out in a team meeting, "So, Chelsea, what did you do this weekend? Let me guess: You went to church" or "Chelsea is the Holy Roller—she went to church." It escalated to the point where Chelsea avoided all conversations about her weekend, feeling faith-shamed. The bottom line: It's on all of us to think before we speak, smirk, shrug, joke or remain silent. It's on all of us to notice and call out microaggressions, whether in the moment or after the fact. We don't need any more A-holes in the office.

Another thing to remember: Everyone's job, whether they're in the C-suite or part of the basement mail crew, serves a purpose. Everyone deserves to be seen and hear words like *hi, please* and *thank you*. No matter what. I cannot tell you how many people I've come across who take a different approach or only remember this when convenient.

I've also seen firsthand how energizing and meaningful it is when those in senior positions carpet-bomb the workplace with respect and weave it into the culture. When I worked at *Self*, then-editor Lucy Danziger made everyone feel like more than a cog in the machine: Generous with attention, thoughtful in her words and always on your side (even if she disagreed with you!), she made us feel like we and our work mattered, which motivated us to work harder. So make a point to tell everyone, especially those saddled with the most thankless tasks, "I appreciate you." Include others in conversations and solicitations for ideas and input. Smile and say hello. These simple acts go a long way.

Put People First, Work Second

Right before I started my gig at *Woman's Day*, the new digital director told me she needed surgery and would be out for six weeks. My initial thought: *This is going to screw me.* It's normal to operate with blinders on and think first about how things affect us, and it's easy to forget that coworkers have lives outside of work that aren't conducive or convenient for your plans.

Thankfully I caught myself. My coworker needed empathy and compassion first; no one wants hip surgery! It hurts! She needed someone to help her figure out how to recover *and* ensure work got done. I've been on her side before—with sick kids, a sick dad, my own pneumonia, the need for a mental health day. When we minimize or ignore what coworkers are going through outside of work, or if they're forced to soldier on or over-compartmentalize, it creates conflict between their two "lives." And research suggests that can lead to feeling less energized at or about work and reduced feelings of meaning, which hurts everyone. We also miss opportunities to foster better relationships at work and help colleagues in ways that can make our own job feel more meaningful.

You can't enable people who will take advantage of your kindness, of course, nor do you need to run yourself ragged covering for a coworker or have long heart-to-hearts if that's not in your emotional bandwidth. I'm saying that a little grace and understanding is fertilizer for work relationships and a positive work culture. A supportive word or note can mean the world to a coworker and do you both good.

If You Can't Say Something Kind, Zip It!

After I found a publisher for this book—a longtime dream and the result of more than a year of hard work—I had a colleague tell me my book wouldn't sell and wouldn't be worth my time. I had another tell me the concept and content were played out. In both instances, I stood there thinking, *WTF?* I didn't expect a parade, but I certainly didn't expect to be run over by a semitruck of negativity.

Although these are extreme examples, rude comments or backhanded compliments sneak into work conversations all the time. And they usually come from a place of insecurity or jealousy. It's not uncommon for us to feel that if someone else wins, it means we lose. Or that someone else's success diminishes our shine. Resist that thinking. Instead, recognize and accept your emotions—insecurity, envy, jealousy, whatever. They're powerful and totally normal. Also recognize that you can feel their fire without burning someone else's house to the ground.

Instead, explore what's fueling the flames. When I'm hit with jealousy, I try to see it as a gift or at least a message. Is it trying to tell me something about myself—what I want, what I'm valuing at the moment, where I think I might be falling short? Then I put my fire into addressing *that*.

Give Out Gold Stars

When GoodHousekeeping.com hit 45 million unique digital page views, Kate Lewis, the company's chief content officer, gave us all pencils that said *Best Day Ever*. It was a small and simple gesture, but it felt just as the research suggested it would: When we're recognized, valued and appreciated, it helps work feel more meaningful and we feel more engaged. Recognizing accomplishments is good for the person giving kudos, too. It's a form of gratitude and allows everyone to savor the good, which strengthens relationships and overall good vibes.

You can't necessarily control how well or often your boss or coworkers acknowledge success or hard work, but you *can* always shine a light on others, no matter your rank. For example, I've emailed head honchos to congratulate them on awards and messaged the whole office highlighting the work of amazing assistants. That light then reflects back on you and helps create a culture and environment where recognizing people and their accomplishments is the norm. And that floods the entire workplace (virtual or real) with sun.

Appoint Yourself Workplace CSO

Whether you're in a leadership position or not, look for ways to up the fun factor among your colleagues—or at least buy into someone else's attempt. I used to work with a guy who would rally the office around a March Madness pool. John would set up the game online, give us all baller nicknames and send out hilarious update emails after each set of matchups. I knew nothing about basketball, never watched the tournament and do not gamble, but I loved playing. During those weeks, the energy around the cubicles felt different; the game fostered a special kind of camaraderie and sense that I was part of the group and in on the fun.

Big sporting events create easy opportunities to build camaraderie, but you can do it through any type of game or shared focus on something fun or exciting. Think games or pools around award shows or what everyone is watching on TV. Even DIY games work, like the "plank-offs" we used to have with my *Self* coworkers. These things take otherwise superficial water cooler (or Slack) chat to a fun new level—and even though there might only be one winner, everyone wins.

Show Off Your Company Pride

Polyester golf shirts with the company logo aren't winning anyone style points, but there's something to be said for repping your job, employer or profession in a public way. Think about it: We proudly don gear that touts our alma mater, kid's school, sports teams, favorite bands. It shows the world what's meaningful to us and identifies us as a fan or part of that tribe. Shouldn't we, at least ideally, want to feel that way—proud, excited—about what we do or where we work? Repping it publically can help you connect more to those feelings.

Thankfully, a golf shirt isn't the only way to go about it. You needn't even be so obvious. I'm known for my monthly manicures inspired by the covers of my magazines; it's a super-fun way to rep my work and lets me proudly talk up the cover and content inside.

Go the Extra Mile for Milestones

Celebrating birthdays and other personal milestones may seem superfluous, but it sends the message that work isn't all about work and that people matter beyond their performance. Just don't force it. If you work/worked in an office, chances are you experienced at least one painful Zoom happy hour or virtual party during lockdown. Whether we'll ever celebrate in conference rooms again, who knows; regardless, follow this rule of thumb: Keep video conference parties small and conference room parties big—and both infrequent and as fun and meaningful as possible.

The Good Housekeeping digital team knows what's up: Before the shutdown, they schooled our whole floor in the art of the office party. Rather than individual celebrations, which get tiresome, force small talk and feel obligatory, they throw one big monthly birthday bash everyone can look forward to, complete with a theme, decorations, fun treats and, best of all, entertainment: a funny slideshow of that month's birthday crew.

Bring More of Yourself to Work

We can't build meaningful relationships or help work feel personally mean-ingful if we don't share who we really are with our coworkers. The trick is finding small and simple ways to let others into your world—your sense of humor, what's important to you, your likes and dislikes. Not everyone will join your fan club, no biggie. Still, opening up makes it easier to connect with everyone, which will be even more important for those of us who end up working remotely at least some of the time post-pandemic.

For example, I used to work with an advertising rep known as the "citrus guy" because he kept a bowl of oranges on his desk for the taking. People loved him for this generous gesture, and because he loves citrus, it was a way of sharing something about himself that also invited connection and conver-sation. Try it: What do you like and want to be known for at work? Food was always a good one, and now maybe it's a giant vat of hand sanitizer or tacking up a funny meme or inspirational quote.

You can even try a virtual version of this. Put a different quote or picture at the bottom of your emails or try different backgrounds or fun outfits for your Zooms. My go-to: personalized out-of-office replies. Who decided those things had to be so formal and boring? When I don't have a chance to answer someone, that's exactly when I want to make more of a personal, good im-pression. So I share something about me and try to deliver a smile to the sender's face. One recent one:

> Yay! You found me, but I'm OOO until Tuesday, October 22. I'll be slooooooooow on email, but if you miss me, tag along on social at @meaghanbmurphy.
>
> Note: I will give preferential response time to all emails including the name of your favorite Halloween candy!

I know I certainly get impatient when I can't get a quick reply because someone's OOO. These messages help counter that reaction. Rather than feeling put off or annoyed, I hope the sender sees me as a (gasp!) human with a life outside of work who *also* cares about those she works with.

Talk to People—with Your Actual Voice

Email, Slack, text—all straight-up gifts to humanity. Except in how they tend to keep us from actually making meaningful contact with humanity. Once in a while, instead of letting your fingers do the talking, pick up the phone or, if you can, walk over to someone's desk. These more personal inter-actions do all sorts of good things for your energy—and they're more import-ant than ever when working remotely.

Talking to coworkers might even help you do your job. Research suggests people are a lot more willing to do something when asked face-to-face (or, I'd imagine, screen-to-screen) compared to over email or text. One study pegged it at an incredible *thirty-four times* more effective; it showed asking six people for a donation in person netted roughly the same results as sending an email to 200. So, while I have certainly been in meetings that could have been emails, we might be better off if some of our emails were meetings, chats or phone calls.

Forget Work-Life Balance

The idea of balance was a joke even before the coronavirus shutdown and now, in the midst of it, well, it's so funny I could cry. (No, really.) Here's the problem with balance: It implies some degree of equality or even distribution of energy, time and importance. Trying for that is like trying for perfection—and we all know how that turns out. My job will never be as important as my family, but I sometimes *have* to sacrifice Team Murphy because my job is *also* important. Plus, the demands of life/family and work are so different and shift on a dime. How the heck can you keep score when everybody's playing different games and the rules keep changing?

You don't. I'm not the first to recognize that the concept of balance is crap, of course. Researchers like Steger, the expert on meaningful work, and business leaders including Jeff Bezos, have all talked about work-life *harmony* instead, where different parts of life (work, family, faith, fitness/health, hob-bies, etc.) function like instruments in an orchestra, all playing their part to create beautiful music—i.e., well-being, health, happiness, a good life.

That's a nice analogy, but I think the idea of synergy is better. Maybe it's semantics, but to me, harmony implies all the elements stay mostly separate, doing their own thing—a violin and cello can't share strings, for example. Synergy allows for separation *and* the combining or sharing of resources or elements when doing so adds even greater value. That's what I strive for; I *want* different parts of my life to understand the others so they can cooperate, not only play together in the same orchestra. Because that helps me feel stronger, more equipped and like the whole, complex, multifaceted person I am.

I don't have perfect answers on how to achieve synergy—and I definitely don't always succeed at it. And what success looks like is a personal thing dependent on an infinite number of factors. There is one main thing that has helped, though.

Bring Your Work Home and Vice Versa

I was at the salon once, my highlights setting under foil, when my colorist came over to introduce her husband over FaceTime. She said she likes him to see her in action, meet her clients and share this (big) part of her life. It struck me as so sweet—and similar to what Pat and I try to do with our kids. We bring them to work and talk openly and honestly about our jobs so they understand that our time away is important, why (and when) we have good days and why (and when) we're struggling on bad ones. Likewise, at work, I talk about my family. I talked about my dad's death. I talk about the importance of my morning workouts and family getaways and this book.

However you can, find ways to integrate and connect other parts of your life with your job. It will help you feel more like a person (versus a worker bee or robot), and everyone will better understand who you are. That allows all your different parts not only to coexist, it helps them cooperate more effectively. For me, that looks like my kids being much more chill when I have to spend the weekend prepping for a TV segment or take a call on the way to soccer practice, and my coworkers are more understanding when I decline an invite for a 6 p.m. happy hour.

Be a Hard-Ass About Boundaries

While blurring the lines between work and life help you in some ways, when it comes to the nitty-gritty of actually *doing* work, full-on compartmentalization can save your energy and sanity. Years ago, I knew a mom who kept her nanny cam feed open on her desktop and constantly fielded texts from home. It was hard to watch and torture for her to straddle these two worlds all day long—sort of what this shutdown has felt like for many of us working parents.

Whoever said you can have it all just not at the same time was perhaps talking big picture, but it applies to the day-to-day, too. You often *need* to completely shut out other parts of life so you can fully focus on work and vice versa. That means, when you're working, be fully present *to work*, including presetting parameters around potential overlap if needed—like scheduled check-ins with the kids or babysitter. Likewise, when home, *be home* as much as possible, whether you designate phone-free hours or otherwise shut off work. Ironically, the more rigid you are under normal circumstances, the easier it may be to be flexible when absolutely necessary.

It's not easy, and during the pandemic many of us didn't have a choice but to multitask (poorly, in my case). And the experience made the need for strict boundaries crystal clear. Keeping my fingers in all these pots at once wasn't fair to anyone, most of all me; it kept me from fully doing what energizes me and from being my true self—the woman who is present and engaged with her kids *and* the one who takes pride in and enjoys her work and derives great satisfaction and meaning from it.

Build a Village, Not an Island

I don't do it all, I do it almost. And by *it*, I mean *everything*. I'm lucky to have a village (who I missed *hard* during the shutdown) that picks up the slack—a great babysitter, two involved grandmas, a cleaning lady, friends, a husband who cooks, a competent team at work. Even if you don't have a demanding job or kids, we need village-esque support. Even if you're a stay-at-home parent and work *is* home. Actually, especially if you're a stay-at-home parent, for whom "work" can feel like a 24/7 gig. I know a lot of moms who believe they should be able to take care of everything—it's their job after all! But then who's taking care of you?

These days, research suggests moms spend more time with their kids than ever before (yay!) *and* that we're more stressed and less happy while caretaking than in the past (nay!). Yet research shows it's not the quantity of time you spend with your littles that benefits them most, it's the quality. So if you're exhausted or stressed because you're overextended or burned out, you're not doing you, your kid, your work or anything else any favors.

There's so much more to say on this topic than I can cover here—and so many nuances and bigger-picture issues at play, especially with childcare. But take these few tips to heart:

Shamelessly Ask for and Accept Help

If you can afford a babysitter once in a while or a cleaning service, grocery delivery or anything else that frees up time and/or mental space for you, and you don't take advantage of it, why not? Are you valuing less important things over your energy? Can you look at your budget and reallocate something?

And if your funds are truly tight (or even if they're loose, we all find ourselves strapped for time or energy sometimes), try this radical strategy: Ask for help, because you're likely to get it; research shows we seriously underestimate how willing people are to do us a favor. So talk to a fellow parent or a friend about taking your kid sometimes. Or barter—trade off dinner prep or babysitting so you each get time to yourself.

Along the same lines, if someone *offers* help, *take it*. Do not "feel bad"— you've won the lottery! I've heard so many women say they feel bad when offered kindness. Think how silly that is: It ruins the experience for you and diminishes the kindness of the person offering help. Likewise, don't wave off an offer because you think it's insincere. It is not your job to parse someone's motives. Wouldn't we all benefit from being more honest with each other? That can't happen if we don't take people at their word. Accept the favor, express heartfelt gratitude, then do what you need/want to do. Period.

Trust Your Village

If you get or hire help of any form, for it to truly boost your energy, you have to give up some control. Yes, that can be extremely scary or hard, especially when the stakes are as high as kids. For example, if you get a babysitter or a friend to watch your kid and you dictate every second of time or worry and check up on them often, you haven't lightened your load, you've added a new one.

We trust bus drivers and train conductors to safely get us places. We trust restaurants not to poison us. We trust so many people we've never even met with lots of different things. Trust yourself! Trust that you've done due diligence and whoever you're trusting is trustworthy and that you've made your needs and expectations clear. Will everything always go perfectly or exactly how you want? Probably not. They'll probably still be perfectly fine.

It may even go better than planned. Research on micromanaging and meaningful work suggests that when people feel empowered to do their jobs *their* way, it benefits everyone. Even in stressful jobs (ahem, nannies and daycare staff), those with freedom and control over their work and decisions are healthier and happier. Isn't that what you want from, say, a babysitter? On the other hand, micromanaging kills morale and productivity and increases the chance that the person and those around them (i.e., your kids) will be unhappy and dissatisfied. And they're more likely to quit. Micromanagers (i.e., *you* if you don't trust your village) are also at a higher risk for burnout.

Support Your Supporters

Along with trusting your village, show them they matter—through gratitude, respect, kindness and every other way possible—and everything will go much more smoothly. That means communicate well and give people the same level of support and recognition they give you or that you want. At the minimum, recognize birthdays and holidays, be respectful, considerate and generous. In other words, be a decent human.

I have a friend who tried to be all those things for her kids' babysitter, who, it seemed, appreciated the autonomy, trust and bonuses. And it earned my friend loyal and dependable childcare, and her kids got a loving, engaged caregiver. On the other hand, the family this babysitter worked for after my friends' kids were grown nickeled-and-dimed her at every turn, often showed up late and wouldn't even salt the icy walkway for her in the winter. Two weeks in, she was unhappy and looking for another job.

Ask for What You Need

What would help you feel like you are or could be achieving more or more meaningful goals? What would help you feel less stress and more "hell yes!" about work (i.e., productive, engaged, satisfied)? Have you ever thought to ask for those things in concrete terms?

I spoke at a conference for working moms where one of the panelists urged women to shoot for the moon when negotiating work arrangements, and not only in terms of pay and title—in flexible hours, responsibilities, collaboration and support, mentorship opportunities, even simple stuff like a good office chair. Later, an advertising executive stood up and told everyone what happened when she did exactly that: Burned out, she had decided to resign, and when she did, her employer asked what it would take for her to stay. With nothing to lose—she'd already quit—she asked for a "preposterous list of demands." They agreed to everything.

Let her be your inspiration. Even if you don't want to resign and even if you like your job, if you've proven yourself valuable, you've earned more equity than you might think. At the very least, you've earned the right to ask for what will help you do your job more effectively, enjoyably and synergistically with other life priorities.

So buck up, recognize the value you bring and make it incredibly easy for your manager to say yes to whatever you're asking for, whether it's flexibility or taking on new responsibilities or doing your job differently. Here's what to bring to the meeting:

- **Specific, thoughtful and realistic requests.** You might think open-ended asks or conversations send the message that you're agreeable and flexible. What you're really doing: creating work for your supervisor if she has to figure out details or problem solve. And that can trigger a lightning-speed "No, sorry."
- **Specifics on why you deserve what you've asked for.** Sell yourself, and as the cool kids say, bring the receipts. Remind your boss why you're such a superstar and that it's in his or her best interest to keep you happy, productive and thriving.
- **Specific plans.** Even if your boss is receptive, she still has to make sure work gets done and answer to *her* boss or the HR policy or your coworkers. Tell her how you'll meet your job duties and arm her with talking points; explain why it's a win for her *and* you. You may not get everything you want, but don't let the chance of one *no* stop you from getting any *yes*es.

Hack Your Confidence
No matter how self-assured, well prepared or experienced you are, moments of self-doubt are normal. Maybe you freak out before a big meeting. Maybe

you're stricken with imposter syndrome. Whatever hijacks your self-esteem, some simple mental trickery can help shoot it down ASAP.

First, think about how everyone is rooting for you—it's how I prep before a big presentation, TV segment or anything else that makes me nervous. It's a simple trick, and common sense says that's kind of what's going on: Nobody *wants* you to waste their time or see you flub. They want to be wowed, entertained, hear a thoughtful comment, see you get the job done. It's in their best interest to root for you. I find that settling and energizing, even if they aren't mat-talking me like the squad from Netflix's *Cheer*.

Another trick: Keep a flattery file. Bosses, colleagues and work contacts have probably told you at some point that you and your work are amazing. Whether it comes via email, text, scribbled note or other form, save it in a folder on your computer or in your email. Snap a picture of a note or jot down what someone says and email it to yourself. Then, during a confidence crisis, review your file and come face-to-face with your fabulousness. I've been doing this for years, and recently, a former colleague randomly told me it works for her, too. Not only does it turn around a crap day, she said it reminds her to be extra generous with adoring emails to her own team.

Chase Challenges

There are moments we all need or want to coast in our jobs or careers. For me, it came at varying times when my kids were little and my dad was sick. When certain parts of life are a hot mess or soaking up inordinate amounts of brainpower and energy, a boring work routine and doing enough to get by are as good as gold.

However, if your confidence takes a dip, you start wondering whether you're achieving enough, or you question your role or just feel unmotivated and restless, it's possible you aren't being challenged or challenging yourself enough. With nothing tangible to strive for, there's little incentive to push yourself to achieve. And without a chance to rise to any occasion, it's harder to remind yourself how much you actually *can* achieve.

That's kind of how I felt at the end of my tenure at *Good Housekeeping*. I was proud of my achievements over the six years I was there. But it felt like I was starting to coast when I could have been racing. I wondered if I was doing enough. Then the opportunity to lead *Woman's Day* came up. Hello, challenge!

Lots of people thought I was nuts for jumping at the job considering print magazines (not to mention OG editors like me) are an endangered species. Plus, the brand needed an overhaul. Didn't matter. After my first meeting and an overwhelming data dump, I felt completely reenergized. Sure, there was a chance I'd fail no matter how hard I tried, but somehow the only thing running through my mind was, *I can't wait to surprise everyone.*

Bottom line: If your confidence is teetering, force yourself to jump into a new challenge and prove to yourself and everyone else you can fly. I've always looked up to people who fully embraced uncertainty and hard, new or different challenges. (Shout-out to Andra, my right hand at *Woman's Day*, who took the job during a pandemic, when I couldn't officially give her a title or salary bump.) They aren't always the people who start out the most confident, but they usually end up being the most successful.

Find Ways to Save the Day—or Profits, Morale or Something Else

As the longtime textiles director at the Good Housekeeping Institute, Lexie Sachs was responsible for testing things like sheets and towels, awarding the Good Housekeeping Seal to the best products and helping readers make smart buying decisions. Then, as the magazine industry changed, and as profits narrowed and revenue sources shifted, it became clear that boosting digital traffic was a necessity to keep the lights on.

With GHI's reviews already online, Lexie turned her scientist brain to figuring out how to drive more eyeballs their way, even though this was well outside her job scope. She researched search categories, analyzed traffic patterns and became an SEO ninja, and soon GHI reviews were landing at the top of search results. Traffic and clicks spiked, new revenue streamed in and her work won her a company award.

The lesson here: If you're stuck in a rut or feel like your job lacks meaning, look for opportunities to shine. Ask yourself what *you* can do, where you can add value, what problem or challenge you can use your skills to solve or what improvements you can make—even if they're outside your job duties or seem relatively small. Doing so can feed your sense of capability and accomplishment in ways that will make work feel more meaningful.

Give Yourself a Break

Inside the *Good Housekeeping* kitchen lives a magical thing called the Fresca fridge, which is stocked with cans of the refreshing (and underappreciated, IMO) grapefruit soda. It's just far enough from where the editors sit that it requires an almost-as-refreshing three-minute stroll to get to it. While the fridge itself is a luxury, the Fully Charged powerhouses in the office know that the break "Fresca o'clock" provides is actually a secret weapon for staying productive, sharp and successful. (Aya Kanai, the former editor of *Marie Claire*, and I even had a virtual Fresca break during quarantine!)

No matter how much you think you can power through an hours-long task, piggyback smaller to-dos onto each other all day or fill every second between meetings, your brain does not function best in nonstop mode. Over time, your brain feels slower and your thinking seems jumbled. If you ignore the signs and push through, the quality of your work suffers and you get less done. However, if you take a few breaks throughout the day (around five to fifteen minutes each), the opposite is true, even after accounting for "lost" time.

All you have to do: Nothing. Let your mind wander. Go for a walk. Have a snack. Have a Fresca. Stretch. You know those brilliant ideas or aha moments that pop into your head in the shower or right before you fall asleep? You get them because your brain finally got a break, which it used to process information and form new ideas. Give it that same kind of break *while* you work—and no, answering emails or doing less challenging tasks aren't breaks. Truly bench your brain so it can rest and reset.

BEWARE THE ENERGY VAMPIRES

Burnout

Meaningful work can be a powerful charge, but it has the potential to blow your fuse. Think about it: If you feel work is super important/meaningful and you're extra committed, you might easily find yourself doing, caring and working more . . . and more and more until you're overdrawn at the energy ATM. That's burnout: mental, physical and emotional exhaustion, often with a side of apathy or negativity.

So avoiding burnout requires a careful balancing of your energy bank account, setting withdrawal limits and priority spending on what pays dividends—things you do purely for fun or relaxation that charge you. Try these tips:

- **Take ALL the vacation days.** Half of Americans don't use all theirs, and when they are off, many are on—emailing or working in some capacity. Not smart; research shows vacations are essential for preventing burnout, as well as for success, productivity and otherwise feeling energized and happy at work and in life. Fun and rest is as much an investment in your emotional health and professional success as the work you do.
- **Shut down after fifty-five hours a week.** Long hours may earn you a reputation as a hard worker, but it might be for nothing. Research suggests productivity drops significantly after fifty hours a week, and after fifty-five hours, it drops so much you're better off giving up.
- **Choose hobbies and downtime carefully.** You'll feel more refreshed on Mondays if you use weekends to offset the demands on your brain and energy during the workdays, according to research. For example, if you flex creative muscles at work, spend days off doing non- or less-creatively-taxing stuff. Or, if your job is super-social, plan for alone time.

Perfectionism

Although perfectionism can live in different realms, for many of us, it pops up most around work and raising kids. What is perfectionism anyway? Elizabeth Gilbert called it "a high-end, haute couture version of fear." That quote truly gets at the heart of what's going on when we kill ourselves trying to meet some (impossibly high and subjective) standard—fear of failure, of being exposed as an imposter, of losing work or screwing up our kids. But those fears are almost always constructed by us, not based in reality, and their energy cost is high: increased risk of depression, anxiety and other mental health disorders, plus anger and irritability.

If your perfectionism feels debilitating, which it can be, it's worth seeing a therapist. Otherwise, when you feel yourself chasing perfection, remind yourself that your experience, skills and knowledge got you where you are—you are not an imposter. Remind yourself that you learn and earn experience through mistakes and getting feedback. Trying for perfection right out of the gate is like trying to find your way to the bathroom, blindfolded and after five shots of tequila.

Then set limits or boundaries—on the amount of time you work, on what you set out to do, whatever. Lower your standards a smidge. My friend the author, speaker and entrepreneur Marie Forleo uses this rallying cry: Progress not perfection. I think of that often, along with a few other *P* words to strive for, like *potential* (to learn or feel energized), *positive experience* (rather than an exhausting and futile one) and *proficiency* (good enough is good enough).

Then, finally, give yourself a reality check. If you do reach some pinnacle in your mind—maybe not even perfection, but close enough—ask yourself: Will you have actually succeeded or will your performance truly be "perfect" if whatever you produced or accomplished left you stressed, sick and un-happy, forced you to sidetrack other things or set you back in other ways? Are those worthwhile trade-offs for not facing fear?

Early in my career, I chased perfection a lot at work. I'd stay late every night obsessively tweaking copy. After having kids, suddenly I couldn't stay late. I had to reshuffle how I spent my time. And you know, the quality of my work didn't suffer. If anything, it improved because I was getting more feed-back and saw it as that, not an affront to my effort. If you can find value in acceptable, perfection won't seem so important.

Toxic Colleagues and Bosses

They can be know-it-alls or do-nothings, steal your ideas, talk over you, be overly competitive, condescending, rude or radioactive in some other way. Whatever type of toxicity you're dealing with, research from Harvard Busi-ness School and elsewhere suggests they hurt productivity, morale, job satis-faction and your health. Think of them like an injury; they're painful to deal with and make things harder, but with a few adjustments, you can manage the damage and come back stronger. Here's what to try:

- **Keep things professional.** Personal relationships and interactions serve you well at work *except* with energy vampires. Email, text and Slack—as good as a garlic necklace. Also, give and request only as much information as is needed to do your job.

- **Ignore the bait and bite your tongue instead.** Relationship expert Terri Cole calls it being unprovokeable; whatever nastiness someone spews— or tries to drag you into—it's not worth getting involved in, nor is it your problem to fix.
- **Kill 'em with kindness.** When Michelle Obama talked about going high when the others go low, I took it to mean also go kind, go generous, go helpful. Even if it kills a little piece of your ego in the process.
- **Hustle until the haters ask if you're hiring.** Staying above the fray gives you more brain space, energy and focus to do your job and do it well. That's a powerful force field against toxicity—so powerful, haters may soften up and want in.
- **Go on the record.** Managing toxic people does not mean letting them walk all over you. If needed, talk to your boss or HR. Avoid bad-mouthing the person; rather, stick to your experiences and how this person impedes your productivity or well-being.

MURPHY'S LAWS

Fast-track hard conversations

I once edited an interview with Shonda Rhimes in which she dropped a gold mine of advice. The one nugget I now follow constantly: Have hard talks ASAP. Don't wait for a "good" time. Don't wait to see if things sort themselves out. Don't wait so you can obsess over the right approach. It's going to be tough regardless, and all waiting does is weigh you down with extra anxiety or fear.

Respond to every email

Even if it's just a quick "Got it. Thanks!" Yes, it's time consuming. It's also a professional courtesy and special brand of kindness that makes a heck of an impression and may help you later. Whenever I'm tempted to delete emails en masse, I remember the PR rep who once introduced me by saying, "Meaghan *always* responds to my emails—it's the best." That's a reputation I want.

Say "I do" to a work wife or work husband

While all work friends help you feel good about work, it's even better to have at least one extra-special someone, roughly the same seniority, who always has your back and whom you trust the most. Even Steve Swartz, the CEO of Hearst (which owns *Woman's Day*), said he had a few; I asked during a roundtable discussion and he spoke beautifully about what their support and guidance means to him.

Be a connector

Helping others is strongly linked to meaningful work. One simple way to do it: opening doors. When I first had the idea for this book, for example, a friend graciously offered to connect me with an agent. The rest is history. The more you help connect people, the more you get back in unexpected ways.

Clear physical and digital clutter

Our work environment impacts how we think, feel and behave, and clutter can trigger stress, anxiety and lack of focus. The first thing I do before getting down to business: clear my in-box and clean my desk.

Take it easy . . . or hard

Although productivity experts disagree on what you should tackle first to be most productive—easy tasks or hard ones—I'm in the easy-first camp; it gives me what's called a "completion high," which builds momentum and confidence. I also like having fewer items on my to-do list. Experiment with both to see what works best for you.

The Health Charge

The groundwork for all happiness is good health.
—LEIGH HUNT

*I*f you've gotten this far, you've seen that to live Fully Charged, you have to get out there and, well, live—actively participate in life and do things that spark happiness and generate positive energy. And to do anything beyond the bare minimum, beyond the things you already do, it requires a certain degree of raw, physical energy and endurance, plus mental and emotional stamina. That's what the Health Charge delivers.

Think of it this way: All the other charges can give you the energy you need to believe you can run a 5K or even a marathon. They can motivate you to put together a training schedule and feel pumped and ready to start running. They can even give tired legs a boost mid-run. But what I've learned through both my own experiences and as a certified personal trainer, is that the other charges alone won't get you across the finish line. You need physical health and endurance to actually carry you the distance.

Living a Fully Charged Life is a lot like an endurance event, and physical activity and quality sleep literally give you energy—the energy needed to participate *and* win.

What's so cool is that along with physical energy, the Health Charge produces a powerful mental and emotional charge. Exercise and sleep both slay stress, giving you extra patience and headspace to deal with the road-blocks and detours of life. They balance your mood and flood your brain with feel-good chemicals that help you enjoy and appreciate the scenery along the way. And this combo of physical, mental and emotional energy makes you unstoppable.

I couldn't do half of what I do in a day if I didn't work out regularly and log around seven hours of sleep a night. I might be able to give work my all, but I'd have little left for my family, friends, sanity, side projects and everything else that creates a life I love. Or I could give my family all my (limited) energy, but at work I'd be dragging my butt from meeting to meeting (or snoozing through my teleconferences) and dropping balls and turning down opportunities left and right. Heck, I probably wouldn't even have the option to turn down anything because I would have missed whatever event, meeting or extracurricular that opened the door or inspired me in the first place.

I refuse to make those trade-offs. Decide now to prioritize your health and you won't have to make them either. Because the alternative—choosing to be sedentary, treating sleep like it's optional—means choosing to put limits on your energy, happiness and life. It may not seem like that's what you're doing, but your choices will catch up to you. And the longer you wait, the fewer choices and the less potential for energy you have.

So much of our energy and mental state depends on our physical health, and what you do now can set off a chain reaction that either creates complications or opens you to opportunities.

Even beyond maximizing your day-to-day energy, consider all the unexpected things that knock you off your feet when you least expect it—illnesses, accidents, injuries, stress and emotional or mental strain. Hello COVID-19! You can't spend your life worrying you'll be stricken, but know this: The healthier you are when you're "healthy," the harder you can fight and the better shape you'll be in when something tries to take you down.

When I got pneumonia a few years back, the doctor said if my heart and lungs hadn't been in peak form from regular workouts, I'd have ended up in the ICU. Same with one of my besties and fellow fitness fan Candee, who beat breast cancer not once but twice, in part because of how strong she was (and still is) physically and mentally. Some of the first research to come out about COVID-19 even suggested people who exercised regularly were at lower risk for fatal complications.

HEALTH IS WEALTH, AND YOU CAN GET RICH QUICK

If you're currently not feeding your body and mind the activity and sleep it needs to be strong and energized, why not? Think about your reasons: Are they actually excuses in disguise? Because in the long term and big picture, chances are none of those things are as important, will make you feel as good or will prepare you as well for life and all its unknowns and uncontrollable variables as much as moving your body even a little most days and getting just a little more sleep.

For that reason, working out is a nonnegotiable for me. For years, I've been waking up at the butt crack of dawn five days a week and sweating for an hour—boot camp, yoga, Orangetheory, boxing, Pilates, indoor cycling. I'm not bragging; I'm saying this because exercise is as essential as breathing. It gives me the physical energy my life requires and keeps my mood up and emotions on an even keel, which helps me weather life's storms *and* take full advantage of every bit of sunny sky. Exercise is also true self-care. That hour in the morning is the one thing I consistently do that's 100 percent all about me. Of course I want to stay healthy for my family, but if I'm forced to skip a workout for whatever reason, it feels as if I don't matter as much—not okay!

DO IT YOUR WAY

You do not have to love exercise or work out like I do to get the Health Charge. It doesn't matter what you do or how long or where. If you never want to set foot in a gym, don't. Hate running? Join the club! Group fitness not your jam? That's cool—it's mine, and I'll explain later why you might want to give it a go, but you do you. However, to live Fully Charged you must move your body most days and in some way that gets your blood pumping and muscles working. And you must get enough sleep, which your body and mind need to rest, recharge, repair and process everything you've experienced in a day. Both are proven ways to help you live each day as the healthiest, most energized version of yourself.

Outside of that, you've got a ton of wiggle room to figure out exactly what exercise and sleep look like to you and how they fit into your life. You don't need to overhaul your entire schedule or swear off late-night parties or that blissfully quiet time after everyone's asleep and you finally get a moment to yourself. Most need only make a few tweaks and positive choices that put your health and energy first—not even all the time, just sometimes.

> **We get so many chances every day to make healthier, more energizing choices. Start by making just a few simple ones.**

Healthier choices may seem hard at first because they're different or because they force you to be different. However hard they seem, the energy you invest will pay off in huge dividends. I could nerd out on the science all day, since it's so convincing. But I'll keep things short and super-sweet.

MOVEMENT: THE MAGIC BULLET

You already know exercise is good for you. You learned about it in school or your doctor mentioned it. Maybe you've read articles. Perhaps your mother, sister, friend, Instagram feed or someone else in your orbit can't shut up about how great this or that workout is. (Guilty.) Let me cut through what may have become noise and explain a few things:

- **Exercise is the ultimate medicine and multivitamin.** Just about every doctor, mental health professional, health expert, life coach and otherwise successful, happy, Fully Charged person I've ever met asserts that exercise guarantees a wide range of both immediate and long-term physical and mental benefits. Exercise has even been proven more or as effective than a lot of medications currently being used to treat common conditions, including depression. It's also a pretty great insurance policy against a lot of ailments and diseases, including thirteen types of cancer. Yes, it is *that* good for you.

- **Exercise delivers the raw materials for energy.** Physical activity improves how efficiently your heart and circulatory system work. And better blood flow delivers more nutrients to cells that use them to produce energy. Physical activity also triggers the release of growth factors that help produce new mitochondria, the tiny organisms within cells that act as the cell's "power plants." It's mitochondria that manufacture adenosine triphosphate (ATP), the *actual liquid energy* that powers every cell in your body. So the more you have, the healthier and more functional your muscles, brain, heart, immune system and everything else in your body.
- **Exercise energizes emotions, too.** Physical activity controls your stress response, and it initiates the release of endorphins and other natural feel-good neurotransmitters in the brain like serotonin that boost feelings of well-being and other good vibes. And, of course, when you feel good and stress is under control, you tend to naturally feel energized, plus more open, friendly, focused and motivated.
- **Exercise = any type of activity.** From walking to sprinting, gardening to high-intensity interval training—anything that gets you moving and your heart pumping counts.

A Little Goes a Long Way

It's worth reiterating that to get all those benefits, you do not necessarily have to work out like a maniac. A study that measured people's activity levels, mood and how energetic they felt a few times a day found that when they were just a little more active during one check-in period, they reported feeling happier and more energized at the next check-in. They weren't necessarily even exercising in the traditional sense. Similarly, researchers at the University of Georgia studied healthy young adults with unexplained fatigue. After being active for just twenty minutes a day—even walking or casual biking—three times a week for six weeks, ratings of fatigue plummeted 65 percent. The participants also felt more energized and invigorated overall.

Additional studies show exercise boosts other measures of energy, like motivation and productivity. For example, on days people worked out at their office gym, they reported a 41 percent jump in motivation to work, plus said they were better able to concentrate and finish tasks. The scientists concluded that the emotional boost attained on exercise days was likely responsible.

While you'd be hard-pressed to find someone who finishes a workout and thinks, *Boy do I feel worse (or more stressed or blue) than before*, the long-term mental-health benefits of exercise are equally striking. Piles of research show how being active equates to a lower risk of depression and anxiety and higher levels of psychological well-being. One study that reviewed data from more than a million Americans found that regular activity is as good for well-being as a $25,000 per year salary hike. *Cha-ching!*

Another study from the University of Michigan shows just how little exercise you actually need to see changes in happiness. Researchers reviewed twenty-three different trials, pooled data from more than a half million people and found that those who exercised just ten minutes a day (or for longer periods on fewer days) were markedly happier than their couch potato peers. Of course, the more exercise people got, the bigger their happiness gains, up to 150 to 300 minutes a week. Even better, it didn't matter how people split up activity. You can do a little every day, break it up throughout the day, or log a longer workout a few times a week.

SLEEP: YOUR SUPERPOWER

Given all I do in a day, people always ask if I sleep. Hell yeah I sleep, and you should, too. It is a legitimate superpower that gives you mega energy, makes you smarter, stronger, happier and healthier—and we're all born knowing exactly how to do it. I cringe when someone talks about "needing" only like five hours of sleep, as if it's a point of pride or makes them superior. Nope. It's likely making them less productive, happy and healthy and more stressed. It's likely making everything feel harder. What they're really saying is they can *get by* on five hours. But why not get one or two more and thrive?

That's the message more and more business leaders and other objectively energetic, successful people have started spreading. *Yay!* Like Arianna Huffington, my sleep hero. It took collapsing from exhaustion in her office—the result of routinely logging only four to five hours per night—for her to make a change. And when she did, she says everything in her life improved. She became one of the first baller women to push for smarter conversations around sleep, to talk about its role in success (at work and in life) and to advocate for extra hours in bed rather than the office.

Don't Snooze? You Lose.

The research on sleep is unequivocal: Skimping even a little or not getting quality sleep makes you irritable and stressed, increases risk of depression, anxiety and burnout, messes with your immune system and can leave you overall dragging ass all day. On the flip side, one study even suggests that during a good night of sleep, ATP (what your cells use for energy) may flood areas of the brain you exercise the most during the day, helping replenish those cells.

You've probably experienced the effects of a rough night (or several) firsthand, so I won't waste time convincing you sleep is critical. What I *will* try to convince you to do: Prioritize sleep if you're not currently getting seven to nine hours a night. That's the range science suggests the vast majority of us need to be our healthiest and happiest. And the good news is you don't necessarily need to upend your entire life to get there—or at least close.

Research shows crazy-amazing benefits of getting just one extra hour of sleep per night. One hour! In one study, reporters at the BBC partnered with the University of Surrey's Surrey Sleep Research Centre to test what happened when people got either 6.5 hours a night for a week or 7.5 hours. Turns out, when subjects got less sleep, they struggled more with mental tasks, plus five hundred different genes associated with higher risks for disease and poorer stress management were affected. Getting more than seven hours a night kept those genes in check.

Another study put a price tag on an extra hour of z's. Researchers determined that going from six to seven hours a night is linked with a 16 percent bump in salary, which they reported was due to the improvement in memory and focus extra sleep provides. Other research shows an extra hour may energize you during exercise and improve athletic performance and lower your risk by a third of developing dangerous calcium deposits in arteries.

I could fill dozens more pages with eye-popping studies that convince you of the overwhelming benefits of exercise and sleep. But that's ultimately probably not what's going to get you to work out more or go to bed earlier. The actual secret to going from "OMG, yes, okay, I really want to get my butt in gear" to "OMG, *yaaaassss*! That workout rocked! See you tomorrow!" is in the how-tos. And when it comes to your health, making better choices and adopting new habits are most successful when those how-tos are as simple and straightforward as possible. So here we go . . .

THE HEALTH CHARGE TOOL KIT
Program Your On/Off Switch

Long ago I put my body on a sleep schedule, and now I pretty much automatically shut down by 10:17 p.m. and power back on, often without an alarm, at 5:03 a.m. (when I get up most mornings for workout classes). And I protect that schedule as if my life depends on it because, honestly, it does. In the past, when I left my bedtime open-ended, there was always *just one more thing* I wanted or needed to do. The trade-off was later nights, which turned into bleary-eyed mornings, caffeine-fueled afternoons, yawn-filled evenings and a cycle of low-grade exhaustion known as "getting by." When I really thought about what I was staying up for, those things rarely mattered as much as feeling good for morning workouts and everything else that followed, right up to about 10 p.m.

The thing is, getting restorative, restful sleep isn't only about making sure you log the requisite hours. Our circadian rhythm, which rules so many biological processes, especially sleep, thrives on predictability and routine. A study published in *Sleep* found that when two groups of people slept for 7.5 hours a night for a full month, the group that went to bed and woke up around the same time every day felt more alert and awake during the day than those who tucked in and got up willy-nilly. So while there are plenty of times for spontaneity, don't make your bedtime or wake-up time two of them.

To set my on/off switch initially, I worked backward from the time I would get up for the gym (5:03 a.m.) and figured I needed to be asleep by 10:03 to net a full 7 hours. But being asleep by 10:03 meant getting into bed before 10, and that felt too dang early. So I started getting ready for bed at 10 and crawled under the covers about 10 minutes later. Here, a few other tips to help you set your own schedule:

- **Balance what's best with your best.** Figure out what time you should turn in based on the time you need to get up, but allow for flexibility.

In my case, I'd love to get 7 hours every night instead of 6 hours and 46 minutes. But going to bed before ten didn't feel right. I didn't want to risk blowing up a good routine over fourteen minutes. What's more, your schedule can vary a bit. Sometimes I wake up earlier for an earlier fitness class, and on weekends I sleep until at least 6:30 to even things out. With sleep, as with so many other things, practicality beats perfection.

- **Consistency counts.** Sticking with a (mostly) regular sleep-wake schedule—even on weekends—makes it easier to fall asleep because it sets your circadian rhythm. And when your internal clock knows when it's time to downshift, it sets off the biological changes necessary to make it happen. A consistent routine before bed—washing your face, putting on moisturizer or whatever else you do before closing your eyes—also conditions your body and sends the signal it's sleepy time.

It took about three weeks before my body got on board with my schedule. Now, years later, I get twitchy if it's 10:14 and my face isn't washed and I'm not in pj's. My husband told me he sometimes asks, *"Can we just talk about [X] before you shut off?"* but if I've been horizontal for more than three minutes, there's a good chance I'm already passed out.

If you struggle with insomnia, tinkering with sleep habits and falling asleep isn't so easy, of course. Establishing and maintaining regular bed and wake times and following the same nighttime routine is a good place to start, though. Regardless, all this advice doesn't mean you can't sometimes stay out late or sleep in; just make sure whatever you're doing is 100 percent worth it.

- **Find your magic number.** You may need more than seven hours to feel your best—between seven and nine hours is the range—and it may take trial and error to find your sleep sweet spot. Go by how you feel when you wake up. Ideally you want your eyes to pop open just before your alarm, and to feel legitimately rested. If that's not happening after about seven hours asleep, shift your bedtime by ten or so minutes for a few nights at a time until you get there.

HOW MANY DAYS DOES IT TAKE TO CREATE A HABIT?

There are all sorts of claims about how long it takes for new habits to stick. Years ago at *Self*, an expert told me the magic number was nineteen days. Other sources claim it's twenty-one days. Another study determined it took an average of sixty-six days for an action to feel automatic. In general, though, the latest research suggests what we all instinctively know—that easy behaviors become habits faster, harder ones take longer—and lots of other factors play a role. What you can bank on: The more you do anything and the more you integrate a new habit into your existing lifestyle or habits, the faster it will become part of your routine and the easier it will eventually feel. Will it always be easy? Not necessarily. But it can become more doable or even automatic.

Quit Your Bedroom Shenanigans

A consistent bedtime and routine makes it easier to fall asleep and get enough shut-eye, but you'll get the sleep of your dreams if you treat your bedroom as a sacred space devoted only to sleep (with an exception for sex). That means no laptop or work bag, no piles of laundry, no cluttered nightstand or dresser reminding you of stuff you want or need to read or do or fix. Hide it all away in drawers, closets, the kitchen, the basement—anywhere but your bedroom. The rest of your house can be an unfinished to-do list, but a bedroom that's tidy sends your brain the message that it's a place to clear your mind and truly relax.

Secondly, and this is a tough one for so many, try to swear off TV and especially email, social media, Amazon Prime, Words with Friends or whatever else you're doing on your phone in bed. I know, I know, right before you doze off feels like the *only* time and place in a hectic day you can catch up on Facebook, scroll Insta or reply to emails in peace. I'm sorry to tell you, in the interest of your energy, do it elsewhere.

Even if you don't think your screen's blue glow is messing with you, science says otherwise. It suppresses melatonin, the naturally calming hormone your body produces that helps you fall and stay asleep and throws off your circadian clock. Plus, everything your phone feeds your brain keeps it churning away when what you need is a brain that's bored AF. Even if you might be able to fall asleep out of sheer exhaustion after scrolling (or, ahem, mid-scroll), sleep quality can suffer and you're likely to wake up feeling more groggy. Certainly read before falling asleep if that's part of your routine, but choose a dull or lighthearted book or magazine—actual print materials (remember magazines?!) don't seem to have the same effect as a device.

SLEEPY SECRETS

A clean and screen-free bedroom goes a long way toward better sleep, but if you're still having trouble shutting down or getting quality z's, consider trying these:

Caffeine cut-off

Caffeine blocks adenosine, a natural chemical that builds up in the brain throughout the day and makes you sleepy, and it can also take your body hours to fully flush the stimulant out of your system. If you're having trouble falling asleep when you need to, go for decaf starting in the early afternoon.

A 65-degree room

In order to fall asleep, your core body temperature must drop, which is tricky if the thermostat is jacked up to near-sauna levels. Sixty-five degrees seems to be the ideal temp for quality z's, according to the National Sleep Foundation. Then, adjust your sheet and blanket situation depending on how you feel.

Total darkness

As with scrolling, you may not realize the negative effects ambient light has until you experience how sweet sleep is without it. So try blackout curtains and unplug or cover up anything that glows. And if you make nighttime bathroom trips, invest in a motion-sensor nightlight. When you wake up in total darkness, the bathroom vanity feels like an interrogation lamp and it will jolt your body from sleep mode, making it harder to drift off afterward.

Lavender essential oil

While I'm not convinced oils do everything their proponents claim, I swear by a nightly spritz of lavender water on my pillow. It's one more step in my p.m. routine that tells my brain it's time to shut up and shut down. There's also actual science behind lavender's calming reputation: Research shows microscopic scent compounds may travel up your nose and block receptors in the brain for an "excitatory" neurotransmitter that otherwise makes you feel alert and awake, and it has helped some sleep better. (Note: Lavender can have estrogenic effects, so consult your doctor if necessary.)

A weighted blanket

A few friends and my own daughter (a notoriously awful sleeper) swear by weighted blankets, and although there's not a ton of science behind them, there is some. In one study published in the *Journal of Sleep Medicine and Disorders*, people with insomnia said that a weighted blanket made it easier to settle down to sleep, improved their sleep and helped them feel more refreshed in the morning. Researchers also noticed they slept longer and moved less during the night than with a standard blanket.

Binge-free TV

Watching TV for a few hours right before bed can make you feel more awake and is associated with poorer sleep, according to the *Journal of Clinical Sleep Medicine*. Best practice is to skip TV before bed altogether, but let's get real: That's usually when most of us get to cuddle up with our partners and zone out. I'm not about to give that up, but I do think about the trade-off when I'm tempted to hit "play next" after one episode.

Join the Dawn Patrol

If you already exercise consistently and your routine works for you, *stick with it* no matter when you sweat because the best time to work out is the time you actually work out! But when I hear people say they don't have time to exercise or can't keep a routine—which I hear *a lot*—my response is always: Give mornings a chance.

Early a.m. exercise is the secret sauce for fitting in fitness. Most of us have way more control over our time and attention first thing. If you have kids, they're (hopefully) asleep and you're (hopefully) not getting phone calls or emails for which the subtext is *reply ASAP*. You're also not yet engrossed in any tasks or feeling the tug of the bajillion or so other things that vie for your energy and attention after breakfast.

There's so much stuff and so many people that claim so much of our days—for better or worse—and it will almost always be easier to prioritize those distractions in the moment if you haven't yet fallen in love with fitness or made it a routine. *You* can own your morning! That's the rallying cry of *Women's Health* magazine, and it's a perfect quick, easy and actionable mantra. Beyond fitting in exercise, you're smart to sweat early for a few other reasons:

- **Exercise may feel easier.** Cortisol gets a bad rap as the "stress hormone," but under normal circumstances, it also naturally rises in the morning and gives us energy. Mentally, your willpower and self-control may also be stronger in the a.m. Here's why: Every tough decision (i.e., anything other than lying around eating bonbons) can chip away at your ability to make hard choices later. So if you always end up blowing off evening workouts, it could be because you spent *the whole day* doing the right (but hard) thing, and it's worn you down. (Scientists call it "decision fatigue.") With morning exercise, the only hard decision you have to make first is to get out of bed. And once you're up and at 'em, the rest is a piece of cake.

- **You'll feel more energized and sharp all day.** Given that exercise increases energy, helps manage stress and lifts your mood, sweating in the morning naturally revs you for your day. In one study, people who walked forty-five minutes in the morning were more active the rest of the day, too. Morning workouts also boost a growth factor that maintains and produces new brain cells, and they can increase memory and brain function in areas needed for attention, planning, prioritizing and decision making. And don't underestimate just how good it feels to accomplish something major before most people brush their teeth. That feeling breeds confidence that ripples into your day.

- **You'll sleep better at night.** Exercise helps you sleep better no matter when you're active by reducing stress and maintaining the normal, healthy buildup of hormones and neurotransmitters that initiate sleep. However, working out at 4 p.m. seems to reduce levels of melatonin come bedtime compared to doing the same workout at 9 a.m., according to a study in the *International Journal of Sports Physiology and Performance*.

EXCUSE-PROOF MORNING WORKOUTS

- **Start slowly. Set the bar low.** Rather than aiming for 5 a.m. five days a week right out of the gate, ease into a routine with, say, a twice-a-week goal and vow to stick with it for about three weeks. (I stick by the nineteen-days-to-a-habit theory!) You can do that!

It's only six early mornings out of nineteen days. Afterward, maybe you decide that's all you want to do. Great! Or maybe you love how you feel so much you add in another day.

- **Plan ahead.** On Sunday, decide exactly which days of the upcoming week you'll get up to work out and what exactly you'll do. Write it in your calendar. Sign up for a class—and prepay for it—or arrange to meet your walking buddy. Whatever it is, set it up and write it down. Research shows concretely planning in this way could double or even triple your chances of following through.

- **Set yourself up.** The night before, lay out your clothes and sneakers. Put your keys and bag by the door or set up what you need for a home session. Fill your water bottle, put out a snack, set the coffee maker, pre-apply toothpaste to your toothbrush. Make it *excruciatingly* easy to get up and out as quickly and as hassle-free as possible.

Sweat with a Squad

If you like working out solo, keep doing your thing. But you might be surprised by how much more motivated you are, how much more enjoyable it is and how much of an extra charge you get taking a class once in a while or teaming up with others. Energy is contagious regardless of the setting, and research suggests that during a workout it's no-joke as catchy as "Old Town Road."

In one study of stressed-out med students, for example, those who took group workout classes for six weeks felt less stressed overall and reported higher increases in quality of life (physical, mental and emotional) compared to students who jogged or lifted weights alone or with just one or two other people. Another study found that rowers' pain thresholds were significantly higher when they worked out together versus on their own. Researchers credited the added boost in endorphins that comes from the social aspect of group sessions.

Believe in True (Fitness) Love—and Cheat When You Want To

Finding the right workout for you—one you truly love and enjoy enough to *want* to do it—is a lot like finding a husband or wife. You've got to "date" until you match with *the* one (or ones . . . exercise polygamy is highly encouraged). That means you might kiss a few dumbbells before realizing Pilates is your prince. Don't give up! Also keep in mind that while you may think you know what type of workout is right, if they all feel like a bad date, change it up and try something completely different.

It sounds obvious, but so many people try to force themselves into a specific regimen or type of workout—like running or CrossFit or cycling—because they think it's what they should do or it's the trendy new thing. I'm guilty of it, too. But if you don't at least enjoy parts of it, the only thing that gets easier is finding excuses to skip. And that can leave you feeling guilty for not going, discouraged or hating exercise altogether, when really you were just in a bad relationship. It's not you, it's the workout! Try these tips to help find what's right:

- **Follow your instincts.** Start by trying workouts that seem cool or sound interesting and fun. Think about the vibe you might need or what you've liked doing in the past. Above all, listen to your gut. Think about how you feel in class and how you feel when you think about going back. If a workout doesn't feel right from the first or second date, break up and move on. But have a mini postmortem. Ask yourself why you didn't like it. Was it the workout itself or the instructor? The music or energy of the studio? Or maybe it was how you were feeling. Use what you learn to inform your next sweat date.

  Here's an example: A few years ago, I used to kick off Monday mornings with yoga, figuring it would help me ease into a stressful workweek. But *om*-ing in the dark amidst a cloud of incense at 5:45 a.m. just annoyed me. I felt *more* anxious trying to force my body and brain to chill. No thanks. I realized I needed to punch my way into the week with a killer boxing class.

- **Leave your ego at home.** Of course trying a new workout can feel a little intimidating. Did I mention I suck at boxing? My brain cannot nail the jab-jab-hook-cross-uppercut before dawn. Who cares?! I throw my heart into throwing punches, and I love it. And the fact that I'm there with friends allows me to laugh off the combos that I completely butcher.

- **Listen to your head and heart.** Consider prohibitive factors when "dating" different workouts. For example, I am in lust with a few workouts in New York by my office, but just as it's tricky to fall in love with someone who lives in a different state, the same goes for far-flung gyms. I want to commit, but it's realistically never going to work for more than an occasional hookup. The same goes for pricier classes. I'm "Mega" addicted to SLT, but I can't afford to go more than once a week.

- **Rekindle an old flame—with new rules.** After breaking up with yoga, I decided to give it a second chance. Except this time, I went to a different studio, one that incorporated more upbeat music and felt more inclusive and playful, and on a Thursday, when I was ready to Zen out. Because when I thought about it, it wasn't yoga that turned me off, it was the environment and my own mindset. Similarly, you might have a better experience with a different instructor. Or come back after a while away. I've sometimes revisited workouts years later—when *I'm* different—and found that what was once a nay is now a YAY!

Find Your Good-Vibe Tribe

It's not easy waking with the roosters and peeling yourself out of a warm, cozy bed—even with a routine, even with a killer class and your workout gear all lined up. Realizing I've got so much—or rather, so many—to get up for is always the extra push I need. Morning meetups with my fitness buddies are like happy hour, except with water instead of cocktails and zit cream residue instead of mascara. I can't wait to get to the gym and feel grateful to see and sweat with them, and am extra motivated knowing they're waiting for me.

I met my tribe almost by accident. We all happened to work out in the mornings at the same few studios around town. Under different circumstances, we probably wouldn't have become friends. We used to lovingly call our pal Courtney "Plus 1" because while most of us were in our thirties and married with kids, she was a single twentysomething. She and the others started out as familiar faces, then recognition turned into *hello*s and high fives, then chitchat and coffee runs, then full-on bonding—over career highs and lows, parenting wins and fails, the pain of losing family members and the joy of an engagement and wedding. At first we just showed up for each other in class. After a while, we showed up for each other in life, and those bonds made us even more devoted to our sweat sessions.

Love the Ones You're With
I'm extremely lucky I found these women. The truth is, gyms and classes and sports clubs and communities all over the country are full of people like them. Like you! If none of your current friends will join your workout tribe, look at where and when you're currently sweating or want to sweat. You already have a shared experience in common, and that's the only opener you need. For example, while I've got my core group of girls, we've added plenty of members along the way. One of them, Lisa, was a sixty-something woman who had exercised on and off her entire life but could never get a routine to stick. Until she started talking to a friend in our group and "joined" our tribe. Now she's hooked.

If you're shy, I get it: Chatting up someone might feel awkward or intimidating. How about starting with "Hi!"? Talk about what you like about the teacher or how the class felt. Is it your first time? Ask for advice or how long the person has been taking the class. Compliment someone's tank top. Ask why they weren't there last week. You already have so much in common!

Facebook groups are also rife with potential workout buddies. A friend told me about a mom who recently moved to her town and posted on her daughter's school parents' page about starting a running club. She got ten responses and ended up with a group of three or four regulars for weekly runs. You may not become good friends after one session, or even a second or third, or maybe not at all. That's okay. Be open to connection, notice friendly and familiar faces and people who notice or say hi to you. You've got nothing to lose and lots of friends and motivation to gain.

Werk Your Workout #OOTD
When I was fitness director at *Self,* we did a TV segment with a woman who wanted to get in shape for her wedding but was struggling. I quickly saw that one big thing bringing her down was an unsupportive bra. She simply couldn't

comfortably exercise. When I suggested a new sports bra, she kind of blew me off, but she took the Enell sports bra I offered, along with some sweat-wicking, high-waisted leggings and tanks. A few weeks later, she was a full-fledged runner, was in a healthier weight range and no longer had near-bloody shoulders from her bra straps. She told me that bra helped change her life.

Let me say that how you look when working out does not and should not matter. But how you *feel* is everything. And lord knows there are enough barriers to working out already. Don't make your clothes one more by wearing stuff that's uncomfortable, unflattering or you just don't like. Life is too short to settle for a crappy bra and a ratty, old, sweat-soaked T-shirt and underwear or leggings you have to keep hiking up. And as for those baggy sweats that make you feel frumpy? They're doing for your motivation the same as they're doing for your tush.

Now think about how you feel when you put on one of your favorite non-workout outfits. Not the sweatpants and washed-a-million-times T-shirt you wore all quarantine long. I'm talking clothes that make you feel like you're winning at life; they're comfortable, stylish, easy, flatter your butt and cover you in confidence. *That's* how you can and should feel when exercising! And great workout gear delivers.

Dress for the Workout You Want

Scientists at Northwestern University researching the power of clothes came up with the term "enclothed cognition" to describe how what we wear influences our psychological processes. They tested their theory with lab coats—universally associated with intelligence and authority (e.g., scientists and doctors)—and predicted that wearing the coat and calling it a "doctor's coat" would boost performance on attention-related tasks. Sure enough, it did. It's not hard to make the jump to great workout clothes and realize how much they can boost motivation, confidence and performance while doing bicep curls or climbing the leaderboard in Spin class. Even beyond the comfort factor.

I feel this every time I get dressed for the gym, as does my tribe—it's why we're more likely to splurge on workout gear than, say, fancy dinners. You've undoubtedly heard the advice "Dress for the job you want, not the job you have." The same applies to workouts, so hear this loud and clear: You do

NOT have to be traditionally "fit" to wear killer workout clothes. Don't wait until you're in better shape to rock Athleta's sweat-wicking, stretchy, flattering fits. Don't wait to see if you stick with a new routine to invest in fun striped and bright K-Deer leggings or a tank you wear only for workouts. It's not vain or showing off. It's taking advantage of anything and everything that inspires you to be active, strong and feel your best. The fact that your butt or back looks amazing is gravy.

FOOD FOR THOUGHT

Wondering why there's no "Eat for Energy" section? It's because there are so many different ways to do it, and the right one for you depends on an infinite number of factors. So rather than get specific, try this: If you know you need to make healthier, more energizing choices or changes, commit to them now. Stepping up your fitness game and sleep habits may make it easier—exercise, diet and sleep all influence one another. For example, research shows people who are more active sleep better *and* tend to make healthier food choices. Meanwhile, those who get enough sleep eat healthier because sleep normalizes hunger hormones. A few other things to consider:

- **Small changes can be huge.** Studies show even modest improvements to your diet—like simply munching a few more fruits and veggies every day—can improve mood and increase feelings of happiness and well-being. Plus, every nutrition expert I've ever talked to has said that, for most people, what matters is how you eat *most of the time*, not at any one meal or night out or vacation.
- **Consider what you're getting, not giving up.** People often think about healthy eating like it's a majorly unfun chore. Or they

focus on what they're sacrificing rather than the good they're doing. That's a mistake; how you think and talk about food shapes your perspective and how you feel and behave. Try reframing healthy choices. If you're eating a salad, love it for what it's doing for your energy and health, and thank yourself for making that choice instead of hating it because it's not disco fries.

- **Ditch the "good" or "bad" mentality.** Yes, certain foods are healthier than others. That does not make any good or bad, nor are *you* good or bad based on what you eat. Do you say or think things like "I'm so bad, I had a huge bowl of ice cream" or "I'm going to be good and order grilled fish"? The more that loaded language infiltrates your brain and speech and the more your emotions and identity get tangled up in food choices, the more you feel bogged down by pursuing your healthy-eating goals.

Give Your Butt a Rest

Sitting has been called the new smoking, and while few habits are as dangerous as puffing away, spending too much time on your behind is linked to all sorts of similar and scary health problems, including heart disease, diabetes and cancer. Beyond the possibility of sitting yourself to death, it's also a huge physical and mental energy suck. It reduces blood circulation, and the lack of muscle movement impacts hormones, the functioning of mitochondria (your cells' power plants) and more. Australian researchers also found that the more time people spend sitting, the greater their risk for severe depression and anxiety.

On the other hand, standing more—not even moving, just standing—can boost focus, brain power and productivity. In one study, call center employees given adjustable desks sat for only about an hour and a half less over the course of the day than those with regular desks, and they were 46 percent *more* productive.

Take a Stand, Take a Walk

I could have written that study. I got a standing desk seven years ago and get more done and feel more creative than I ever did sitting. You don't necessarily need a new desk (although if you can get one or DIY it, DO IT); just decide not to be chairbound. Newton's law absolutely applies to humans—a body in motion stays in motion. And the more you get up throughout the day and move, the more energized you feel. Or at least the less drained and tired. For me, even when I know I'm tired, I don't feel it until I'm forced to sit during a meeting or my commute.

In an office? Don't send an email or text when walking over and talking to someone is a viable option. Or set a timer for at least every hour and stand, stretch or go for a little walk. If you're on the phone a lot, stand or pace. Better yet, take the term *mobile phone* literally. If all else fails, guzzle water all day. You'll be hydrated and *have* to get up to hit the bathroom.

My challenge to you: Try one of those tactics for a week and see how you feel. When researchers put thirty sedentary people to a similar test, the results were amazing. Each person spent one day sitting for six hours (the control), one day walking for thirty minutes in the morning and a third day taking a five-minute walk every hour for six hours. On both days people walked, they said they had more energy and vigor. On the days they took the five-minute-walk breaks, they *also* got a mood boost and felt less fatigued. Just by walking for five minutes every hour.

BEWARE THE ENERGY VAMPIRES

A Misery-Loves-Company Friend

I used to have a friend who would essentially bully me into eating too much crap food and drinking too much rosé. After hanging out, I'd drag my pickled, bloated body home and crash, then wake up feeling drained and terrible the next day. I never felt guilty about overindulging necessarily; it was more that I couldn't stand up to her pushing to consume and do things I didn't want to. I wasn't in high school, for Zac Efron's sake!

Most of us have probably been around these kinds of people. Sometimes it comes across as bullying—pushing food or drinks or trying to get you to skip workouts or stay out late—or it manifests as backhanded compliments (e.g., "You went to Spin class *again*?! You're making the rest of us look bad!"). Either way, it's exhausting.

If you find yourself in a similar situation, realize most disparaging or bullying comments are more about that person than you. Meet them with empathy, then match their snark. When they joke about your dedication, for example, say something like "Come with me to Spin next time so you know how good it feels!"

Also try removing triggers. Instead of meeting over food or drinks at 8 p.m., suggest manis and pedis at 3 p.m. or hit up a museum—and set an end time that you stick with no matter what. (Stay strong!) Or talk to them about how you feel. But if you have nothing else in common or your friend isn't supportive or willing to accept what's important to you, maybe they're better kept at arm's (or Facebook's) length.

Comparing Yourself to Beast-Mode Friends

On the flip side of pusher friends are the hardcore—whether they work out all the time or are extremely disciplined and vocal about their health habits. While those people may sometimes inspire and energize us, sometimes they have the opposite effect. That's what happened when my husband committed to a keto diet. When I realized it wasn't a phase—this strict way of eating worked for him long-term—I was impressed. I also thought, *Man, I could never do that.* And somehow his unfailing rigidity made me less motivated to maintain my more relaxed approach to healthy eating.

Our psyches are weird; I didn't even *want* to eat keto. I believe in balance and carbs and sugar. And yet I felt less than. It was like, *Welp, I'm never going to be that perfect, so what's the point?* Whether I could or couldn't or even wanted didn't matter. His routine made me feel less content and energized in my own goals and by my own accomplishments.

An all-or-nothing mentality can kill energy by itself, and it's extra danger-ous when coupled with comparing—especially to someone who isn't that different from you except that they're succeeding at the "all" you're not. If comparison is the thief of joy, as the saying goes, in these situations it's also the sneaky pickpocket of motivation and small victories.

What helped me: I went all-in on Pat's superstar status. It sounds funny, but I started thinking of him as the LeBron James of keto. (Stay with me here. . . .) Even objectively good ballers don't compare themselves to LeBron—he's in a league of his own. They don't let the fact that they'll never be as good as LeBron stop them from playing. I would never be as disciplined as Keto Pat, but it was okay; Keto Pat was LeBron, and I could still be good at *my* game.

MURPHY'S LAWS

Never miss a Monday
No matter how many days you work out, make one a Monday. Just as exercising first thing in the morning sets the tone for your day, a start-of-the-week sweat session can set the tone for the next six days and help slay both Sunday scaries and Monday blues.

Hide-and-see
You're much more likely to choose healthy food if it's *right there*, front and center in the fridge or out in plain view on the counter. Ditto with workout clothes, sneakers or other gear in your closet or home; seeing them can be the gentle nudge you need to stay or get active.

Detox your thinking
Your body isn't toxic, nor does it need to "detox." Here's what to detox from instead: the idea that you need pricy supplements, juice blends or powders, or to cleanse at all. Think instead about resetting by eating *all* the veggies and lots of other whole, unprocessed foods. Every meal or snack is an opportunity to start fresh.

Veg out
Pizza, sandwiches, burgers, pasta—greenwash anything with an unhealthy-ish reputation by piling on or in the veggies. When I

worked at *Self*, a favorite tip around the office was "always fit a salad into your sandwich." The same idea can apply to other foods and even sweets. The extras—nuts, fruit, veggies—help bulk up your treats, leaving you more satisfied.

Go to the doctor already!
Just as you put on your own oxygen mask before helping others, prioritize your health. Have that weird symptom checked out. Get a physical. Schedule your mammogram or prostate exam. Taking charge of your health can be incredibly empowering—and energizing. Knowing the facts, even if it's hard, usually feels better than living under the weight of uncertainty.

CHAPTER 6

The Extra Charge

If you're sad, add more lipstick and attack.
—COCO CHANEL

A while back I was walking through Penn Station on my way to work when I saw a woman dressed almost head to toe in various shades of orange, my all-time favorite color. She had on a fiery red-orange hat with a furry pom-pom on top, a fuzzy coat in a rich shade of marmalade, a chic apricot leather handbag and carrot-colored UGGs. Amid the endless flow of commuters in black and brown, she was a beautiful sunset, and I couldn't help staring.

As a longtime orange fanatic, I also wanted to find out what kind of woman she was. We're used to seeing celebs on the red carpet go all-out with bright colors, but it's not every day you see it on the terrazzo tile of the train station during rush hour. Even in New York City. I see plenty of fashion risk-takers, for sure. She was different. It really seemed like she wasn't trying to make a statement, take "a risk" or follow a trend, or get anyone's attention. She seemed like a super-cool sixty-something lady who was owning her love of orange. And I was into it.

After catching up to her, I told her how great she looked, how happy she had made me and how fun it was to see a kindred color spirit out in the wild. She laughed and said, "Thanks," then I overshared about my orange couch and orange front door. We talked for a minute, geeking out over this joyful color. She said it's her favorite, too, because it's such a bright, happy shade. The impression I got: She picked her clothes precisely for that reason; winter is dreary, and oranging out, especially on the stuff she wears every day like a coat and boots, makes it feel less so. Her outfit delivered her a dose of happy energy. And it did for me when I saw her. That's how the Extra Charge works.

Color, fashion, beauty, your home or environment and other external or frivolous-seeming extras in life can deliver a real energy and emotional boost, making them anything but frivolous.

You probably know what I'm talking about at least in a sense. Most of us have experienced the whole look-good, feel-good phenomenon. It's why we walk out of the hair or nail salon feeling Lizzo-level good as hell and why we get done up for a night out. Science shows there's something there, that beauty and fashion can indeed boost self-esteem and give us a measurable lift. One study, for example, showed that when women wore makeup during a mock exam, they performed better than those who listened to positive music and those who did neither.

Our environment likewise impacts our mood, overall well-being and even our behavior. For example, almost three-quarters of people who say they're happy with their homes report being happy in life, and your home may account for up to 15 percent of happiness. Meanwhile, visual art can reduce stress, while clutter may spike it. And if you happen to be stuck in the hospital, a nice view from your bed has been shown to help people recover faster and feel less pain. Bright colors in our homes also convey a sense of joyfulness that can make us feel happy.

HOW DO YOU WANT TO FEEL?

That's the question we should be asking when making decisions about the "extras" in life—home decor and setup, beauty, fashion. I realized later why exactly my orange crush at the train station seemed so stinkin' cool—and why I kept thinking about her days later: how it seemed she approached her outfit. Although she was (probably) also trying to look good, I got the sense that her sartorial decisions originated from the opposite direction—based more on how orange made her feel or how she wanted to feel, and the joy that comes with expressing herself out loud.

That's what this chapter is really about: realizing the extent to which you can use life's extras to explicitly *feel* more energized and express yourself, rather than simply or accidentally backdoor-ing your way into it by focusing first on how you or your home looks.

SAFE CHOICES ARE MISSED OPPORTUNITIES

Designer Ingrid Fetell Lee, author of the book *Joyful*, has spent more than a decade studying how our surroundings, design, color, ordinary objects and aesthetics in general can be used to elicit happiness and joy. On her blog, *The Aesthetics of Joy*, she made a similar point about leading with how you want to feel. Writing about home design, she said that when decorating or renovating, people tend to think about and make decisions based on how things look. Will the space look good or tasteful? Will everything go together? Does it look dated? Is this piece of art/hardware/rug/whatever right for the space?

Coming at it that way can overwhelm you, Fetell Lee said. Because lots of stuff *looks* good. I've experienced this in my own adventures in renovations; Amazon, Wayfair, Crate and Barrel, Pottery Barn—all filled with stuff that looks good. As a result we go the safe route, choosing neutrals over color, simple over impactful, style over substance, ordinary over extraordinary or interesting. Or we copy what we see online or from others—most of which tends to look pretty similar and similarly safe.

I think that feeling of overwhelm can also sometimes drive us to make no choice—it's the true path of least resistance. Like how I lived with the same generic, builder-grade, boob-like light fixtures in my house for seven years. I've hated them since day one, but could never pull the trigger on replacements.

According to Fetell Lee, because of our safe decisions (or indecision), our homes often lack character and personality. The same could be said about safe or your standard, go-to clothes and beauty choices. They might be easy, comfortable and look good but are rarely energizing. Has beige ever set your heart ablaze with Yay? Going the safe route is kind of like going to the gym and only drinking a smoothie from the juice bar—better than nothing, but a missed opportunity to impact how you actually feel.

To be clear, we all need to make the safe choices sometimes. Like that

safety-rated minivan in an off-the-lot, dirt-camouflaging black. But how energizing would it be if, once in a while, you could ditch the van and hop into
the back of a truck with all your friends and go for a joyride? Unlike tum-
bling around the back of an F-150, making some energizing, Yay-inducing
choices for your home, clothes and beauty is low risk, high reward. Your life
isn't on the line, but you'll probably end up feeling more alive.

EMBRACE THE EXTRA

I love how the definition of *extra* has gone from a vague modifier and adverb
to this perfectly descriptive noun that means (if you're not up on the slang) a
sort of atypical over-the-top-ness. Like, my orange-clad commuter friend was
extra. It perfectly describes someone who, more than anything (and to stay in
the realm of slang), evokes a #mood, not only a look.

I've gotten the sense that some people think being extra or caring too
much about beauty, fashion, home decor and other extras is silly, frivolous or
self-indulgent. Like, with so much crap happening in the world and with
everything else you've got going on with work, kids, bills and pandemics,
why waste time, energy and money on superficial stuff? Well, all the crap,
stress and obligations are precisely *why* we should be frivolous and extra.
You're not ignoring what's going on to concern yourself only with mani/pedis
and new throw pillows. It's that indulging in frivolity helps us feel good; it's
a fun, lighthearted distraction that can soften the impact and sharp edges of
all the hard and stressful stuff in life.

So forget about seeming indulgent or superficial. I think of that quote I
mentioned earlier about true self-care and how it's creating a life you don't
need to escape from. Prioritizing anything that helps you feel energized and
happy counts. After all, we prioritize exercise and time with our families and
meaningful work because they energize us. And if a funky manicure, a thirty-
seven-step skincare routine or an orange fuzzy coat (or four of them) can do
that, too, then they're not really frivolous, are they?

Paying attention to the extras in life also sends the message that you care
about you *enough* to prioritize what makes you feel good. That's energizing all
on its own, apart from the effects of your clothes or space. Think of the extras

as a quick and temporary hit of joy or fun—as good as icing on a cake or a cappuccino at the end of the meal.

THE EXTRA CHARGE TOOL KIT
Make Your Bed

I do this every morning without fail—whether I'm running late for work or have a rare day off. Smoothing the covers, arranging the pillows—these are small acts that are easy to let go, but I never do. Apparently neither do lots of other happy, energized, successful and well-rested people.

Retired Admiral William H. McRaven, a former U.S. Navy SEAL, literally wrote the book on the power of this simple chore, *Make Your Bed: Little Things That Can Change Your Life . . . and Maybe the World*. Part of his reasoning is that the task gives you a sense of control and achievement and sets off a motivational domino effect. The satisfaction and accomplishment act like a shot of energy, prompting you to take on the next thing, which feeds your motivation for the next, and so on.

Indeed, one survey found that 82 percent of bed-makers say the task helps them feel more productive. They're also more likely to get to work right away upon arrival, and more report striving to do their best work versus only what's required.

McRaven also explains that making your bed and doing it well—military corners optional, I imagine—drives home the idea that details matter. And if you can focus on and do little things well, you're more likely to get the big things right, too. Perhaps that's one reason when Gretchen Rubin, who wrote about bed-making in *The Happiness Project*, asks people which habits in her book made the biggest difference, bed-making is one of the most common answers.

A made bed might even help you sleep better. Bed-makers report they fall asleep more easily, are more likely to stay asleep and wake up feeling more well rested. They're also less likely to snooze in the morning. Think of it like presetting your relax mode. Bottom line: Yes, I wrote a whole page about making your bed: IT'S THAT IMPORTANT, and I wanted to fully express just how big an impact this teeny habit can have.

Just Add Color

When I worked at *Cosmo*, we used to do these color stories where we'd find studies or interview psychologists or other experts about what different colors conveyed or were supposed to make you feel. We reported the truth—what the pros or research said—but honestly, it often felt like a stretch. (Sorry, *Cosmo* readers of the early aughts.) I remember feeling skeptical that a color would have this universal effect. Like, does yellow really boost *everyone's* mood and is red actually "sexy"?

And, in fact, when taken as a whole, the research is more nuanced. Red, for example, *is* universally stimulating because it's the color of alarms, fire and blood. But it can have either positive or negative connotations depending on the person. Green is particularly confusing; the color of nature, it's been found to be refreshing and relaxing while other research has linked it to tiredness and guilt. *What?!*

Here's some research that actually rings true: Color, period, especially bright, main colors (green, yellow, blue, orange, red) are stimulating, energizing and feel happy and joyful precisely because they're bright. They're also usually associated with positive emotions like happiness, excitement and hope more than neutrals.

Fetell Lee, for example, has explained that vivid shades are energizing and enlivening in part because of the way they reflect light; they literally send excitable molecules to your eyeballs. Our experiences and associations also play a role. People wear dark colors to funerals and in corporate America because they're serious occasions and the colors have always been associated with somber, serious stuff. Now consider the vibe of a kids' birthday party or a daycare playroom; it's like rainbows have thrown up all over the place.

Try baby-stepping your way to a more colorful life. What colors give you the biggest lift? What are you drawn to? Think about what shades make you feel good when you see them—in a room, on a friend. Then sprinkle in candy colors wherever you can and in doses that feel good, even if a little different.

If your home or closet is filled with neutrals or muted tones, pops of color—in art, pillows, jewelry, shoes, eyeliner, a single "party nail" on your next mani—are as sweet and enlivening as the M&Ms in trail mix. The home of Rachel Shingleton (@pencilshavings on Insta), for example, is awash in shades of blue, but every room is punctuated with a different bright shade or shades—a yellow light fixture here, orange chairs over there, a fuchsia pattern rug down below—and it's one of the most joyful places I've ever seen.

COLOR YOUR FEED

Instagram and Pinterest are full of inspiration. But if your feed is filled with images that look as if they've been filtered through wheat, of course that's what you'll gravitate to IRL. Expand your color views by following pros who peacock a bold love of color and let them inspire you, like my friends and fellow human rainbows Christine Bibbo Herr (@nycpretty) and Rachel Pitzel (@xorachel), plus Courtney Quinn, the self-described Color Queen (@colormecourtney).

Control the Clutter

Organization is my love language. Even if it's not yours, consider this: Home is the launchpad of our lives, and if yours is suffocating under the weight of stuff and disorder, your energy, brainpower and well-being are suffering the same fate. Even before Marie Kondo hit the scene, research revealed just how life-changing a tidy home can be.

For example, a clutter-filled house has been linked to procrastination and, among those in their fifties, life dissatisfaction. Studies show it spikes stress hormones in working moms and may encourage overeating. Neuroscientists discovered through MRI tests that when there's too much clutter, your brain has trouble focusing and processing information—which is why it may cause you to feel distracted and unmotivated. And it can ding your memory, trigger anxiety and, at the very least, cause you to waste precious minutes and energy searching for the f#%*! [fill in the blank] that always goes missing.

Recently I've been following the (inspiring) decluttering journey of my pal Liz Vaccariello, the editor in chief of *Real Simple*. A true member of the Fully Charged sunshine squad, she runs a tight and tidy ship at work, but at home, she's married to a man she (lovingly) refers to as #clutterhusband. Around the time she took the reins of *Real Simple*, she began taking back her home one small move at a time.

Obviously there are different degrees of clutter. If you're more of a "keeper of stuff" than a KonMari convert, there are professionals who can help (like @itsorganized, @theprojectneat or @doneanddonehome). For the rest of you who, like Liz and me, struggle with just keeping on top of the enormous influx of randomness that materializes when you stop paying attention, the best thing you can do is declutter daily. Spend five to ten minutes either at the end of the night or first thing in the morning tidying, putting away or doing whatever you need to start seeing more surfaces again.

QUICK CLUTTER FIXES

- **Try a tray.** One of the first things Liz did to turn #clutterhusband into #herohusband: Corral all the little stuff that collects in various spots (counters, entry tables).
- **Give everything a home.** Homelessness is the leading cause of clutter. Decide where things should live (or make a home for them) and get out the label maker so everyone can drop stuff off where it belongs.
- **Keep a giveaway bag at the ready.** You never know when the urge to purge will strike, and having a home for castaways makes it effortless. For me, that means a ThredUp bag in my closet and a shopping bag for the Salvation Army by the front door.
- **Send stuff to purgatory.** Kids given only four toys to play with stayed occupied and engaged twice as long as kids given sixteen toys, according to one study. It's also estimated most people wear only 20 percent of their wardrobes most of the time.

Pack a bunch of stuff—clothes, accessories, toys, etc.—away and every few months "shop" the box.
- **Outsource.** One reason clutter increases working moms' stress is because they often feel responsible for staying on top of it. Get everyone in on that sweet declutter action. (Insanely detailed chore charts have worked for us!)

Holiday Hard

My mom, a former teacher and current Fully Charged badass, has always been holiday house #goals. When I was growing up, she'd decorate for every holiday like it was her job and she was gunning for employee of the month. What stuck with me more than what the house looked like was what it felt like: A warm hug and a huge party all at once. The rotating collections of tchotchkes and DIY decor created a vibe that there was always something worth celebrating and that doing so can be part of everyday life.

So for Christmas, Thanksgiving, Valentine's Day, St. Patrick's Day, Easter, Mother's and Father's Day, Independence Day . . . we go to extremes (over)decorating for every single one at Team Murphy HQ. My style's a bit different than my mom's, but the big-party energy is the same, maybe even bigger. I'm talking garlands, table runners, lots of crafts, seasonal pillows, outdoor flags, festive ice cube trays, string lights, chair backers and much, much more. We even decorate the pantry and kids' rooms. And as such, decoration days—when we swap out the decor for one holiday with the next one's—are major events.

The actual holidays are almost secondary—an excuse, really. It's the decorations that matter; they're deliberate, obvious and intentional ways of reminding yourself to have fun. Plus, they prolong the party vibe; waking up or coming home after a long day to a house that feels celebratory, fun and full of character is a natural high. It's why my friends, our babysitter and even my Instagram followers now all holiday harder. One stranger even wrote me to say that it's filled her life "with so much JOY and YAY!"

The thing is, you don't have to go over the top like I do. Do whatever

#extra means to you. My friend Angela, for example, is extra about her holiday mantel and keeps the rest of the house low-key. Even if you're on a tight budget, even if you're a minimalist, you might be surprised how much of a lift you get from a DIY holiday centerpiece, some dollar-bin finds and a few strategically placed seasonal ribbons.

Celebrate Everything

Major holidays are easy to celebrate—they recognize worthy things like tradition, family and religious beliefs, plus gratitude, giving, love, mothers, fathers, independence. Don't stop there. Embrace the minor and made-up holidays, and the ridiculous and random ones, too. They offer opportunities to recognize and appreciate simple and silly things in life. Think Taco Tuesday, National Donut Day, the Super Bowl. (A holiday that celebrates snacks, parties, polarizing halftime shows and, oh yeah, sports? Yes please!) One year, I showed up for my April first workout in head-to-toe boring black and everyone kept asking if I was okay before I yelled, "April Fool's!" (Need inspo? We started posting a weekly calendar of excuses to party at @womansdaymag every Monday.)

The point is, if you live your life looking for reasons to celebrate and have fun, you'll find them—and a lot of happiness, too. Celebrating something makes regular days and the usual routine feel special and more fun. It's essentially positivity in practice—an excuse and a way to focus on and savor what's good. And, as I talked about back in the Positive Charge chapter, savoring gives you an extra shot of happiness.

I know people find rando holidays frivolous. But the harder things are or the more the world disappoints us, the more we need a reprieve. "Holidays" like National S'mores Day or Groundhog Day give you permission to prioritize fun, even just for a minute. It doesn't take much effort or time to, say, get excited that graham crackers, marshmallows and chocolate found each other and we can eat 'em together. And those little hits of happiness are one more thing to help stop the world's dumpster fires from burning up your energy and joy.

And for the cynics out there saying these holidays are commercial ploys: Of course they are. So what? Does it matter who reminded who of the deliciousness of donuts or s'mores and suggested you treat yourself? People profit from everything these days, and you can profit in fun, the delight of a treat or a chance to connect with someone.

Tap into Flower Power

I hope you know how good it feels when someone gives you flowers. Now see how good it feels to buy them for yourself on the regular. Harvard researcher Nancy Etcoff found that people who had fresh-cut flowers at home not only felt less negative, worried and anxious overall, they reported feeling happier and had more energy and enthusiasm at work that day. Rutgers researchers found similar results: Flowers not only made people happy in the moment, they led to people reporting later that they felt less depressed, anxious and agitated and had higher levels of life enjoyment and satisfaction.

I buy a grocery store bouquet every Monday to offset and cope with my happiness hangover after fun weekends. Maybe for you, Fridays make sense—buy them to celebrate the end of the week and enjoy the blooms at home all weekend. Maybe you pick random days or when you need a boost. Doesn't matter. What does: that you're worth it.

Dress Up to Feel Up

Clothes can act like a venti cup of coffee for your energy or like a tranquilizer— a long-held belief I temporarily cast aside during the stressful first weeks of the coronavirus lockdown, when I became a walking meme about daytime and nighttime pj's and elastic waistbands. The day I blow-dried my hair, put on real clothes (still with an elastic waistband . . . baby steps) and a little makeup, I instantly felt more motivated, normal and calmer than I had in a while. It sent the message to my subconscious that it was time to work and that I could, in fact, homeschool and make a magazine and finish a book and record a podcast . . . and better manage my stress. Or at least want to keep trying.

What we wear really can influence how we feel and behave, according to research. Remember when I talked about "enclothed cognition" in relation to workout clothes? It applies to other clothes, too. Studies show certain outfits may help us focus and feel more confident and upbeat. The key: What constitutes "dopamine dressing" or "power clothes" seems to depend mostly on you and whether you associate them with joy, power or anything else.

So when getting dressed, use your associations and choose clothes that give off a vibe you *want* to feel, and there's a good chance they'll help you get there. Down in the dumps? Need a confidence boost? Put on your version of a rainbow or power suit. Overall, though, bright colors and playful patterns and styles tend to be universally uplifting.

Wearing them may give you more of a boost than you think. Say you put on something cheery and feel good. You're then more likely to treat others well and your positive energy rubs off on them. Even just seeing *your* cheery clothes can brighten someone's day. I can usually count on at least a dozen smiles from strangers when I wear my orange raincoat versus my navy trench. Those kinds of reactions *double* the Yay you get from wearing it.

What's more, good vibes stick to clothes like Scotchgard, according to a cool study in the journal *Qualitative Research in Psychology*. When you get a compliment on something you wear, the next time you see it in your closet or put it on, the happy memory of the compliment and positive emotions you felt rush back and give you a charge.

Pick a Power Color, Symbol or Style

Aside from choosing happy outfits, up your clothes' and accessories' Yay potential by picking and wearing a power color, symbol or style—and broadcasting it loud and proud. Like how I never shut up about orange and I cover my body in lightning bolts any chance I get. For my husband, it's goofy socks with his suits. He's all business until he sits down and you get a glimpse of dancing avocados or bacon and eggs. For Shiona Turini, a stylist and costume designer (*Queen & Slim, Insecure*), she once wrote on Instagram that she'll "crop top on any block" in her signature, a crop-top-high-waist combo; and she's as consistent and vocal about it as she is insanely cool and chic.

Whatever you choose, go a little over the top. Own it, and talk about it. You'll get a lift from wearing and talking about what you love and what's meaningful, personal and energizing, and your signature will set you apart as an individual. What's more, people will start recognizing and identifying it as your *thing*, and you'll attract more of it into your life. I get all kinds of Yay-worthy orange and lightning-bolt gifts and pictures from friends that read, for example, "channeling you in this outfit!" It's a fun way to connect, and knowing someone thought of you feels really freakin' nice, even if it's over something superficial like a lightning bolt sweater.

Make a Statement

"No bad days." That's the mantra Cristian, a CrossFit coach in Garwood, New Jersey, decided he wanted to live by. He knows bad stuff happens, but also that how we react to it ultimately makes the day good or bad. To help him keep this mantra top of mind and share it with others, he decided to make T-shirts. Then a beaded bracelet. Then artwork.

Mantras are an important and effective tool for reinforcing a feeling, thought or behavior. But for them to work, they have to play on repeat in your mind, which isn't always easy. Like Cristian, I found wearing positive messages or seeing tangible reminders works. It's an in-your-face reinforcement, plus I like that it invites others to be part of the messaging. It tells the world something about you and your mindset that might spark a conversation or connection. It might even offer an uplifting message to someone who needs it. That's good mantra mojo.

Splashing your inner thoughts across your chest not your thing? Find another way to take your mantra or message out of your mind and to the forefront of your life. Maybe you have it engraved on jewelry or printed on a coffee mug. Make it your screensaver or write it on a Post-it note and stick it to your computer or mirror. Even if it seems silly, it might be the nudge you need to go from trying to manifest the message to making it happen.

Delight in Details

I once shared an elevator with the most stunning woman wearing the classiest tailored camel coat I'd ever seen. She was the definition of sophisticated, understated elegance—what minimalist dreams are made of. Then I spotted her initials quietly monogrammed on the collar. I think I actually said out loud: "Oh!" I had never seen a monogram on a coat like that, and it was so surprising and looked so cool. It also seemed so on-brand for her.

Unlike me, not everyone wants to wear the equivalent of an energy drink all the time. Or ever. Details like the monogram let your clothes and accessories bring the Yay without the usual bold colors or patterns or mantras.

Maybe you derive sartorial energy from a stress-free, everything-goes-with-everything capsule wardrobe or jumped on the uniform dressing bandwagon. Maybe your job requires an actual uniform. Maybe you already have a signature style and it's jeans and a white tee or all-black everything. Take a cue out of this lady's playbook: Add surprising and fun details like a monogram, a pin or patch, a patterned lining, a tassel tied to your bag or anything else that makes your outfit—and, by extension, you—feel special.

Prioritize Feeling Be-you-tiful

Let me start by stating the obvious: You are beautiful just the way you are, and your value as a person is not tied to how you look. We can't hear or internalize that message enough because the world will try to convince you otherwise at every turn. It's also true that how we look is part of who we are—how we see, define and express ourselves—and that what we think and feel about our appearance can influence how we act and feel overall. For example, research shows not only that makeup may help women feel and act more confident (coined the "lipstick effect"), but also that acne is linked to lower self-esteem and depression and it can impact quality of life.

Why are things like lipstick and clear skin confidence fuel? Why are we driven to make *any* changes to our appearance? The answers are complicated, and not only about vanity. For starters, it's part of our evolutionary drive to find and attract a mate; we want to send signals we're a healthy, good choice of partner. Our culture's long-ingrained expectations and norms play a big role, too, of course. But instead of wringing our hands over society's standards or feeling handcuffed by a definition of beauty pushed on us, embrace and use products and treatments in a way that best serves *you*: to express yourself, to feel cared for, to look and feel like the best, healthiest, most energized version of *you*, as dictated by *you*.

Tune Out the Noise

Maybe you couldn't give a rat's ass how you look. Maybe you need a full face of makeup and every hair in place to slay your day. Maybe you fall in between. How we feel about our appearance and what we do to it are deeply personal and nuanced decisions and usually evolve as we do. Yet lots of people have opinions about how we should look or what we should or shouldn't do beautywise. What's worse is hearing messages like *Be yourself! Do what makes you feel beautiful!* then *still* being judged. Decide now to stop listening to anyone except yourself. You have better things to do and care about.

And you know, if those better things are a mani, pedi and blowout, great! Or eyelash extensions and Botox? Super! Too often we feel conflicted, like if we care about our looks, we can't also rage against society's obsession with appearance and youth. Or it feels at odds to love makeup and beauty services *and also* hate that appearance so often dictates how women are perceived, treated and paid. Those conflicts don't make you a hypocrite. Embrace what makes you feel good, call out and fight against what feels unfair and don't waste energy trying to parse or square the two.

Book a Standing Beauty Appointment

My friend's mom has gotten a manicure almost every week for the past forty years. She began splurging on the service back in the eighties, when her fiery red nails complemented the shoulder-padded powersuits she wore working her way up the ranks at an advertising agency. And she's kept it up, even now that she's a seventy-six-year-old retired grandma on a fixed income.

She keeps these appointments in part because it's an "extra" that helps her look and feel her best no matter what else is going on. For me, my "essential extras" are sunny blond highlights and a fun gel mani. For another friend, it's professionally shaped brows. Whatever it is, can you treat it as a nonnegotiable part of your schedule and budget, even making regular appointments far in advance? Even if money is tight or salons close down again, can you block out time for the DIY version?

The act of making time for and spending on something "extra" sends a signal to your heart that you are a priority and how you feel matters. I believe that's at least partly responsible for the boost in self-esteem and confidence that comes from beauty. Sure, beauty treatments sometimes come off as clichéd #selfcare, but consider if what you're really doing is showing authentic self-love.

Do Go A-Changin'

I never had acne as a teenager, but in my early forties, it hit me with a vengeance. My skin became so red, blotchy and cystic-bumpy that people would ask me what was wrong, thinking I had a rash. I hit a breaking point when, before a TV segment, a morning-show makeup artist looked me square in the zit and said, "What am I supposed to do with *that?*"

I spent a good year trying different things before a new dermatologist suggested the right mix of topicals and Rx meds that cleared up my skin. (Of course it took a Fully Charged, single momma of two, super-derm Dr. Shari Marchbien to figure it out.) It wasn't cheap or easy, but how I feel now compared to then is priceless. Every time I look in the mirror or leave the house without makeup on, I remember how heavy and exhausting those moments used to feel, and what a gift it is to look on the outside how I feel on the inside. That feeling convinced me to then get a few drops of Botox to help me look more awake and refreshed. Again, not to fight my age, but to help me feel more like me, like the best version of me.

Even though attitudes are starting to change, people still believe making bigger changes to their appearance—whether it's Botox or a laser treatment or even a boob or nose job—means you're vain, indulgent or buying into some unrealistic beauty ideal. But if there's something about your appearance that doesn't match how you feel or who you want to be, and you want to and are in a position to change it, why not do it? Why judge someone else for doing it?

I realize I'm in a very privileged position to even afford Botox. It and other more permanent procedures also aren't for everyone. The question is, where do we draw the line between what's okay or acceptable and what goes too far? *We* don't—*you* do. It's up to each of us, based on our own priorities, budgets, beliefs and feelings. And if any change you want to make—whether it's putting on lipstick, dyeing your hair or undergoing surgery—is about enhancing who you are (rather than trying to hide or reject it), then it's something that ultimately will charge you.

BEWARE THE ENERGY VAMPIRE
Never Feeling [Fill in the Blank] Enough
Maybe you don't feel young or thin enough. Maybe your clothes aren't stylish enough or your car nice enough. Maybe your furniture isn't Houzz-worthy

enough. We've all probably felt these energy assassins creeping in the corners (or forefront) of our minds. And envy and inadequacy not only can leave us drained, they can mask deeper issues.

For example, plastic surgery might be exactly what some people need to feel like their true self. For others, it might be an expensive, painful Band-Aid on low self-esteem. Similarly, a designer bag might be a special, hard-earned reward. For others, it doesn't relieve the heavy load of inadequacy, envy, discontent or entitlement. The solutions aren't simple, but here are a few ideas to try:

- **Imagine it forward.** Picture yourself getting whatever you think you want or need, and use it as a litmus test for whether this thing truly matters and will make a meaningful difference. Ask questions like, *What will happen if I get this thing? How will I really feel? How will it change or improve my life?* When I find myself eyeing fancy cars around town and considering an upgrade, I start asking why I'd want to pay for luxury when I don't drive much. I think about whether the status of it is really that important, and if the stress over a ding in the door would be worth it. Suddenly, I don't really want it anymore.

- **Rank priorities.** Consider how this thing you want lines up with other priorities. With my car example, I think about the extra money we'd have to spend on payments, and what we'd have to give up to afford them—top priorities like vacations and the freedom to do what energizes me. Is the status and luxury worth it? Not even close.

- **Get a gratitude and pride fix.** Research links feelings of gratitude with lower materialism, envy, as well as narcissism. Because looking at your life and what you do have through a lens of gratitude, plus taking pride in what you've accomplished, earned and who you are, makes it nearly impossible to feel that you or your life is lacking. Use that power to tamp down the vampire-ish voice telling you that you need more or aren't enough.

MURPHY'S LAWS

Decorate with love

Take the mementos—from vacations, special occasions or your kids' childhood—that would otherwise languish in a box and put them on walls or display or use them in some way. Physical mementos help us retrieve, reflect on and savor good memories, which research suggests can buffer stress and boost mood. One of my favorite things is the "Adventure Board" full of magnets from places Team Murphy has traveled that's hanging in our mudroom.

Have fun

Whether for girls' nights or weekly Zoom calls or, you know, Tuesday mornings, give your overworked beige eye shadow a break and swipe on green. Or try mixing patterns or putting together colors you normally wouldn't or channel a friend with out-there style. Clothes, makeup, hair—you can change these things every day if you want to, sometimes multiple times a day! Give yourself permission to play and experiment.

Pick a theme

Themes make regular days and standard stuff feel special—and make it easy for everyone to get in on the fun. During quarantine, my friend's five-year-old suggested her family celebrate Fancy Fridays, where everyone dresses up for dinner, they set the table with good china and make a special meal. And it was a blast.

Share the cheer

I'm constantly trying to recruit friends and neighbors into my Holiday Hard cult, so for hostess, birthday and other gifts, I always give energy in the form of holiday flair or decor.

CHAPTER 7

The Recharge

*Sometimes you have to let go of the picture of what you thought it would
be like and learn to find joy in the story you are actually living.*
—RACHEL MARIE MARTIN

I had planned to start this chapter talking about the death of my dad from
pancreatic cancer in 2016. The idea for The Recharge was born out of those
months leading up to and after losing him, and I put nearly all the tips you'll
read here into practice during that time. Then, in mid-March of 2020, as I
started writing this final chapter, everything changed. And it kept changing—
every day, it seemed—as the coronavirus spread and tightened its grip on the
world, upending life as we knew it.

Up until this point, my dad's illness and death had been the hardest,
scariest and most draining experience of my adult life. Now here was this
new, different thing that was even scarier, harder and more draining on so
many fronts. When I wrote this, it felt as if we were all reeling from an un-
precedented, collective cocktail of fear, panic, anxiety, stress and grief. And
disbelief, in a way. We were struggling under the weight of so many unknowns, half knowns and hard facts—overrun hospitals, models predicting
nationwide deaths in the six figures that sadly became a reality, economic
ruin, global instability—along with the stress and emotions brought on by
each of our own immediate new realities, whatever they may be.

Most of us were also mourning—for people who died, health, feelings of
safety and control, certain freedoms, lost businesses, livelihoods and jobs,

schooling, hugs and human contact, canceled experiences, events and celebrations long planned, looked forward to and worked hard for. We were mourning the loss of normalcy and routine. It was all taken away so swiftly and unexpectedly that it didn't seem real.

As the pandemic first unfolded—the day I was told not to come back to the office and that schools would close—I sat at the kitchen table trying to wrap my head around what was happening, how bad things might get and what I now faced: finishing this book while putting out my first issue as editor of *Woman's Day* from my house without a single photo shoot while coordinating the homeschooling and virtual classroom schedules of my three elementary school kids while trying not to completely lose it over what felt like impending suffering and doom. I felt so stressed and scared, sad and helpless—for myself and our family, and especially for those I knew had it or would have it much worse than me. I was lucky; I couldn't imagine what people like healthcare workers, grocery store clerks, restaurant staff and small-business owners were going through.

My optimism and positivity are usually off the charts, but bad things happen and life can knock you on your butt no matter what you do or how energized or positive you start out. And this pandemic had dealt us all a TKO. I had many dark moments since that first day, and I expect to have more because, as of now, even as there are flashes of hope, it's not over and nobody knows what the (likely messy) aftermath will look like or what the future holds.

Here's what I do know: A Fully Charged approach to life and all the tips I've shared up to this last chapter build a solid foundation of well-being and positivity that can help us immensely during times of crisis and heartache. It's helped me so much during these weeks and will continue to do so. I also know there are times those tips feel as woefully inadequate as our country's initial supply of PPE, testing kits, ventilators and, inexplicably, toilet paper. I—we, you, everyone—often need more; big things happen or reality strikes us in a way that overwhelms our usual charging tools. That's when we need a recharge.

The Recharge delivers specialized jolts of energy that help you cope during times of extreme stress or tragedy or when dealing with intense grief or other negative emotions.

**The Recharge helps you make room for positivity during times
when you question whether it even exists anymore.**

We all have days when we feel overwhelmed, drained, stressed or negative. During a crisis or tragedy, it's different: like after the death of a loved one
or, you know, a global pandemic. It might be a major accident or trauma, the
loss of a job, relationship or home. It could be anything that shatters the idea
of what you thought life would be like or shakes you in a way that you're on
the brink of collapse. And when the grief, anxiety, stress or other tricky emotions we feel seem so unwieldy or heavy, we need to treat ourselves differently.
We need to take different actions.

This pandemic has proven that life will test us in ways we cannot imagine. And while our struggles and the reality of what happens to us can be soul
crushing, every moment doesn't have to be. They may drain us to nearly
nothing, but we don't have to live in the emotional gutter. If the Fully
Charged Life takes a glass-is-refillable approach, the Recharge is for those
times when something big barrels through and knocks the glass to the floor.
It helps you pick up the broken pieces, glue them back together and start re-
filling from the bottom up.

THE BRILLIANCE OF RESILIENCE

Although a little different from the other charges, the Recharge is still rooted
in the basic principle of positive action. Taking action is a requirement of
resilience—officially defined as the process of adapting well in the face of
adversity, trauma, tragedy, threats or other significant sources of stress. We all
have a certain degree of resilience that helps us manage day-to-day twists and
turns. When the road leads you not just around a turn but straight into a
brick wall or off a cliff, that's when we find out how resilient we truly are.

Research on resilience shows what you might expect: It's closely linked to
greater well-being, happiness, life satisfaction, success, lower stress and other
markers of health. For example, corporate executives with high resilience
were four times less likely to suffer from depression and three times less likely
to have anxiety compared to those low in the trait. Resilience keeps you physically healthier and helps you recover more easily from illness or injury. In

one study, older adults who scored high on resilience needed fewer healthcare interventions and felt healthier overall over time. Many of resiliency's positive effects seem to stem largely from an ability to effectively manage or buffer extreme stress—to neutralize or deal with it before it overwhelms and damages your mental and physical health.

When it comes to traumatic life events, some studies report humans tend to be a pretty resilient bunch. We might struggle for a bit, but most bounce back relatively quickly. However, researchers from the University of Arizona, who analyzed data with greater nuance, concluded we likely need more help than once thought. Meaning, we don't only need time to adapt to a new normal post-tragedy, we could really benefit from specific tools and support that build resilience and coping strategies to make that long limbo stage between acute suffering and feeling stable and good again more productive and healthy for us.

LEARNING TO BEND, NOT BREAK

Your level of resilience is partly determined by genes and inherited traits, as well as environment and upbringing. Regardless of where you start, though, you can build your resilience muscles with targeted strategies, according to psychiatrists Dennis S. Charney, MD, dean of the Icahn School of Medicine at Mount Sinai, and Steven M. Southwick, MD, professor emeritus at Yale, two leading resilience experts and authors of *Resilience: The Science of Mastering Life's Greatest Challenges.*

After years of research, interviews with survivors of all types and their own experiences (Charney was shot by a former colleague and Southwick suffered from cancer), Charney boiled things down to a handy ten-point "Prescription for Resilience":

Resilience Rx
1. Optimism, or maintaining a positive attitude
2. Reframing negative or stressful thoughts
3. Developing a moral compass
4. Finding a resilient role model
5. Facing your fears

6. Developing active coping skills
7. Establishing and nurturing a supportive social network
8. Prioritizing your physical health and well-being
9. Training your brain
10. Playing to your strengths

Over time, practicing these specific ways of thinking and behaving can trigger changes in your brain that naturally improve your ability to cope and adapt to life's everyday challenges and its biggest tragedies, traumas and hardships. You don't even need to hit all ten—focusing on just a few can help.

Many of Charney and Southwick's strategies are related to key components of living Fully Charged that I cover in earlier chapters. So if you're already using the tips in this book, you're ahead of the game. For example, The Health Charge (chapter 5) gives specific ways to prioritize physical health, while the Love Charge (chapter 3) offers strategies to nurture social support and relationships—both of which help you navigate extreme stress and distress.

SILVER LININGS ARE GOLDEN

Reframing or reinterpreting your thoughts, aka cognitive reappraisal (which I talk about in chapter 2, The Positive Charge), plays an especially vital role in resilience by helping prevent negative emotions from completely running amok. That's important because, left unchecked, negative thoughts and feelings act like gremlins—they can multiply, intensify and overwhelm you; the more you focus on how bad you feel or how bad a situation is, the worse off you are and the harder it can be to adapt and continue moving through life, much less feel happy or energized. On the other hand, finding flashes of positivity or positive meaning in hard or tragic situations helps balance or stabilize emotions.

During a crisis, this obviously looks different than during, say, a fight with your spouse or a setback at work. We often need more time to face what's happened or is happening, to grieve or react and process emotions. However, the more you can take moments to notice the good, the more it can help you. For example, at a funeral, noticing the outpouring of support rather than only focusing on the loss. Thinking back to when the pandemic was raging, nobody could ignore what was happening, and there was nothing good about people dying, overwhelmed hospitals and a tanking economy, but if that's primarily all you focused on, you likely felt paralyzed and struggled a lot during that time. Maybe you're still struggling.

On the other hand, I think many of us tried turning to uplifting stories—and there were so many—of people helping each other and stepping up in big and small ways. Maybe we found ourselves reaching out to or connecting with people even more (from at least six feet away, of course). Likewise, how incredible to be reminded, even if through the virus's wreckage, how connected we all are and how our actions can affect so many around us.

When my dad was dying, I remember waking up many mornings thinking it was a bad dream. When reality set in after a few blinks, so did a weird mix of emotions—many poisonous but also tempered by, for example, the relief of knowing he'd soon be out of pain. A similar thing has been happening lately. The fear and sadness gets so prickly, then, in waves, I get relief thinking of the gift of this time with my kids and how amazing it is to be home for family dinner every night, which I never was before. At some point I'll probably commute into the city again, but it won't be every day if I have a say in it, and I plan to be home by six as often as possible. I'm not sure I would have gotten here on my own, and for that I'm forever grateful.

OPTIMISM, ACTIVATE!

The ability to find positive meaning in something traumatic also builds resilience because it forces you to acknowledge and provides hard evidence that good things can come from bad. Rewriting the narrative of a tragedy and attaching value to it, whether in the moment or through reflection, imprints the proof on your brain. Then, the next time you're faced with something terrible or even slightly challenging, it's easier to believe there's good to be found there or that it can be an opportunity for growth. And of course to see that you will come out of it okay—maybe even better in some ways.

Sounds like optimism and a positive attitude, right? Cognitive reappraisal, or reframing, is an effective way to practice and build optimism, which holds the top spot on Charney's ten-step Resilience Rx. In studies of former prisoners of war during Vietnam and earthquake survivors, for example, optimism was one of the main predictors of who was able to come away from those horrific experiences without severe post-traumatic stress issues. Optimism also helps predict which college students better weather the stress of their freshman year.

To be clear, I'm not talking about Pollyanna-type optimism. What matters most during and after a tragedy, same as during everyday challenges and stress, is realistic optimism: You register what's happening (even how bad it is) *and* the hope and belief you'll be okay. Specifically, the most resilient people see the whole ugly picture, then quickly separate out the things they can't control and what doesn't matter, and focus on what they can control, what actions they can take and what they need to know to maintain hope. That helps drive them to do what's necessary to come out the other side. In fact, lots of research shows that optimism not only is closely linked to well-being and health, it's also consistently associated with the ability to deploy active and healthy coping strategies—another ingredient in the Resilience Rx.

If you haven't noticed already, there's a lot of overlap in the strategies on Charney and Southwick's list. Just as reframing (#2) encourages and builds optimism (#1), optimism helps grow social support (#7), which is an active coping strategy (#6), as is exercise (#8). You get the point, and it's heartening: There isn't only one way or path to build resilience; rather, there are many interconnected ways that feed off of and nourish the others.

COPING FOR THE BEST

In a sense, each Rx ingredient itself can function as an active coping strategy. In a paper in the *European Journal of Psychotraumatology*, Charney and coauthor Brian M. Iacoviello wrote that resilient individuals "act and create their own resilience" through active coping. Just like I talked at the beginning of this book about how we can *do* positivity, we *do* resilience. Active coping means doing something, even if it's small, to address stress, the situation and our feelings head-on, through either our behavior or thought processes. And research shows when we do that, the process helps us not only feel better in the short-term, it also increases our ability to adapt and feeds overall well-being.

Passive or avoidance coping (e.g., withdrawing from life or trying to avoid your feelings or what's happening) does the opposite. Of course after a tragedy or during a crazy-stressful time, you may need to spend time in survival mode. You may want distractions or want nothing to do with facing your feelings. That's okay! Don't ask too much of yourself at first.

When ready, though, if we want to be resilient and build strength and energy, we have to be active participants in unloading our layers of hurt and heavy emotions. That's what active coping is all about. And there are a lot of ways to go about it, including many of the tips in this book, because doing anything that cultivates positive emotions seems to help us. But when caught in the eye of a storm, even skilled sailors need targeted skills. That's what I needed when my dad was diagnosed and after he died, and it's what I need now, off and on in the midst of the COVID-19 crisis. And that's what the Recharge tips deliver.

These strategies are neither a complete list nor a comprehensive plan for treating severe depression or managing trauma or all-encompassing grief. They're not meant to replace professional or group therapy, which many of us still need. They're a start—suggestions and ideas that nudge you in the direction of well-being, positivity and resilience. They're baby steps, and baby steps are how we learn to walk and eventually run.

THE RECHARGE TOOL KIT
Precharge
When your emotions feel insurmountable or all over the place, first turn inward before doing anything else. These three steps have helped me get to a place where I can truly start to recharge, and I've come back to them every time I need a reset.

Acceptance: Be Okay with Not Being Okay
Give yourself time and opportunity to feel your feelings. Emotions are messages, so listen up! Whatever bubbles up, notice it and tell yourself it's okay. Think about them. Accept that what's happening f*#!ing sucks, that it's terrible or hard, that you're hurting or angry. Accept that you might hate your feelings. Maybe you hate how much you hate them or maybe you're conflicted. Whatever your feelings, before trying to do something about them,

be okay with having them. Mindfulness and acceptance of negative feelings actually can help blunt their intensity and increase well-being and life satisfaction over time, according to research.

Often acceptance includes understanding that while other people have it worse than you, your feelings are still valid. In these days of COVID-19, many of us struggle with stress, fear and sadness as well as pangs of guilt. As in: *I know my problems are nothing compared to others; my family is healthy, we have jobs, we have space to spread out and Joe Exotic to distract us.* Listen up— you're *still* allowed to feel bad. This isn't the hardship Olympics. We can be empathetic toward those in dire situations, feel grateful for what we have *and* validate our feelings of loss, disappointment and fear.

On the flip side, it's okay to think you actually have it *the worst.* Losing your job, overdue bills, losing a spouse or a child or any loved one is devastating, and it's okay if you resent those in better circumstances. People may not understand. They might try silver-lining you before you're ready. Tune them out. Don't try to manage your emotions or let anyone else before you've had a chance to sit with them.

Acknowledgment: Recognize That Life Isn't Always Okay

No matter what we do, almost nothing is guaranteed. We might know this intellectually, yet when faced with tragedy or terrible things or events out of our control, it won't feel fair. Accept that you feel that way, then try to acknowledge that life itself isn't fair. There's often no rhyme or reason for who suffers the worst or why good people can be dealt such bad hands.

That's one message resilience researcher Lucy Hone, PhD, director of the New Zealand Institute of Wellbeing & Resilience and author of *Resilient Grieving*, drives home in her work and experienced personally. She had been studying resilience, and shortly after completing her master's degree, her twelve-year-old daughter, Abi, Abi's friend and her friend's mother were killed in a car accident.

In a TED Talk and accompanying article, Hone explained how recognizing that none of us are entitled to an easy or tragedy-free existence helped her come to terms and start coping with what happened. After Abi died, she thought: *Terrible things happen. . . . This is your life now—time to sink or swim.* In other words, instead of getting caught up in the unfairness of life or of trying to understand why this terrible thing happened to *you*—which is usually a pointless exercise anyway—release the idea that you somehow deserved better.

If you are a victim of, say, a crime, then yes, you *did* deserve better. In many other situations, you *do* deserve better. Still, if you can try to redirect your brain from a "why me?" to an "okay, this happened" mentality, it may give you the clarity that can help you better figure out what to do next and how to cope.

Action: "Okay, Let's Go"

I'm not exactly a religious person; I haven't been to church on a non-holiday or prayed before bed like Little Meaggy in too long. I believe strongly in the power of something bigger than all of us, including the collective "all of us." I believe in the power of hope, of people's goodness and, most of all, in the power of positive action. In my moment at the kitchen table, hours before lockdown began in earnest and turned life upside down, I was so overwhelmed and stressed, I wasn't sure what to do. But I was ready to do something.

I got up and walked down to the Presbyterian Church at the end of my street. Weeks before, on the lawn, they'd put up a simple wooden cross between two poles with wire strung back and forth between them. Tied to the wires were dozens of purple ribbons on which people had written prayers and words of hope. I had driven past it dozens of times, and now I was writing down my own hopes for peace and health. I tied my ribbon to the wire and walked home, crying my eyes out.

This small, simple action was cathartic. Still stressed and sad, it helped me feel not so helpless. In doing something that represented and expressed hope and positivity, I felt a charge of energy, and the tiniest bit of momentum that kept me moving. In your most trying times, think about what action might do that for you. What could give you a gentle push to feel like, *Okay, I'm ready now?* Maybe for you it's got nothing to do with hope or positivity; you need to punch a pillow or scream. Maybe it's a deep breath, a workout or a hug. There's no right answer—except action.

Get Outside

Sad? Tired? Stressed? Unmotivated? [Insert any related emotion here]? Stand up. Open the door. Go outside. Walk. Stroll. Pace. Shuffle. Sprint. Be active if you can, or don't. Sit on the front steps or concrete. Lie on the grass. Just surround yourself with fresh air and nature as much as possible; it is as close to an emotional pain reliever as you can get. I cannot understate how much research has shown the benefits of being outside, especially amongst grass, trees and other natural terrain, especially when you're hurting and trying to heal. Here's a small sample of what lies just outside your front door:

- **Vitality.** Researchers use this word to describe a combo of physical and mental energy—that feeling of aliveness, enthusiasm and energy. Multiple studies have found that being in nature gives you a big, healthy dose of vitality; people report feeling more alive, engaged, more energetic, less stressed, and healthier and better overall. What's more, these vital states are linked to more effective coping and resilience.
- **Healthier thoughts.** People who walk through nature areas report less anxiety and don't ruminate on negative experiences as much as those who walk in concrete jungles. In one study, brain scans showed reduced activity in an area linked to risk for mental illness.
- **Life satisfaction, health and well-being.** People feel more satisfied with life on days they spend more time outdoors. And two hours per week in parks or natural environments (all at once or split up) is linked to a significant boost in psychological well-being and physical health.
- **Less stress, more positive emotions.** Walking in nature versus in urban areas lowers heart rate and other markers of stress. It improves mood and elicits other feel-good emotions like gratitude, awe, generosity and kindness.
- **Mental clarity.** Over the course of a day, so much vies for our attention that our brains get fatigued. Several studies show taking in nature (even green spaces in urban environments and even through windows) helps reset or restore attention and focus. It makes us more meditative, creative and open, which may help us better deal with hard times.
- **Lower PTSD-related symptoms.** More therapists are turning to nature-based therapies even for severe trauma. One study of military veterans

reported that after a four-day rafting trip, PTSD symptoms dropped an average of 29 percent, stress was down 21 percent and life satisfaction and happiness increased. The results may be at least in part due to eliciting awe. (Check out page 39 for more on awe.)

- **Emotional, mental and physical healing.** Several studies show that gardens, trees and other landscaping and even good views out of a hospital window reduce pain and speed healing, plus offer emotional and mental benefits to patients and caregivers.

For many of us in nonurban areas, stay-at-home orders have ironically pushed us outside more than ever, and it's been a true bright spot in this ordeal. For me, that first week home, I was missing my morning gym along with much of my sunny optimism and positivity, and felt stuck, metaphorically and literally, between my little home office and the kitchen table/classroom. So at the start of week two, I got up early and jogged (something I hadn't done regularly in years) around Echo Lake Park—through lots of trees, past a waterfall, around a pond. Everything was so still and quiet, and it woke me up. I felt freer than I had in a while.

When our problems and feelings seem so big and scary, if we can step out and take in the largesse of the world—the trees, the sky, the dirt, the chipmunks—as well as its size and see that the world is still turning, it opens us up. That helps us surrender some of our negative emotions and heaviness. I didn't think I would ever run outside again, but I plan to keep it up even after gyms open, along with afternoon family dog walks, coffee on the patio and cocktails on the porch.

Cry It Out

I'm a big crier, as are lots of other Fully Charged folks I know. Because while living Fully Charged means getting in touch with and growing your well of positive emotions, it requires paying attention to *all* your emotions. So just as my big Yay energy is out there, my tears flow freely. Crying also helps push an emotional reset button. It's as if each tear sheds a bit of anger, sadness, hurt or anxiety, and releasing those bits leaves space to fill with more positive things.

While some science backs up the crying-as-catharsis theory, newer research suggests that, like a lot of things, it's subjective: What *you* believe about crying may be the most important factor in whether it helps you feel better or worse. The experts also found that people who are more in tune with their emotions and regularly express a range of them tend to think crying is more beneficial.

I don't love crying in front of others, although there are times I can't avoid it. For better or worse, most of us have learned that it makes us seem vulnerable or weak. So I usually save my tears for the shower or the car. My friend Christine, a nurse who can't fall apart at a patient's side nor wants to with her kids or friends, likewise told me the shower's been her safe space since her mom died years ago.

It's actually perfect tear territory if you think about it. You're naked and can't hear much, and thus already somewhat vulnerable, plus it's a mostly distraction-free zone, all of which can help you get into your feelings and open the floodgates. The water and cleansing also serve as nice metaphors for tears and healing. So hop in and think of your tears or the water washing away some pain or other hard feelings. You may just emerge feeling a little more refreshed and open to brighter moments.

Initiate Operation Good Grief

My dad was just sixty-six when he died. Pop wasn't ready to say goodbye, and his family wasn't either. We needed more years on the receiving end of his signature gesture we called The Point, where he'd point at you in his Pop way and give you a look that made you feel instantly recognized, important and understood. We needed more family parties where he'd dole out scratch-off lotto tickets and holler "Winner!" or "Weiner!" And we needed more summers of him filling his pockets with store-bought sea glass to scatter along the beach so he could watch his grandkids "discover" it.

Pop was the best. He was *my* guy, the one in our family I had always been closest to. And watching him go through chemo and radiation, get sicker and eventually pass away drained me like nothing had before. It tested my usually sunny outlook and all the Fully Charged skills that previously had helped me ride through hardships. One day I joined him for chemo and cuddled up to him in his giant vinyl recliner, and he told me not to be so negative. I forget what I said to elicit that response; I only remember trying to be present, realistic and accepting of the situation. I do remember his remark hitting me like a truck.

I wasn't a negative person! That's not me! He needed the Fully Charged Miss Meags more than ever, and it took him saying that for me to realize I did, too. His comment helped me see that even though the future looked bleak for him, and for me without him, there were still good things in the world and positivity to be had. Acceptance and optimism aren't mutually exclusive; I could live with what felt like a stabbing pain in my chest and still be okay, even smile. Even if he died.

After that day, I decided to work hard to find the good bits of life and flex all those resilience muscles I'd built over the years. I started by thinking about how his illness had given us a few months to try on the idea of losing him if it came to that—a chance to ask big questions, take advantage of and savor every moment and, should the time come, to properly say goodbye.

It was around then I committed to finding at least one good thing about life every day, taking a picture and posting it to Instagram with the hashtag #operationgoodgrief. I chose things like an oasis of daffodils at the end of a walkway, the magical foam on a latte, an "It's Raining Tacos" dance party with my kids. I've since had several people tell me they've tried #operationgoodgrief and it's helped them, too.

Optimism in Action

Operation Good Grief works because it sparks positive emotions in the moment and has far-reaching implications for how we grieve and feel down the line. It forced me to live and look beyond my grief to find joy amidst the pain and sadness. An example of the cognitive reappraisal and "meaning-finding" that's an essential part of resilience, it helped me uncover positive meaning in the hardest moments of my adult life. And, as the research shows, people who are able to reframe extreme stress are less likely to experience depressive symptoms, and they experience more positive emotions, which, as I talked about in chapter 2, lead to all sorts of positive outcomes for energy and well-being.

During bereavement, specifically, research shows positive emotions can lead people to develop more abstract, long-term goals. And, along with positive emotions, those goals predict greater well-being a year later. In other words, reappraisal and meaning-finding can make you more optimistic.

A friend once told me about her friend Shannon, who had struggled for years with infertility. After six miscarriages, she and her husband stopped trying for a child. After some time, she started deliberately focusing on what was good about her life as it was, even though life was painfully different from what she wanted and expected. Having always loved to travel, she embraced the freedom to take spur-of-the-moment trips and plan adventure getaways. She also took the worst experience of her life and turned it into something good to help others: She started a local support group for women dealing with similar grief and eventually a fertility counseling business and a podcast, *Happily Ever After (Without Children!)*.

Then, at forty-five years old, without "trying," she got pregnant and gave birth to a healthy baby. A few weeks before, though, her father-in-law suddenly passed away. Just as she had in the aftermath of her miscarriages, she saw that in this tragic situation—that her father-in-law would never meet this long-anticipated grandson—there was also hope. As one life ended and grief set in, her baby would bring so much joy to the family.

Shannon's story shows twice over how looking for what's good even in the worst times is a way to practice optimism. Even if the positive emotions you summon feel like a temporary salve, the mere action of looking is itself hopeful—hope that there are bright spots out there, you might find them and you'll feel better.

Find Teachers

The day my dad was diagnosed, I went to an Orangetheory class to literally work out some emotion. I was such a hot mess that I broke down on the treadmill, and the woman next to me asked if I was okay. After telling her why I wasn't, she said: "I lost my dad to pancreatic cancer a few years ago." After class, we talked, cried, bonded and became real friends.

Connecting with Tracey was a gift. I had friends who supported me, but none knew what a death sentence pancreatic cancer was or what I was going through like she did; with her, I didn't have to get into the gory details. More than a friend, she became a loss mentor, giving me advice—like making sure

I got videos with Pop's voice—and showing what it looked like to come out the other side of this terrible thing. In her, I saw how you can never stop missing your person and still continue living. That didn't feel possible at first; she helped me believe it.

Nearly all the highly resilient people Charney and Southwick studied named at least one person they looked to for cues on how to behave, think about and approach extreme stress. Your role models can be literally anyone—friends, family, kids, famous people or someone you heard or read about. They can be those who suffered similar tragedies or fought a different fight. The important thing: In the face of adversity they embody the resilience you want and act in a way that inspires and shows you a way forward.

You can also have more than one. I looked to Tracey, who had been through exactly what I was going through. I also found strength in Brandon Farbstein, who has a rare form of dwarfism and, at barely twenty years old, has emerged as one of the most inspiring speakers of our generation. Picking up books and reading articles about how people overcome hardships can be incredibly helpful, too. Right now, as I'm struggling with work and home-schooling and fear over the virus, I'm finding ideas and comfort in stories of how others are coping. Like my friend Lindsay Powers, author of the book *You Can't F*ck Up Your Kids*. Her approach has helped me chill out considerably.

Whomever you choose, watch and model these teachers. From the time we're babies, we learn so much through observation—so observe with a thoughtful eye on resilience. What coping skills do your role models employ and how do they talk about stressful times? How do they think about the future? What "rules" do they follow? Modeling is especially effective at helping us learn coping strategies and how to reframe. And optimism is especially catchy—one of the best ways to become more optimistic is to hang out with other optimists.

Be Needed

I remember reading in the *New York Times* about a cancer patient who had suffered for years with depression. He had been caring for his ill mother, and when she died, he felt adrift and aimless. He later told his doctor that during that time he wouldn't have cared whether he died, but now, Sadie needed him. Sadie was his cat. Something in him clicked when he began caring for his furry friend.

When tragedy strikes or you're struggling, it's okay to be needy, to feel listless and to not want to think about anything. But being needed, even if it feels at times like a burden, can give you a sense of purpose and give your life meaning. It can push you (in a good way) to seek out healthy, active coping strategies. Sometimes fulfilling the needs of others is itself an effective coping strategy.

After my dad died, I wanted to crawl into a hole. Good thing I had three tiny humans who needed to be fed, bathed and loved. They were a big part of what kept me going—to workouts, to work, to the attic for holiday decorations and to the grocery store floral department. The research on having purpose in life shows it's incredibly healthy, both mentally and physically. It's linked to increased resilience, well-being, stress management and longevity.

Like grief itself, purpose is personal; you must find something meaningful to you. As the story from the *Times* showed, pets can fill that role by making you feel needed and loved. Even hamsters, finches and fish can give life meaning and a sense of stability, suggests one study. Aside from purpose, other research shows animals reduce feelings of loneliness, which itself increases resilience and well-being.

Volunteerism and community engagement also increase sense of purpose. Research shows it may have an especially significant impact after trauma, during life transitions and for depression. After my dad died, my mom threw herself into rehabbing Jackson Woods, a vast acreage near her house that suffered in Hurricane Sandy. A few weeks after Pop's funeral, Hurricane Kathy hit—she had the mayor on speed dial, was applying for grants and mobilizing volunteers. I could see the change in her almost immediately and a fresh spark with each new development or event.

Do Good

There's a family in my town, the Roofeners, who cover their house in insane balloon art and other huge decorations at Halloween. Anyone who wants to tour the balloon fantasy land, hang in the VIP tent or spin the prize wheel is asked to leave a donation for the Crohn's and Colitis Foundation. Last year's take: a blowout $30,000. They started the tradition as a way of coping after their nine-year-old was diagnosed with the disease. During quarantine, they put up weekly balloon displays—from a giant stethoscope saluting our healthcare heroes to an oversize apple to high-five teachers—as a way to support their friend's business and shower Westfield with positivity.

This is one of countless stories of how people channel pain into a new purpose of doing good and find relief or healing in the process. Like volunteering, kindness, altruism and simple helping behaviors are strongly linked to a greater sense of purpose, resilience and well-being. They boost happiness and positive emotions and help us feel more connected to people, which in turn give our lives more meaning and strengthen relationships.

Research suggests our own suffering may even make us more empathetic, driving us to *want* to do good for others. Consider the outpouring of support during large-scale tragedies like what we're dealing with right now. We're all suffering, in a way—even if not as much as those on the front lines in hospitals and grocery stores—and all those good deeds are worth double; they help those in immediate need, and we end up improving our own lot. You don't need to make grand gestures. Even just sending a thank-you note to someone who impacted your life increases happiness and feelings of meaning. So start small. Write a note, donate time or money to a cause, pay for coffee for the person behind you—it's worth it.

Laugh It Off

"The buttons on my jeans have started social distancing from each other."

"Alexa, homeschool my kids."

Those were two of the memes I got via text during the first week of lockdown from my pal Lara, a teacher and meme machine. I was so grateful for the hilarity, and when I found out the incredible personal hardships she was dealing with at the time—as well as major ones she'd overcome in the past—I admired her and appreciated the humor even more. She later told me that memes—and other types of humor—give her brain a break and lift her mood in times of stress. They also give her something to relate to, and a means to laugh and bond with friends.

Lara pretty much summed up what the research says about how and why humor helps us cope, reduces distress and encourages resilience. Humor is a hit of pure pleasure that spikes dopamine and other feel-good brain chemicals and increases positive emotions, which broaden our thinking. And with a more open mind, it's easier to engage in the reappraisal and perspective-shifting that helps us deal with trauma, tragedy and intense stress. Humor has been linked to lower anxiety and catastrophizing thought patterns. And, as Lara pointed out, it helps you feel closer to others, which shores up your support network, another big factor in resilience.

Memes or any jokes that directly take aim at pain points (*ahem* home-schooling under house arrest) can be especially soothing because they manage to combine both positive (laughing, humor) with the negative (tragedy). That helps with reframing and offers a safer, more palatable way to face tragic, hard and scary stuff. Think about it: If a joke belittles an awful situation, it's easier to feel more in control of it. A coronavirus meme is akin to making fun of the schoolyard bully; it takes away some of this scary, stressful thing's power and transfers it to you. And that can increase your capacity to cope and adapt.

Even when depressed, we likely don't lose our appreciation of humor, research suggests. We may just have to try harder to find the funny. So watch a comedy or stand-up special, follow meme accounts on social media, call your funniest friend, hang around with kids and focus on the ridiculous stuff they say. Anything about yourself you can laugh at, too?

Tell Your Stories

One afternoon while hanging an Easter wreath on our door, I saw my neighbor and we started talking. I asked her why she didn't decorate her house for holidays anymore. She told me her dad died two years before, and she didn't feel like celebrating—it didn't feel right to celebrate without him. She opened up about other things, too. She cried. We laughed a little. I shared a bit about my experience losing my dad, about Operation Good Grief and how much our family always loved seeing her house dressed up in its Easter (and Christmas and Halloween) best.

A few days later, I saw carrot decorations on her front porch. I certainly didn't do anything special except ask questions and listen. She made the choice to open up, and it seemed to make a difference for her.

When we're hurting, turning to and getting support from others is like emotional steroids; it gives us strength to better cope and adapt to trauma, tragedy and a host of negative feelings. Research has shown again and again that positive relationships and support help people come away from adverse life events mentally healthier—less risk of depression, less likely to suffer PTSD symptoms, higher markers of well-being.

One big way we get support from others *and* how we can support ourselves: Tell our stories. Here are four tips for how to do it in ways that help you better process emotions and build resilience:

Expand Your Audience

If someone asks how you're doing and you feel comfortable with them, answer honestly. While nothing beats talking to our nearest and dearest, if you've been telling the same story to the same people, or you stopped telling it because everyone close to you already knows, you can easily feel stuck and get stuck in your head.

Sharing your story with someone new or unexpected who doesn't know the details—like my neighbor did or like I did at Orangetheory—may help you think about, explain or process your experiences, feelings and ways of coping in new or different ways. And that may help you continue to heal, even if just enough that you put out your equivalent of carrot decorations.

Share Your First Draft—Early and Often

Whatever you're dealing with, talk about it or write about it. Just get it out. Happiness researcher Sonja Lyubomirsky and her colleagues conducted a study for which they had people either talk, write or think about their worst experience. They found that writing and talking help you process negative experiences better than merely thinking about them, and that doing so leads to improved mental and physical health and increased life satisfaction.

The researchers explained that translating thoughts to words forces you to organize and analyze problems and emotions in a way thinking doesn't—in a way that can better facilitate a solution or at least greater acceptance. You create a narrative that "often leads to searching for meaning, enhanced understanding and identity formation," write the researchers. Chronicling your hardships externally also, of course, helps you unburden yourself.

All of this is not to say thinking about your experiences isn't helpful. It's just that talking or writing may help you process them better. It may also save you some pain. Ironically, thinking about traumatic experiences is closer to reexperiencing them, which makes it more painful than talking about them.

Revisit the Prequels

When I ran my first marathon and my blistered feet started bleeding around mile 20, I got through it, in part, by thinking about how I clawed back to health from anorexia. During childbirth, I thought about that marathon. When I had pneumonia and felt sicker than I ever had and was forced to slow down and miss three weeks of work, I thought about childbirth and maternity leave.

These days, when I find myself in a dark place over the pandemic, I think about getting through pneumonia. I also think about 9/11. The fear, the uncertainty, the everything-feels-different-ness of that time is so similar to these pandemic vibes. But I eventually took the train again and went back to work, and taking my shoes off at airport security became normal. And someday, I trust that going to Trader Joe's won't be so scary and wearing a mask won't feel so weird.

Our past holds an incredible amount of strength and potential optimism that we can use to help get through a difficult present and imagine a better future. When times get tough, unlock it: Think back to past adversity and hard things you've done; they're proof you can do hard things now. Think about what it felt like to come out the other side. Feel proud of it. Tell yourself you're strong now because you did x, y and z then. And, of course, remind yourself that the pain and struggle was temporary and everything turned out, and it will this time, too.

My friend Allison is a therapist—a "worry coach" to her kid clients—who told me when clients get scared or anxious, she tells them to "Use their logic." Remember that whatever you're going through now, even if it's the worst or scariest thing that's ever happened, logic tells you that before this, you went through another worst or scariest thing. You're still here. And you can deal with this. This too shall pass.

Revise and Rewrite

As I talked about in the beginning of this chapter, you can reframe and spin your story in lots of different but still truthful ways. So when you're ready, tell your story with a new perspective. Don't edit out the bad stuff, try to work in the good. The best books, movies, TV shows, great plays—they all have elements of tragedy and triumph, pain and joy. That's how this experience can be.

For example, when I tell people or think about how much I miss my dad now, I include how lucky I was to have a dad who left a gaping hole in my heart. And when I think back to all these weeks at home, I think about how hard it's been, but also how I haven't been stuck here; I'm safe here. I'll remember the extra time with my kids and the outpouring of kindness.

I'm also editing the ending. I'm choosing to believe that when all is said and done, when I've mourned the losses both massive and piddly, this time at home will end up being a gift I didn't want and didn't necessarily need but will nonetheless become one of my most cherished. There was a post making its way around Facebook in the early days of lockdown that talked about some what ifs on the horizon for our kids. It asked: What if, instead of lagging behind in school, our kids come out ahead because of this? Ahead because they spent more time playing, more time with family, more time doing simple things at home and at a slower pace. And what if they have more empathy, learn to value teachers more, feel more grateful for playdates and see once-invisible workers as essential heroes? It perfectly exemplified this idea that we can revise and rewrite even the hard stories.

Consider how you might end up ahead of whatever you're going through. Even if you've experienced great loss or immeasurable pain and feel left behind by the world, can you think of one or two ways you *might* come out ahead? If you can do that, you're already there.

Do Something Scary

A few days after Pop died, I took my kids to Liberty Science Center, slipped into a safety harness, climbed up to a steel I-beam eighteen feet in the air and walked across it—no small feat for someone scared sh*tless of heights. My palms pumped out sweat, my heart raced and I could barely breathe. After losing Pop, I was so numb and terrified of what life ahead would look like, I weirdly wanted to do something that terrified me in a different way. Given the science center was one of his favorite spots, this seemed like the exact right something.

Facing fears head-on can help build resilience. By exposing yourself to what is, in a way, a safer or more manageable stressor or fear, it can increase your sense of control and lower your anxiety in the face of other types of stressors and fear. It's kind of like how a vaccine works; you expose your immune system to a little bit or different form of the virus in order to teach your army of immune cells how to deal and shore up your defenses.

Ideally you do a scary thing before a more traumatic experience, which is kind of what I did. I knew Pop was going to die, so that wasn't quite as traumatizing as what was coming: learning to live without him and with this pain in my chest instead. The experience was thrilling, horrible and wonderful, and it helped me feel alive, invigorated and a little more able to handle everything that came next, including the funeral, the eulogy, going back to work and my kids', my mom's and my own grief.

BEWARE THE ENERGY VAMPIRES
Emotional Hijackers

After or during a tragedy, our feelings can swing wildly day to day, moment to moment—and so can our needs. But what you always need: nonjudgmental, flexible and receptive support and the freedom to process grief and other intense emotions on your own timeline and in your own messy way. That's not always what we get. Knowingly or not, people may try to hijack your emotions in ways that leave you feeling worse.

You can't stop anyone from being insensitive or thoughtless. You can notice what's happening and walk away or directly signal that person's acting like a creep. Here are three common hijackers, and ideas for how to shut them down:

- **The Feelings Police.** They'll try to enforce a set of rules for how *they* think you should be feeling or acting. Maybe they think some arbitrary grief expiration date has passed. Or they gloss over what happened or don't get why you're (still) struggling. Either be direct or shine a sarcasm-filled light on their shocking lack of compassion and empathy.

For example, if someone says: "Wow, you're *still* really upset, huh?" Try a reply like: "Yeah, I guess I should find a new therapist. Are you available?" Or if they don't get why you're so torn up over, say, losing a pet because Fluffy was "just a dog," try a version of: "Lucky you, you must have never lost your best friend."

- **The Grief Thief.** This is a person who jumps in to tell their own related story of pain or even tries to one-up you or tell you all the things you *should* be doing. However it goes, the interaction ends up being all about them. For example, say your sister is sick. The Grief Thief launches into a long story about when her friend had cancer. Or maybe it was her sister's boyfriend's cousin. And she ended up dying. Or she didn't because she took special herbs, and cut out sugar and *blah, blah, blah.*

  Grief Thieves' hearts may be in the right place, but it backfires. So extricate yourself ASAP, or try a curt: "That must have been awful *for you*" or "I'll be sure to *ask* if I need more advice" before walking away.

- **The Pain Pusher.** There are certain times or certain people with whom you don't want to talk about your feelings or what's going on. Maybe you're doing okay that day or want to be distracted. Pain Pushers try to lure or pull you back into your sad place by treating you like a wounded bird or constantly asking if you're okay. Like Grief Thieves, their intentions, although potentially good, are tone-deaf.

  In those cases, spell it out for them: "I was feeling good today, but I guess that's not the vibe I'm giving off." Or a simple "I really don't want to talk about it."

MURPHY'S LAWS

Netflix and nada
Accepting your feelings, reframing, finding purpose, telling your story—if the work of recharging feels like too much, take a break. Find a distraction or escape or turn off your brain for a bit. (TikTok

scroll, anyone?!) Avoidance is like the pizza pig-out of resiliency; do it every day and you'll feel gross, but once in a while, it's perfect and exactly what you may need.

Call your people

After two weeks of lockdown, I hit a wall. I called my sister, and we talked for forty minutes about nothing, which we hadn't done in years. Neither of us cried. Nobody was too into her feelings. We each knew the other was struggling, but we didn't talk about it; we just talked. And it was amazing—like being wrapped in the comfortable blanket of normalcy.

Put joy on the calendar

Shortly after my dad died, I planned for my daughter and me to get our ears pierced. Then we planned a vacation. Even amidst the corona confusion around summer 2020, we made plans—for parties, beach days, a friend's September wedding in Ohio. When faced with a bleak present, planning future fun is a simple way of practicing optimism; it creates Yay in the moment through anticipation and almost guarantees it down the road.

Create a smile pile

I've kept a little collection of stuff on my desk for the past fifteen years: a piece of orange ribbon from my wedding dress, a doily from a trip to France, a pack of Squirrel gum my brother gave me (a nod to an inside joke) and other random things that give me warm fuzzies. I dive into it whenever I'm caught in a moment of major stress or anxiety. Few things feel so grounding and uplifting at the same time as these mementos.

A FINAL YAY TO TAKE WITH YOU

As I was wrapping up work on this book, an Instagram follower randomly DM-ed me a picture of her Snapple cap, telling me the "Real Fact #1445" printed on the inside reminded her of me. It said, "A single lightning bolt contains enough energy to cook 100,000 pieces of toast." *Whaat?!* Well, this supercool factoid got me thinking about how every tip in this book is, in its own way, a mini lightning bolt, each glowing with energy and the potential to do amazing things. And just like we have a choice to focus on the negative or to look for the positive, you can choose to let the sparks fizzle out when you put down this book, or you can decide now to use them to cook up a life more amazing than a truckload of toast—more awesome than you could even imagine. I hope you choose the latter.

Acknowledgments

To Pop: It really stinks that you don't get to hold this book in your hands, because it's electric, and it's for you, my forever cheerleader. You fanned every creative flame (and collaged it in the basement) from my Hallmark rip-off "Meaga Cards" to my first published article (a newspaper clip about an exterminator?!) and every one after. As I cry-write this, I'm so grateful that losing you led me to #operationgoodgrief and the realization that I *had* to write this book.

Big Nana: I miss you every darn day, too. You were the OG holiday over-decorator. (Oh, that light-up ceramic Christmas tree was everything.) I realized and fell in love with the power words have to connect us (and the magic of swirly cursive) thanks to our weekly letters, now bundled in my attic. Don't worry, I'm not working too hard.

Mom/Nana: You're third, but that means you're breathing—yay! I want to be you when I grow up, minus those things we've talked about. I will forever admire your relentless confidence that made me believe everything is always possible.

Erin and Kevin: My sibs! You complete our Circle of Five. Bones, you are my younger and wiser best friend—my first call when I need to ask, "Am I being Mom?!" Kev, you're Pop, and your best friend makes a pretty amazing husband.

That's you, **Patrick!** I know public praise is not your thing, but can I gush a little? I can! It's my book! You are my logic, my reason, my hunky chef, the man who made me a leprechaun Murphy and a mama.

Charley, James and Brooks: I love you sooo much! Team Murphy—you're in here a lot, a lot, and for good reason: You're the ultimate charging station.

There are a lot of other people I'm not related to who made this book possible and who I need to thank, starting with super-agent Laura Nolan. We had coffee.

I cried. She *still* signed me! We pushed and pulled at my proposal for what felt like forever, then took it shopping. She managed to sell it to editor extraordinaire Marian Lizzi and power publisher Lindsay Gordon Bezalel even though I said in our pitch meeting, like the uncool fan girl I was, "I really, really like it here, and I really, really want to be a Penguin Random House author." (Hey, Michelle Obama's book cover was on the wall—I geeked out!) Thank you, Team YFCL for believing in me and cheering on the Yay every step of the way.

Now I'm screaming *THANK YOU* to my collaborator Beth Janes O'Keefe in all caps, and it's still not loud enough. There is a hamster on a wheel running nonstop in my head. She put that hamster on an actual course with a beginning, middle and end . . . on deadline. Just Beth. Mic drop. THANK YOU.

Of course, magazine editors are some of the smartest, funniest, most interesting people I know, and my twenty-plus-year career has received a jolt from each of these powerhouses: Lucy Danziger, Jane Francisco, Kate Lewis, Michele Promaulayko, Lori Majewski, Carla Levy, Dana Points, Lauren Purcell, Cindy Searight, Tula Karras, Ellen Levine, Joanna Coles, Liz Baker Plosser, Aya Kanai, Leah Wyar, Kim Cheney, Lisa Bain, Stephanie Dolgoff, Rachel Rothman, Lexie Sachs, Carolyn Forte, Jaclyn London, Betty Rose Gold, April Franzino, Kristen Saladino, Birnur Aral, Susan Westmoreland, Nicole Saporita, Andra Chantim, Leah Rocketto, Peter Hemmel, Kate Merker, Catherine Lo, Madeleine Frank Reeves, Meredith Rollins, Susan Spencer, Donna Duarte-Ladd, Sarah Smith, Devon Tomb, Laura Brounstein, Jessica Knoll, Jackie Risser, Elisabeth Egan, Courtney Rubin, Sara Austin, Laura Kalehoff, Erin Hobday Ferguson, Liz Miersch, Sheila Monaghan, Jaclyn Byrer, Marissa Stephenson, Ellen Seidman, Elizabeth Goodman Artis, Liz Vaccariello, Lindsey Benoit O'Connell, Kate White, Isabel Burton, John Searles, Lesley Rotchford, Sally Lee, Christina Ferrari and TK more (that's a publishing joke).

And finally, a big, HUGE thanks to the Yay humans who've sparked and supported me, sometimes without even knowing it: Marie Forleo, Karena Dawn, Katrina Scott, Kate Northrup, Candace Cameron Bure, Paula Faris, Kate T. Parker, Maria Menounos, Kevin Undergaro, Laurie Gelman, Vern Yip, Norma Kamali, Joan Lunden, Brandon Farbstein, Terri Cole, Kendall Toole, Jillian Michaels, Kim Constable, Denise Austin, Blessing Adesiyan, Debbie-Ann White, Sarah Friar, Nora Fleming, Dasha Libin, Sarah Politis, Heather Stillufsen, Meredith Sinclair, Meghan Linsey, Jill Koziol, my *Off the Gram* podcast posse: Jamie Hess, Christine Bibbo Herr and Heidi Kristoffer; Amy Jo Martin, Ali Feller, Kafi Drexel, Dorothy Beal, Danielle Shine, Marigo Mihalos, Marisa Brahney, Kathleen Butler Smith, Dina El Nabli and Liz Snyder. I'm LIT . . . with gratitude!

Notes

Introduction: Lightning Bolts

xviii **our brain's evolutionary instinct:** Baumeister, Roy F., Ellen Bratslavsky, Catrin Finkenauer and Kathleen D. Vohs. 2001. "Bad is Stronger than Good." *Review of General Psychology*. December 5(4): 323–370. https://doi.org/10.1037/1089-2680.5.4.323.

xx **if well-being increases:** Unanue, Wenceslao, Marcos E. Gómez, Diego Cortez, Juan C. Oyanedel and Andrés Mendiburo-Seguel. 2017. "Revisiting the Link between Job Satisfaction and Life Satisfaction: The Role of Basic Psychological Needs." *Frontiers in Psychology*. 8: 680. https://doi.org/10.3389/fpsyg.2017.00680.

xx **impact physical health:** Mastroianni, Karen, and Julie Storberg-Walker. 2014. "Do work relationships matter? Characteristics of workplace interactions that enhance or detract from employee perceptions of well-being and health behaviors." *Health Psychology and Behavioral Medicine*. 2(1): 798–819. https://doi.org/10.1080/21642850.2014.933343.

xx **major life stressors:** Ozbay, Faith, Douglas C. Johnson, Eleni Dimoulas, C.A. Morgan III, Dennis Charney and Steven Southwick. 2007. "Social Support and Resilience to Stress: From Neurobiology to Clinical Practice." *Psychiatry* (Edgmont). May 4(5): 35–40. https://www.ncbi.nlm.nih.gov/pmc/articles/PMC2921311/.

Chapter 1: Take Charge

3 **more positive state:** Fredrickson, Barbara L. 2013. "Positive Emotions Broaden and Build." In *Advances in Experimental Social Psychology*. Edited by Patrica Devine and Ashby Plant. 47:1–53. Elsevier. https://doi.org/10.1016/B978-0-12-407236-7.00001-2. Layous, Kristin, S. Katherine Nelson, Jaime L. Kurtz and

Sonja Lyubomirsky. 2017. "What triggers prosocial effort? A positive feedback loop between positive activities, kindness, and well-being." *The Journal of Positive Psychology*. 12(4): 385–398. https://doi.org/10.1080/17439760.2016.1198924.

4 **early concepts and research:** University of Pennsylvania, Authentic Happiness. "Barbara L. Fredrickson, Ph.D." Accessed on May 17, 2020. https://www.authentichappiness.sas.upenn.edu/faculty-profile/barbara-l-fredrickson-phd.

4 **broaden-and-build theory:** Fredrickson, Barbara L. 2001. "The Role of Positive Emotions in Positive Psychology: The Broaden-and-Build Theory of Positive Emotions." *American Psychologist*. March 56(3): 218–226. https://doi.org/10.1037/0003-066X.56.3.218. Fredrickson, Barbara L. 2013. "Positive Emotions Broaden and Build." *Advances in Experimental Social Psychology*. Edited by Patricia Devine and Ashby Plant. 47:1–53 Elsevier. https://doi.org/10.1016/B978-0-12-407236-7.00001-2.

4 **getting better and better:** Fredrickson, Barbara L. 2001. "The Role of Positive Emotions in Positive Psychology: The Broaden-and-Build Theory of Positive Emotions." *American Psychologist*. March 56(3): 218–226.

4 **"A positive emotion may loosen":** Fredrickson, Barbara L. 2001. "The Role of Positive Emotions in Positive Psychology: The Broaden-and-Build Theory of Positive Emotions." *American Psychologist*. March 56(3): 218–226.

5 **build and strengthen relationships:** Saphire-Bernstein, Shimon, and Shelley E. Taylor. 2013. "Close Relationships and Happiness." In *Oxford Handbook of Happiness*. Edited by Ilona Boniwell, Susan A. David, and Amanda Conley Ayers. https://doi.org/10.1093/oxfordhb/9780199557257.013.0060.

5 **get you interacting:** Sandstrom, Gillian M., and Elizabeth W. Dunn. 2014. "Social Interactions and Well-Being: The Surprising Power of Weak Ties." *Personality and Social Psychology Bulletin*. Jul 40(7): 910–922. https://doi.org/10.1177/0146167214529799.

5 **made the bold statement:** Seligman, Martin E. P. 2011. "Happiness Is Not Enough." Accessed on May 17, 2020. https://www.authentichappiness.sas.upenn.edu/newsletters/flourishnewsletters/newtheory.

5 **called a "helper's high":** Luks, Allan. 1988. "Helper's high: Volunteering makes people feel good, physically and emotionally." *Psychology Today*, 22(10), 34–42.

6 **call it emotional contagion:** Dezecache, Guillaume, Pierre Jacob and Julie Grézes. 2015. "Emotional contagion: its scope and limits." *Trends in Cognitive Science*. Jun 19(6): 297–9. https://doi.org/10.1016/j.tics.2015.03.011.

6 **seven hundred thousand Facebook users:** Kramer, Adam D.I., Jamie E. Guillory and Jeffrey T. Hancock. 2014. "Experimental evidence of massive-scale emotional contagion through social networks." *PNAS*. June 111(24): 8788–8790. https://doi.org/10.1073/pnas.1320040111.

7 **simple habit and routine:** Miller, Kevin J., Amitai Shenhav and Elliot A. Ludvig. 2019. "Habits Without Values." *Psychological Review*. 126(2), 292–311. https://doi.org/10.1037/rev0000120.

9   **"True mental self-care":** Leaf, Caroline (@drcarolineleaf). 2019. Instagram.
    November 16. https://www.instagram.com/p
    /B48pTvHA9P5/.

10 **when Martin Seligman:** University of Pennsylvania, Authentic Happiness.
    "Martin Seligman, Ph.D." Accessed May 17, 2020. https://www
    .authentichappiness.sas.upenn.edu/faculty-profile/profile-dr-martin-seligman.

10 **was only "half-baked":** Lopez, Shane J., and Matthew W. Gallagher. 2009. "A
    Case for Positive Psychology." In *Oxford Handbook of Positive Psychology.* Edited
    by C. R. Synder and Shane J. Lopez. 3–6. New York: Oxford University
    Press, Inc.

10 **What's *right* about:** Seligman, Martin E. P., and Mihaly Csikszentmihalyi.
    2000. "Positive psychology: An introduction." *American Psychologist.* 55: 5–14.
    https://doi.org/10.1037/0003-066X.55.1.5.

10 **"families" of strengths:** Park, Nansook, Christopher Peterson and Martin
    E. P. Seligman. 2004. "Strengths of character and well-being." *Journal of Social
    and Clinical Psychology.* 23(5), 603–619. https://doi.org/10.1521/jscp
    .23.5.603.50748.

10 **called the PERMA theory:** University of Pennsylvania, Positive Psychology
    Center. "PERMA™ Theory of Well-Being and PERMA™ Workshops." Accessed
    on May 17, 2020. https://ppc.sas.upenn.edu/learn-more/perma-theory-well
    -being-and-perma-workshops.

11 **known as prioritizing positivity:** Catalino, Lahnna I., Sara B. Algoe and
    Barbara L. Fredrickson. 2014. "Prioritizing Positivity: An Effective Approach to
    Pursuing Happiness?" *Emotion.* December 14(6): 1155–1161. https://doi.org
    /10.1037/a0038029.

12 **feeling good prompts people:** Fredrickson, Barbara L. 2001. "The Role of
    Positive Emotions in Positive Psychology: The Broaden-and-Build Theory of
    Positive Emotions." *American Psychologist.* March 56(3): 218–226.

12 **psychological well-being and happiness:** Lyubomirsky, Sonja, Laura King
    and Ed Diener. 2005. "The benefits of frequent positive affect: does happiness
    lead to success?" *Psychology Bulletin.* 131(6): 803–855. https://doi.org/10.1037
    /0033-2909.131.6.803.

12 **happier, more optimistic people:** Steptoe, Andrew, Samantha Dockray and
    Jane Wardle. 2009. "Positive Affect and Psychobiological Processes Relevant to
    Health." *Journal of Personality.* December 77(6): 1747–1776. https://doi.org
    /10.1111/j.1467-6494.2009.00599.x. Hernandez, Rosalba, Sarah M. Bassett,
    Seth W. Boughton, Stephanie A. Schuette, Eva W. Shiu and Judith T.
    Moskowitz. 2007. "Psychological Well-Being and Physical Health:
    Associations, Mechanisms, and Future Directions." *Emotion Review.* 10(1):
    18–29. https://doi.org/10.1177/1754073917697824.

12 **most optimistic women:** Lee, Lewina O., Peter James, Emily S. Zevon, Eric S.
    Kim, Claudia Trudel-Fitzgerald, Avron Spiro III, Francine Grodstein, and Laura
    D. Kubzansky. 2019. "Optimism is associated with exceptional longevity in 2

epidemiologic cohorts of men and women." *PNAS* 10. 116(37): 18357–18362. https://doi.org/10.1073/pnas.1900712116.

16 **"7 Secrets to Happiness":** Buchan, Meaghan. 2005. "7 Secrets to Happiness." *Cosmopolitan.* June. 180–184.

19 **neural plasticity at work:** Shaffer, Joyce. 2012. "Neuroplasticity and Positive Psychology in Clinical Practice: A Review for Combined Benefits." *Psychology.* 3(12A): 1110–1115. http://dx.doi.org/10.4236/psych.2012.312A164.

Chapter 2: The Positive Charge

23 **most profound insights:** Duckworth, Angela. 2020. "Attention Is Selective: Self-control 202." January 19. Accessed on May 17, 2020. https://characterlab .org/tips-of-the-week/attention-is-selective/.

24 **PERMA theory of well-being:** Seligman, Martin. 2011. Excerpt from *Flourish: A Visionary New Understanding of Happiness and Well-Being.* Accessed on May 17, 2020. https://www.authentichappiness.sas.upenn.edu/learn /wellbeing.

24 **in-the-moment good vibes:** Cohn, Michael A., Barbara L. Fredrickson, Stephanie L. Brown, Joseph A. Mikels and Anne M. Conway. 2009. "Happiness Unpacked: Positive Emotions Increase Life Satisfaction by Building Resilience." *Emotion.* 9(3): 361–368. https://doi.org/10.1037/a0015952. Fredrickson, Barbara L. 2000. "Cultivating Positive Emotions to Optimize Health and Well-Being." *Prevention & Treatment.* 3(1a). https://doi.org /10.1037/1522-3736.3.1.31a.

25 **construal theory of happiness:** Lyubormirsky, Sonja. 2001. "Why Are Some People Happier Than Others? The Role of Cognitive and Motivational Processes in Well-Being." *American Psychologist.* 56(3): 239–249. https://doi .org/ 10.1037/0003-066X.56.3.239.

25 **reinforcing their relative unhappiness:** Lyubomirsky, Sonja. "Sonja Lyubomirsky." Accessed on May 17, 2020. http://sonjalyubomirsky.com/.

26 **Lyubomirsky and her colleagues:** Lyubomirsky, Sonja, Laura King and Ed Diener. 2005. "The benefits of frequent positive affect: does happiness lead to success?" *Psychology Bulletin.* 131(6): 803–855. https://doi.org/0.1037/0033 -2909.131.6.803.

26 **A positive outlook, optimism:** Lee, Lewina O., Peter James, Emily S. Zevon, Eric S. Kim, Claudia Trudel-Fitzgerald, Avron Spiro III, Francine Grodstein and Laura D. Kubzansky. 2019. "Optimism is associated with exceptional longevity in 2 epidemiologic cohorts of men and women." *PNAS* 10; 116(37): 18357–18362. https://doi.org/10.1073/pnas.1900712116.

26 **gratitude are also:** Hill, Patrick L., Mathias Allemand and Brent W. Roberts. 2013. "Examining the Pathways between Gratitude and Self-Rated Physical Health across Adulthood." *Personality and Individual Differences.* 54(1): 92–96. https://doi.org/10.1016/j.paid.2012.08.011.

26 **cut the risk of heart problems:** Kim, Eric S., Kaitlin A. Hagan, Francine Grodstein, Dawn L. DeMeo, Immaculata De Vivo and Laura D. Kubzansky. 2017. "Optimism and Cause-Specific Mortality: A Prospective Cohort Study." *American Journal of Epidemiology.* 185(1): 21–29. https://doi.org/10.1093/aje /kww182. Boehm, Julia K., Christopher Peterson, Mika Kivimaki, and Laura Kubzansky. 2011. "A Prospective Study of Positive Psychological Well-Being and Coronary Heart Disease." *Health Psychology.* 30(3): 259–267. https://doi .org/10.1037/a0023124.

27 **negative emotions don't necessarily mess:** Nowlan, Jamie S., Viviana, M. Wuthrich and Ronald M. Rapee. 2016. "The impact of positive reappraisal on positive (and negative) emotion among older adults." *International Psychogeriatrics.* 28(4): 681–693. https://doi.org/10.1017/S10416 10215002057.

28 **being more mindful:** *Greater Good.* Greater Good Science Center, University of California, Berkeley. "Mindfulness Defined: Why Practice It." Accessed on May 17, 2020. https://greatergood.berkeley.edu/topic/mindfulness /definition#why-practice-mindfulness. Brown, Kirk Warren, and Richard M. Ryan. 2003. "The Benefits of Being Present: Mindfulness and Its Role in Psychological Well-Being." *Journal of Personality and Social Psychology.* 84(4): 822–848. https://doi.org/ 10.1037/0022-3514.84.4.822. https:// selfdeterminationtheory.org/SDT/documents/2003_BrownRyan.pdf.

28 **vitality (i.e., energy):** Wu, Ivan, and Nicole Buchanan. 2019. "Pathways to Vitality: the Role of Mindfulness and Coping." *Mindfulness.* 10: 481–491. https://doi.org/10.1007/s12671-018-0989-x.

28 **In an interview:** Ellen Langer, interview with Krista Tippett. *On Being.* NPR. May 29, 2014. Audio. https://onbeing.org/programs/ellen-langer-science-of -mindlessness-and-mindfulness-nov2017/.

28 **this form of mindfulness:** Feinberg, Cara. 2010. "The Mindfulness Chronicles: On the 'psychology of possibility.'" *Harvard Magazine.* September– October. Accessed on May 17, 2020. https://harvardmagazine.com/2010 /09/the-mindfulness-chronicles.

29 **Meditation is magic:** Garland, Eric L., Norman A. Farb, Philippe Goldin and Barbara L. Fredrickson. 2015. "Mindfulness Broadens Awareness and Builds Eudaimonic Meaning: A Process Model of Mindful Positive Emotion Regulation." *Psychological Inquiry.* 26(4): 293–314. https://doi.org/10.1080 /1047840X.2015.1064294.

29 **stress and anxiety:** American Association for the Advancement of Science, EurekAlert! 2018. "Even a single mindfulness meditation session can reduce anxiety. Experimental Biology 2018." Public release: April 23, 2018. https:// www.eurekalert.org/pub_releases/2018-04/eb2-eas041218.php.

29 **forty-four extra minutes:** Murnieks, Charles Y., Jonathan D. Arthurs, Melissa S. Cardon, Nusrat Farah, Jason Stornelli and J. Michael Haynie. 2019. "Close

your eyes or open your mind: Effects of sleep and mindfulness exercises on entrepreneurs' exhaustion." *Journal of Business Venturing.* 35(2): 105918. https:// doi.org/10.1016/j.jbusvent.2018.12.004.

30 **interviewing Dan Harris:** Dan Harris, interview by Meaghan Murphy, Heidi Kristoffer, Jamie Hess and Christine Bibbo Herr. *Off the Gram*, podcast audio. March 16, 2020. https://podcasts.apple.com/us/podcast/dan-harris-how -to-be-10-happier/id1494608415?i=1000468519068.

31 **Active memory building:** Bryant, Fred B., Erica D. Chadwick and Katharina Kluwe. 2011. "Understanding the processes that regulate positive emotional experience: Unsolved problems and future directions for theory and research on savoring." *International Journal of Wellbeing.* 1(1): 107–126. https://doi.org /10.5502/ijw.v1i1.18.

31 **Savoring good times:** Bryant, F. B., and J. L. Smith. 2015. Appreciating life in the midst of adversity: Savoring in relation to mindfulness, reappraisal, and meaning. *Psychological Inquiry.* 26: 315–321. https://doi.org/10.1080 /1047840X.2015.1075351. Smith, J. L., P. R. Harrison, J. L. Kurtz, J. L. and Fred B. Bryant. 2014. Nurturing the capacity to savor: Interventions to enhance the enjoyment of positive experiences. In *Handbook of Positive Psychological Interventions.* Edited by A. C. Parks and S. Schueller. 42–65. Oxford: Wiley-Blackwell. Tugade, Michelle M., and Barbara L. Fredrickson. 2007. "Regulation of Positive Emotions: Emotion Regulation Strategies that Promote Resilience." *Journal of Happiness Studies.* 8: 311–333. https://doi.org /10.1007/s10902-006-9015-4.

31 **Savoring is related to mindfulness:** Kiken, Laura G., Kristjen B. Lundberg and Barbara L. Fredrickson. 2017. "Being present and enjoying it: Dispositional mindfulness and savoring the moment are distinct, interactive predictors of positive emotions and psychological health." *Mindfulness.* 8(5):1280–1290. https://doi.org/10.1007/s12671-017-0704-3.

31 **goes beyond noticing:** Kennelly, Stacey. 2012. "10 Steps to Savoring the Good Things in Life." *Greater Good.* Greater Good Science Center, University of California Berkeley. July 23. https://greatergood.berkeley.edu/article/item /10_steps_to_savoring_the_good_things_in_life.

31 **negative images trigger more activity:** Ito, Tiffany A., Jeff T. Larsen, Kyle Smith and John T. Cacioppo. 1998. "Negative Information Weighs More Heavily on the Brain: The Negativity Bias in Evaluative Categorizations." *Journal of Personality and Social Psychology.* 75(4) 887–900. https://doi.org /10.1037//0022-3514.75.4.887.

31 **the more you ruminate:** Nolen-Hoeksema, Susan, Blair E. Wisco and Sonja Lyubomirsky. 2008. "Rethinking Rumination." *Perspectives in Psychological Science.* 3(5):400–24. https://doi.org/10.1111/j.1745-6924.2008.00088.x.

31 **physiological stress response:** Aldao, Amelia, Katie A. McLaughlin, Mark L. Hatzenbuehler and Margaret A. Sheridan. 2014. "The Relationship between Rumination and Affective, Cognitive, and Physiological Responses to Stress in

Adolescents." *Journal of Experimental Psychopathology.* 5(3): 272–288. https://doi.org/10.5127/jep.039113

32 **mindful people stew less:** Deyo, M., K. A. Wison, J. Ong and C. Koopman. 2009. "Mindfulness and rumination: does mindfulness training lead to reductions in the ruminative thinking associated with depression?" *Explore (NY).* 5(5): 265–71. https://doi.org/10.1016/j.explore.2009.06.005. Jury, Tasmin K., and Paul E. Jose 2019. "Does Rumination Function as a Longitudinal Mediator Between Mindfulness and Depression?" *Mindfulness.* 10: 1092–1104. https://doi.org/10.1007/s12671-018-1031-z.

32 **Researchers describe rumination:** Nolen-Hoeksema, Susan, Blair E. Wisco and Sonja Lyubomirsky. 2008. "Rethinking Rumination." *Perspectives in Psychological Science.* 3(5): 400–24. https://doi.or/10.1111/j.1745-6924.2008.00088.x.

33 **Fredrickson and a colleague did a study:** Tugade, Michelle M., and Barbara L. Fredrickson. 2004. "Resilient Individuals Use Positive Emotions to Bounce Back From Negative Emotional Experiences." *Journal of Personality and Social Psychology.* 86(2): 320–333. https://doi.org/10.1037/0022-3514.86.2.320.

33 **reinterpret pain as:** Crum, Alia J., and Ellen J. Langer. 2007. "Mind-set matters: Exercise and the placebo effect." *Psychological Science.* 18(2): 165–171. https://doi.org/10.1111/j.1467-9280.2007.01867.x.

33 **workers were shown videos:** Jamieson, Jeremy P., Alia J. Crum, J. Parker Goyer, Marisa E. Marotta and Modupe Akinola. 2018. "Optimizing stress responses with reappraisal and mindset interventions: an integrated model." *Anxiety, Stress, & Coping.* 31(3): 245–261. https://doi.org/10.1080/10615806.2018.1442615.

33 **research shows reappraisal:** Troy, Allison, S., Frank H. Wilhelm, Amanda J. Shallcross and Iris B. Mauss. 2010. "Seeing the Silver Lining: Cognitive Reappraisal Ability Moderates the Relationship Between Stress and Depressive Symptoms." *Emotion.* 10(6): 783–795. https://doi.org/10.1037/a0020262. Troy, Allison S., Anna Brunner, Amanda J. Shallcross, Rachel Friedman and Markera C. Jones. 2018. "Cognitive Reappraisal and Acceptance: Effects on Emotion, Physiology, and Perceived Cognitive Costs." *Emotion.* 18(1): 58–74. https://do.org/10.1037/emo0000371. Nowlan, Jamie S., Viviana M. Wuthrich and Ronald M. Rapee. 2016. "The impact of positive reappraisal on positive (and negative) emotion among older adults." *International Psychogeriatrics.* 28(4): 681–693. https://doi.org/10.1017/S1041610215002057. Garland, Eric L., Susan A. Gaylord and Barbara L. Fredrickson. 2011. "Positive Reappraisal Mediates the Stress-Reductive Effects of Mindfulness: An Upward Spiral Process." *Mindfulness.* 2: 59–67. https://doi.org/10.1007/s12671-011-0043-8.

33 **Mindset shifting:** Crum, Alia J., Modupe Akinola, Ashley Martin and Sean Fath. 2017. "The role of stress mindset in shaping cognitive, emotional, and physiological responses to challenging and threatening stress." *Anxiety, Stress & Coping.* 30(4): 379–395. https://doi.org/10.1080/10615806.2016.1275585.

34 **attach positive meaning:** Fredrickson, Barbara L. 2000. "Cultivating Positive Emotions to Optimize Health and Well-Being." *Prevention & Treatment.* 3(1a)

34 **that are out of your control:** Haines, Simon J., John Gleeson, Peter Kuppens, Tom Hollenstein, Joseph Ciarrochi, Izelle Labuschagne, Caitlin Grace and Peter Koval. 2016. "The Wisdom to Know the Difference: Strategy-Situation Fit in Emotion Regulation in Daily Life Is Associated With Well-Being." *Psychological Science.* 27(12): 1651–1659. https://doi.org/10.1177/0956797616669086.

36 **Taking a few minutes:** Emmons, Robert A., and Anjali Mishra. (2011). "Why gratitude enhances well-being: What we know, what we need to know." In *Designing Positive Psychology: Taking Stock and Moving Forward.* Edited by K. M. Sheldon, T. B. Kashdan, and M. F. Steger. 248–262. Oxford University Press. https://doi.org/10.1093/acprof:oso/9780195373585.003.0016.

36 **Reflecting on good things:** Armenta, Christina N., Megan M. Fritz and Sonja Lyubomirsky. 2017. "Functions of Positive Emotions: Gratitude as a Motivator of Self-Improvement and Positive Change." *Emotion Review.* 9(3): 183–190. https://doi.org/10.1177/1754073916669596.

36 **studies suggest:** Emmons, Robert A., and Anjali Mishra. 2011. "Why gratitude enhances well-being: What we know, what we need to know." In *Designing Positive Psychology: Taking Stock and Moving Forward.* Edited by K. M. Sheldon, T. B. Kashdan and M. F. Steger. 248–262. Oxford University Press. https://doi.org/10.1093/acprof:oso/9780195373585.003.0016. Center for Positive Organizational Scholarship, Stephen M. Ross School of Business, University of Michigan. 2010. "The Power of Gratitude: At-a-Glance." Accessed on May 17, 2020. http://assets.ngin.com/attachments/document/0040/6884/Power_of_Gratitude__At-A-Glance.pdf. Emmons, Robert A., and Michael E. McCullough 2003. "Counting Blessings Versus Burdens: An Experimental Investigation of Gratitude and Subjective Well-Being in Daily Life." *Journal of Personality and Social Psychology.* 84(2): 377–389. https://doi.org/10.1037/0022-3514.84.2.377. Hill, Patrick L., Mathias Allemand and Brent W. Roberts. 2013. "Examining the pathways between gratitude and self-rated physical health across adulthood." *Personality and Individual Differences.* 54(1): 92–96. https://doi.org/10.1016/j.paid.2012.08.011. Seligman, Martin E. P., Tracy Steen, Nansook Park and Christopher Peterson. 2005. "Positive psychology progress: empirical validation of interventions." *American Psychologist.* 60(5): 410–21. https://doi.org/10.1037/0003-066X.60.5.410. Sexton, J. Bryan, and Kathryn C. Adair. 2019. "Forty-five good things: a prospective pilot study of the Three Good Things well-being intervention in the USA for healthcare worker emotional exhaustion, depression, work–life balance and happiness." *BMJ Open.* 9(3): e022695. https://doi.org/10.1136/bmjopen-2018-022695. Fofonka Cunha, Luzie, Lucia Campos Pellanda and Caroline Tozzi Reppold. 2019. "Positive

Psychology and Gratitude Interventions: A Randomized Clinical Trial." *Frontiers in* Psychology. 10: 584. https://doi.org/10.3389/fpsyg.2019 .00584.

37 **healthcare workers at risk:** Rippstein-Leuenberger K., O. Mauthner, Sexton J. Bryan and Rene Schwendimann. 2017. "A qualitative analysis of the Three Good Things intervention in healthcare workers." *BMJ Open.* 7:e015826. https://doi.org/10.1136/bmjopen-2017-015826.

37 **to recovering alcoholics:** Krentzman, A. R., K. A. Mannella, A. L. Hassett, N. P. Barnett, J. A. Cranford, K. J. Brower, M. M. Higgens and P. S. Meyer. 2015. "Feasibility, Acceptability, and Impact of a Web-based Gratitude Exercise among Individuals in Outpatient Treatment for Alcohol Use Disorder." *Journal of Positive Psychology.* 10(6): 477–488. https://doi.org/10.1080/17439760 .2015.1015158.

37 **explained to me how it works:** Emiliana Simon-Thomas, interview with the author. New York City. January 20, 2020.

38 **people indeed underestimate:** Zhang, Ting, Tami Kim, Alison Wood Brooks, Francesca Gino and Michael I. Norton. 2014. "A 'present' for the future: the unexpected value of rediscovery." *Psychological Science.* 25(10): 1851–60. https://doi.org/10.1177/0956797614542274.

39 **taking daily snapshots:** Chen, Yu, Gloria Mark and Sana Ali. 2016. "Promoting Positive Affect through Smartphone Photography." *Psychological Well Being.* 6: 8. https://doi.org/10.1186/s13612-016-0044-4.

39 **is a positivity pill:** Speer, M., and M. Delgado. 2017. "Reminiscing about positive memories buffers acute stress responses." *Nature Human Behaviour.* 1(5): 0093. https://doi.org/10.1038/s41562-017-0093. Bryant, F. B., C. M. Smart and S. P. King. 2005. "Using the Past to Enhance the Present: Boosting Happiness Through Positive Reminiscence." *Journal of Happiness Studies.* 6: 227–260. https://doi.org/10.1007/s10902-005-3889-4.

40 **Studies show awe can make you:** Allen, Summer. 2018. "The Science of Awe." A white paper prepared for The John Templeton Foundation by the Greater Good Science Center at UC Berkeley. September. https://ggsc.berkeley .edu/images/uploads/GGSC-JTF_White_Paper-Awe_FINAL.pdf.

40 **awe helps life feel more meaningful:** Zhao, Huanhuan, Heyun Zhang, Yan Xu, Wen He and Jiamei Lu. 2019. "Why Are People High in Dispositional Awe Happier? The Roles of Meaning in Life and Materialism." *Frontiers in Psychology.* 10: 1208. https://doi.org/10.3389/fpsyg.2019.01208.

40 **a story on awe in *Good Housekeeping:*** King Lindley, Jennifer. 2016. "The Power of Awe." *Good Housekeeping.* January. 69–71.

41 **used to psych herself:** Arzón, Robin. 2019. Peloton Indoor Cycling. "20 Minute 80s Pop Ride." December 5. https://members.onepeloton.com /classes/cycling?duration=1200&instructor_id=c406f36aa2a44a5baf8831f8b 92f6920&sort=original_air_time&desc=true&modal=classDetailsModal &classId=d03f5b0ae86045c6b238ebfc7915152f.

41 **triggers the release:** McGilchrist, Sonya. 2011. "Music 'releases mood-enhancing chemical in the brain.'" *BBC News.* January 9. https://www.bbc.com/news/health-12135590.

41 **during physical tests:** Smirmaul, B. P. 2017. "Effect of pre-task music on sports or exercise performance." *Journal of Sports Medicine and Physical Fitness.* 57(7-8): 976–984. https://doi.org/10.23736/S0022-4707.16.06411-2.

41 **people don't get exhausted:** Karageorghis, C. I., Denis A. Mouzourides, David-Lee Priest, Tariq A. Sasso, Daley J. Morrish and Carolyn L. Walley. 2009. "Psychophysical and ergogenic effects of synchronous music during treadmill walking." *Journal of Sports and Exercise Psychology.* 31(1):18–36. https://doi.org/10.1123/jsep.31.1.18.

41 **listening to music before:** Hole, Jenny, Martin Hirsch, Elizabeth Ball and Catharine Meads. 2015. "Music as an aid for postoperative recovery in adults: a systematic review and meta-analysis." *Lancet.* 386(10004): 1659–1671. https://doi.org/10.1016/S0140-6736(15)60169-6.

43 **due to "backlash avoidance.":** Lindeman, Meghan I. H., Amanda M. Durik and Maura Dooley. 2018. "Women and Self-Promotion: A Test of Three Theories." *Psychological Reports.* 122(1): 219–230. https://doi.org/10.1177/0033294118755096.

43 **who journaled about their accomplishments:** Gander, Fabian, René T. Proyer and Willibald Ruch. 2016. "Positive Psychology Interventions Addressing Pleasure, Engagement, Meaning, Positive Relationships, and Accomplishment Increase Well-Being and Ameliorate Depressive Symptoms: A Randomized, Placebo-Controlled Online Study." *Frontiers in Psychology.* 7: 686. https://doi.org/10.3389/fpsyg.2016.00686.

47 **most of what we worry about:** LaFreniere, Lucas S., and Michelle G. Newman. 2020. "Exposing Worry's Deceit: Percentage of Untrue Worries in Generalized Anxiety Disorder Treatment." *Behavior Therapy.* 51(3): 413–423. https://doi.org/10.1016/j.beth.2019.07.003.

48 **How you carry yourself:** Michalak, Johannes, Judith Mischnat and Tobias Teismann. 2014. "Sitting posture makes a difference-embodiment effects on depressive memory bias." *Clinical Psychology and Psychotherapy.* 21(6): 519–24. https://doi.org/10.1002/cpp.1890.

48 **call it "embodied cognition":** Veenstra, Lotte, Iris K. Schneider and Sander L. Koole. 2017. "Embodied mood regulation: the impact of body posture on mood recovery, negative thoughts, and mood-congruent recall." *Cognition and Emotion* 31(7): 1361–1376. https://doi.org/10.1080/02699931.2016.1225003.

48 **slouching can activate:** Nair, Shwetha, Mark Sagar, John Sollers III, Nathan Consedine and Elizabeth Broadbent. 2015. "Do slumped and upright postures affect stress responses? A randomized trial." *Health Psychology.* 34(6): 632–41. https://doi.org/10.1037/hea0000146.

49 **standing up straight:** Wilson, V. E., and E. Peper. 2004. "The effects of upright and slumped postures on the recall of positive and negative thoughts."

Applied Psychophysiology and Biofeedback. 29(3):189–95. https://doi.org /10.1023/b:apbi.0000039057.32963.34.

49 **Facial feedback research suggests:** Coles, Nicholas A., Jeff T. Larsen and Heather C. Lench. 2019. "A meta-analysis of the facial feedback literature: Effects of facial feedback on emotional experience are small and variable." *Psychological Bulletin. 145*(6): 610–651. https://doi.org/10.1037/bul0000194. Kraft, Tara L., and Sarah D. Pressman. 2012. "Grin and bear it: the influence of manipulated facial expression on the stress response." *Psychological Science.* 23(11): 1372–8. https://doi.org/10.1177/0956797612445312.

49 **Positive or motivational self-talk:** Blanchfield, Anthony W., James Hardy, Helma Majella De Morree, Walter Staiano and Samuele Maria Marcora. 2014. "Talking yourself out of exhaustion: the effects of self-talk on endurance performance." *Medicine & Science in Sports & Exercise.* 46(5): 998–1007. https://doi.org/10.1249/MSS.0000000000000184.

49 **creates psychological distance:** Moser, Jason S., Adrienne Dougherty, Whitney I. Mattson, Benjamin Katz, Tim P. Moran, Darwin Guevarra, Holly Shablack, Ozlem Ayduk, John Jonides, Marc G. Berman and Ethan Kross. 2017. "Third-person self-talk facilitates emotion regulation without engaging cognitive control: Converging evidence from ERP and fMRI." *Scientific Reports.* 7(1): 4519. https://doi.org/10.1038/s41598-017-04047-3.

Chapter 3: The Love Charge

53 **innate and fundamental drive:** Baumeister, Roy F., and Mark R. Leary. 1995. "The Need to Belong: Desire for Interpersonal Attachments as a Fundamental Human Motivation." *Psychological Bulletin.* 117(3): 497–529. https://doi.org /10.1037/0033-2909.117.3.497.

53 **effects can be devastating:** Holt-Lunstad Julianne, Timothy B. Smith and J. Bradley Layton 2010. "Social Relationships and Mortality Risk: A Meta-analytic Review." *PLoS Medicine.* 7(7): e1000316. https://doi.org/10.1371 /journal.pmed.1000316.

53 **fifteen-cigarette-a-day habit:** Holt-Lunstad, Julianne. 2017. "The Potential Public Health Relevance of Social Isolation and Loneliness: Prevalence, Epidemiology, and Risk Factors." *Public Policy & Aging Report.* 27(4): 127–130, https://doi.org/10.1093/ppar/prx030. Health Resources & Services Administration. 2019. "The Loneliness Epidemic." https://www.hrsa.gov/enews /past-issues/2019/january-17/loneliness-epidemic.

53 **higher risk for depression:** Santini, Ziggi Ivan, Paul E. Jose, Erin York Cornwell, Ai Koyanagi, Line Nielsen, Carsten Hinrichsen, Charlotte Meilstrup, Katrine R. Madsen and Vibeke Koushede. 2020. "Social disconnectedness, perceived isolation, and symptoms of depression and anxiety among older Americans (NSHAP): a longitudinal mediation analysis." *The Lancet Public Health.* 5(1): e62—e70. https://doi.org/10.1016/S2468 -2667(19)30230-0.

53 **poor sleep, fatigue:** Bashir Bhatti, Adnan, and Anwar ul Haq. 2017. "The Pathophysiology of Perceived Social Isolation: Effects on Health and Mortality." *Cureus.* 9(1): e994. https://doi.org/10.7759/cureus.994. Novotney, Amy. 2019. "The risks of social isolation." *Monitor on Psychology.* American Psychological Association. 50(5): 32. https://www.apa.org/monitor /2019/05/ce-corner-isolation.

53 **linked to high blood pressure:** Umberson, Debra, and Jennifer Karas Montez. 2010. "Social Relationships and Health: A Flashpoint for Health Policy." *Journal of Health and Social Behavior.* 51(Suppl): S54–S66. https://doi.org /10.1177/0022146510383501. Hawkley, Louise C., and John P. Capitanio. 2015. "Perceived social isolation, evolutionary fitness and health outcomes: a lifespan approach." *Philosophical Transactions of the Royal Society B.* 370(1669). https://doi.org/10.1098/rstb.2014.0114.

53 **hurt we feel over social rejection:** Eisenberger, Naomi I., Johanna M. Jarcho, Matthew D. Lieberman and Bruce D. Naliboff. 2006. "An experimental study of shared sensitivity to physical pain and social rejection." *Pain.* 126: 132–138. https://doi.org/10.1016/j.pain.2006.06.024. Eisenberger, Naomi. 2011. "Why Rejection Hurts." *Edge.* July 6. https://www.edge.org/conversation/naomi _eisenberger-why-rejection-hurts.

53 **casual, low-stakes sort:** Sandstrom, Gillian M., and Elizabeth W. Dunn. 2014. "Is Efficiency Overrated?: Minimal Social Interactions Lead to Belonging and Positive Affect." *Social Psychology and Personality Science.* 5(4): 437–442. https://doi.org/10.1177/1948550613502990.

53 **cut the risk of early death:** Yang, Yank Claire, Courtney Boen, Karen Gerken, Ting Lia, Kristen Schorpp and Kathleen Mullan Harris. 2016. "Social relationships and physiological determinants of longevity across the human life span." *PNAS.* 113(3): 578–583. https://doi.org/10.1073/pnas.1511085112.

53 **slay stress and generate:** Yang, Yank Claire, Courtney Boen, Karen Gerken, Ting Li, Kristen Schorpp and Kathleen Mullan Harris. 2016. "Social relationships and physiological determinants of longevity across the human life span." *PNAS.* 113(3): 578–583. https://doi.org/10.1073/pnas .1511085112.

53 **perceive a hill as less steep:** Schnall, Simone, Kent D. Harber, Jeanine K. Stefanucci, Dennis R. Proffitt. 2008. "Social Support and the Perception of Geographical Slant." *Journal of Experimental Social Psychology.* 44(5): 1246–1255. https://doi.org/10.1016/j.jesp.2008.04.011.

53 **relationships of all kinds:** Amati, Viviana, Silvia Meggiolaro, Giulia Rivellini and Susanna Zaccarin. 2018. "Social relations and life satisfaction: the role of friends." *Genus.* 74(1): 7. https://doi.org/10.1186/s41118-018-0032-z. Fredrickson, Barbara L. 2013. "Positive Emotions Broaden and Build." In *Advances in Experimental Social Psychology.* Edited by Patrica Devine and Ashby Plant. 47: 1–53. https://doi.org/10.1016/B978-0-12-407236 -7.00001-2.

54 **"Other people matter. Period.":** Park, Nansook, and Martin P. Seligman. 2013. "Christopher M. Peterson (1950–2012)." *American Psychologist.* 68(5): 403. https://doi.org/10.1037/a0033380. https://ppc.sas.upenn.edu/sites/default /files/chrispeterson.pdf.

54 **outside our circles:** Sandstrom, Gillian M., and Elizabeth W. Dunn. 2014. "Social Interactions and Well-Being: The Surprising Power of Weak Ties." *Personality and Social Psychology Bulletin.* 40(7): 910–922. https://doi.org /10.1177/0146167214529799.

54 **people at a coffee shop:** Sandstrom, Gillian M., and Elizabeth W. Dunn, 2014. "Is Efficiency Overrated?: Minimal Social Interactions Lead to Belonging and Positive Affect." *Social Psychology and Personality Science.* 5(4): 437–442. https://doi.org/10.1177/1948550613502990.

54 **meaningful daily interactions:** DesHarnais Bruce, Liana, Joshua S. Wu, Stuart L. Lustig, Daniel W. Russell and Douglas A. Nemecek. 2019. "Loneliness in the United States: A 2018 National Panel Survey of Demographic, Structural, Cognitive, and Behavioral Characteristics." *American Journal of Health Promotion.* 33(8): 1123–1133. https://doi.org/10.1177 /0890117119856551. Fingerman, Karen L., Menh Huo, Susan T. Charles, Debra J. Umberson. 2020. "Variety Is the Spice of Late Life: Social Integration and Daily Activity." *The Journals of Gerontology: Series B.* 75(2): 377–388. https://doi.org/10.1093/geronb/gbz007.

54 **social circles naturally start to shrink:** Bhattacharya, Kunal, Asim Ghosh, Daniel Monsivais, Robin I. M. Dunbar and Kimmo Kaski. 2016. "Sex differences in social focus across the life cycle in humans." 3(4): 160097. https:// doi.org/10.1098/rsos.160097.

56 **"feeling connected to others":** Fredrickson, Barbara L. 2000. "Cultivating Positive Emotions to Optimize Health and Well-Being." *Prevention & Treatment.* 3(1a). https://doi.org/10.1037/1522-3736.3.1.31a.

56 **said family gave their life:** Pew Research Center. 2018. "Where Americans Find Meaning in Life." November 20. https://www.pewforum.org/2018/11/20 /where-americans-find-meaning-in-life/.

56 **longest-running happiness study:** Waldinger, Roger. "What Does *The Good Life* Actually Look Like? Lessons From the Longest Study on Happiness." https://robertwaldinger.com/about-happiness/. Mineo, Liz. 2017. "Good genes are nice, but joy is better." *Harvard Gazette.* April 11. https://news .harvard.edu/gazette/story/2017/04/over-nearly-80-years-harvard-study-has -been-showing-how-to-live-a-healthy-and-happy-life/.

56 **Relationships can be the source:** University of Pennsylvania, Positive Psychology Center. "PERMA™ Theory of Well-Being and PERMA™ Workshops." Accessed on May 17, 2020. https://ppc.sas.upenn.edu/learn-more /perma-theory-well-being-and-perma-workshops.

56 **In a past newsletter:** Seligman, Martin. 2011. "Happiness is not enough." *Flourish: A New Theory of Positive Psychology* (Archived Newsletter). April.

Excerpt edited from *Flourish: A Visionary New Understanding of Happiness and Well-Being.* 2011. New York: Simon and Shuster. https://www .authentichappiness.sas.upenn.edu/learn/wellbeing.

57 **spark and grow happiness:** Lyubomirsky, Sonja. 2010. "Happiness for a Lifetime." *Greater Good.* Greater Good Science Center, University of California Berkeley. July 15. https://greatergood.berkeley.edu/article/item/happiness _for_a_lifetime.

57 **release of feel-good chemicals:** Mathers, Nigel. 2016. "Compassion and the science of kindness: Harvard Davis Lecture 2015." *British Journal of General Practice.* 66(648): e525–e527. https://doi.org/10.3399/bjgp16X686041.

57 **protect us from and lower stress** Raposa, Elizabeth B., Holly B. Laws and Emily B. Ansell. 2015. "Prosocial Behavior Mitigates the Negative Effects of Stress in Everyday Life." *Clinical Psychological Science.* 4(4): 691–698. https:// doi.org/10.1177/2167702615611073.

57 **get an emotional boost:** Rath, Tom, and Jim Harter. 2010. "Giving and Your Community Well-Being: People with thriving well-being are often moved by the impact they have had on another person, group, or community." *Gallup Business Journal.* https://news.gallup.com/businessjournal/127217/giving -community-wellbeing.aspx.

57 **And a review of more:** Curry, Oliver Scott, Lee A. Rowland, Caspar J. Van Lissa, Sally Zlotowitz, John McAlaney and Harvey Whitehouse. 2018. "Happy to help? A systematic review and meta-analysis of the effects of performing acts of kindness on the well-being of the actor." *Journal of Experimental Social Psychology.* 76: 320–329. https://doi.org/10.1016/j.jesp.2018.02.014.

57 **which increases self-esteem:** Lyubomirsky, Sonja. 2010. "Happiness for a Lifetime." *Greater Good.* Greater Good Science Center, University of California Berkeley. July 15. https://greatergood.berkeley.edu/article/item/happiness _for_a_lifetime.

57 **kindness and compassion build trust:** Jasielska, Dorota. 2018. "The moderating role of kindness on the relation between trust and happiness." *Current Psychology.* https://doi.org/10.1007/s12144-018-9886-7. Salazar, Ramos. 2015. "Exploring the relationship between compassion, closeness, trust, and social support in same-sex friendships." *The Journal of Happiness & Well-Being.* 3(1): 15–29. https://self-compassion.org/wp-content/uploads/2016/06/Salazar -2015.pdf.

57 **call "prosocial behavior":** Layous, Kristin, S. Katherine Nelson, Jaime L. Kurtz and Sonja Lyubomirsky. 2017. "What triggers prosocial effort? A positive feedback loop between positive activities, kindness, and well-being." *The Journal of Positive Psychology.* 12(4): 385–398. https://doi.org/10.1080 /17439760.2016.1198924.

59 **In a series of experiments:** Epley, Nicholas, and Juliana Schroeder. 2014. "Mistakenly seeking solitude." *Journal of Experimental Psychology: General.* 143(5): 1980–1999. https://doi.org/10.1037/a0037323.

59 **one stranger a day for five days:** Bernstein, Elizabeth. 2019. "The Surprising Boost You Get From Strangers." *Wall Street Journal.* May 11. https://www.wsj.com/articles/the-surprising-boost-you-get-from-strangers -11557567000.

59 **the term "the liking gap":** Boothby, Erica J., Gus Cooney, Gillian M. Sandstrom and Margaret S. Clark. 2018. "The Liking Gap in Conversations: Do People Like Us More Than We Think?" *Psychological Science.* 29(11): 1742–1756. https://doi.org/10.1177/0956797618783714.

60 **cause people to like you even more:** Huang, Karen, Michael Yeomans, Alison Wood Brooks, Julia Minson and Francesca Gino. 2017. "It Doesn't Hurt to Ask: Question-asking Increases Liking." *Journal of Personality and Social Psychology.* 113(3): 430–452. https://doi.org/10.1037/pspi0000097.

60 **asked Brad Montague:** Montague, Brad (@bradmontague). 2020. Instagram. January 28. https://www.instagram.com/p/B74ULy9nFYZ/.

62 **good neighbor relationships:** Mahmoudi Farahani, Leila. 2016. "The Value of the Sense of Community and Neighbouring." *Housing, Theory and Society.* 33(3): 357–376. https://doi.org/10.1080/14036096.2016.1155480.

62 **Volunteering with community:** Yeung, Jerf W. K., Zhuoni Zhang and Tae Yeun Kim. 2017. "Volunteering and health benefits in general adults: cumulative effects and forms." *BMC Public Health.* 18: 8. https://doi.org /10.1186/s12889-017-4561-8.

63 **to want to help others:** Aknin, Lara B., Christopher P. Barrington-Leigh, Elizabeth W. Dunn, John F. Helliwell, Justine Burns, Robert Biswas-Diener, Imelda Kemeza, Paul Nyende, Claire E. Ashton-James and Michael I. Norton. 2013. "Prosocial Spending and Well-Being: Cross-Cultural Evidence for a Psychological Universal." *Journal of Personality and Social Psychology.* 104(4): 635–52. https://doi.org/10.1037/a0031578.

63 **you gotta do a little more:** Lyubomirsky, Sonja. 2010. "Happiness for a Lifetime." *Greater Good.* Greater Good Science Center, University of California Berkeley. July 15. https://greatergood.berkeley.edu/article/item/happiness _for_a_lifetime.

63 **ER nurse Martha Phillips:** Free, Cathy. 2020. "After a rape exam, women's underclothes are often taken as evidence. This nurse buys them new ones." *Washington Post.* February 18. https://www.washingtonpost.com /lifestyle/2020/02/18/after-rape-exam-womens-underclothes-are-often-taken -evidence-this-nurse-buys-them-new-ones/.

65 **emotional or social contagion:** Christakis, Nicholas A., and James H. Fowler. 2013. "Social contagion theory: examining dynamic social networks and human behavior." *Statistics in Medicine.* 32(4): 556–577. https://doi.org/10 .1002/sim.5408.

65 **things like facial expressions:** Deng, Huan, and Ping Hu. 2017. "Matching Your Face or Appraising the Situation: Two Paths to Emotional Contagion." *Frontiers in Psychology.* 8: 2278. https://doi.org/10.3389/fpsyg.2017.02278.

65 **zest for life:** Peterson, Christopher, Nansook Park, Nicholas Hall and Martin Seligman. 2009. "Zest and Work." *Journal of Organizational Behavior*. 30: 161–172. https://doi.org/10.1002/job.584.

65 **passion (the energy with which):** Li, Jingjing, Jian Zhang and Zhiguo Yang. 2017. "Associations between a leader's work passion and an employee's work passion: a moderated mediation model." *Frontiers in Psychology*. 8: 1447–1459. https://doi.org/10.3389/fpsyg.2017.01447.

65 **friends are physically active:** Sawka, Keri Jo, Gavin R. McCormack, Alberto Nettel-Aguirre, Penelope Hawe and Patricia K. Doyle-Baker. 2013. "Friendship Networks and Physical Activity and Sedentary Behavior Among Youth: A Systematized Review." *International Journal of Behavioral Nutrition and Physical Activity*. 10: 130. https://doi.org/10.1186/1479-5868-10-130.

65 **"dynamic spread of happiness":** Fowler, James H., and Nicholas A. Christakis. 2008. "Dynamic spread of happiness in a large social network: longitudinal analysis over 20 years in the Framingham Heart Study." *BMJ*. 337: a2338. https://doi.org/10.1136/bmj.a2338.

65 **even quantified it:** Christakis, Nicholas A., and James Fowler. 2008. "Social Networks and Happiness." December 4. https://www.edge.org/conversation /social-networks-and-happiness.

65 **Terri Cole, a relationship expert:** Terri Cole, interview by Meaghan Murphy, Heidi Kristoffer, Jamie Hess and Christine Bibbo Herr. *Off the Gram*, podcast audio. January 27, 2020. https://podcasts.apple.com/us/podcast /terri-cole-friendship-breakups/id1494608415?i=1000463793680.

67 **memoir *Early Bird*:** Rothman, Rodney. 2006. *Early Bird*. New York: Simon & Schuster.

67 **strengthens relationships more than simply feeling:** Lambert, Nathaniel M., Margaret S. Clark, Jared Durtschi, Frank D. Fincham and Steven M. Graham. 2010. "Benefits of Expressing Gratitude: Expressing Gratitude to a Partner Changes One's View of the Relationship." *Psychological Science*. 21(4): 574–580. https://doi.org/10.1177/0956797610364003.

67 **more comfortable talking:** Lambert, Nathaniel M., and Frank D. Fincham. "Expressing gratitude to a partner leads to more relationship maintenance behavior." *Emotion*. 11(1): 52–60. https://doi.org/10.1037/a0021557.

67 **encourages you to be kinder:** Ma, Lawrence K., Richard J. Tunney and Eamonn Ferguson. 2017. "Does Gratitude Enhance Prosociality?: A Meta-Analytic Review." *Psychological Bulletin*. 143(6): 601–635. https://doi.org /10.1037/bul0000103.

67 **appreciated by their partner:** Gordon, Arnie. M., Emily A. Impett, Aleksandr Kogan, Christopher Oveis and Dacher Keltner. 2012. "To have and to hold: Gratitude promotes relationship maintenance in intimate bonds." *Journal of Personality and Social Psychology*. 103(2): 257–274. https://doi.org/10.1037 /a0028723.

67 **gratitude even once:** Algoe, Sara B., Shelly L. Gable and Natalya C. Maisel. 2010. "It's the little things: Everyday gratitude as a booster shot for romantic relationships." *Personal Relationships.* 17(2): 217–233. https://doi.org/10.1111 /j.1475-6811.2010.01273.x.

67 **tend to underestimate:** Kumar, Amit, and Nicholas Epley. 2018. "Undervaluing Gratitude: Expressers Misunderstand the Consequences of Showing Appreciation." *Psychological Science.* 29(9): 1423–1435. https://doi.org /10.1177/0956797618772506.

68 **A *Vice* article:** Fetters, K. Aleisha. 2017. "Compliments Are Like Mini-Orgasms for Your Brain." *Vice.* February 6. https://www.vice.com/en_us /article/mg9pex/compliments-are-like-mini-orgasms-for-your-brain.

69 **suck at saying sorry:** Schumann, Karina. 2018. "The Psychology of Offering an Apology: Understanding the Barriers to Apologizing and How to Overcome Them." *Current Directions in Psychological Science.* 27(2): 74–78. https://doi.org /10.1177/0963721417741709.

69 **six key points:** Schumann, Karina. 2014. "An affirmed self and a better apology: The effect of self-affirmation on transgressors' responses to victims." *Journal of Experimental Social Psychology.* 54: 89–96. https://doi.org/10.1016 /j.jesp.2014.04.013. Association for Psychological Science. 2016. "Effective Apologies Include Six Elements." May 24. https://www.psychological science.org/news/minds-business/effective-apologies-include-six -elements.html.

70 **apologies are so hard:** Schumann, Karina. 2018. "The Psychology of Offering an Apology: Understanding the Barriers to Apologizing and How to Overcome Them." *Current Directions in Psychological Science.* 27(2): 74–78. https://doi.org /10.1177/0963721417741709.

70 **self-affirming pep talk:** Shumann, Karina. 2014. "An affirmed self and a better apology: The effect of self-affirmation on transgressors' responses to victims." *Journal of Experimental Social Psychology.* 54: 89–96. https://doi .org/10.1016/j.jesp.2014.04.013.

71 **Science suggests that generosity:** Park, Soyoung, Thorsten Kahnt, Azade Dogan, Sabrina Strang, Ernst Fehr and Philippe N. Tobler. 2017. "A Neural Link Between Generosity and Happiness." *Nature Communications.* 8: 15964. https://doi.org/10.1038/ncomms15964.

71 **well-being and even physical health:** Poulin, Michael J., Stephanie L. Brown, Amanda J. Dillard, Dylan M. Smith. 2013. "Giving to Others and the Association Between Stress and Mortality." *American Journal of Public Health.* 103(9): 1649–1655. https://doi.org/10.2105/AJPH.2012.300876.

73 **watched couples discussing:** Gabel, Shelly L., Gian C. Gonzaga and Amy Strachman. 2006. "Will You Be There for Me When Things Go Right? Supportive Responses to Positive Event Disclosures." *Journal of Personality and Social Psychology.* 91(5): 904–917. https://doi.org/10.1037/0022-3514.91.5.904.

74 **spilling the good-news tea:** Reis, Harry T., Shannon M. Smith, Cheryl L. Carmichael, Peter A. Caprariello, Fen-Fang Tsai, Amy Redrigues and Michael R. Maniaci. 2010. "Are You Happy for Me? How Sharing Positive Events With Others Provides Personal and Interpersonal Benefits." *Journal of Personality and Social Psychology.* 99(2): 311–29. https://doi.org/10.1037 /a0018344.

75 **help us feel more connected:** Jung Oh, Hyun, Elif Ozkaya and Robert LaRose. 2014. "How does online social networking enhance life satisfaction? The relationships among online supportive interaction, affect, perceived social support, sense of community, and life satisfaction." *Computers in Human Behavior.* 30: 69–78. https://doi.org/10.1016/j.chb.2013.07.053. Große Deters, Fenne, and Matthias R. Mehl. 2014. "Does Posting Facebook Status Updates Increase or Decrease Loneliness? An Online Social Networking Experiment." *Social Psychology & Personality Science.* 4(5). https://doi.org /10.1177/1948550612469233.

75 **negative effects from it:** Jung Oh, Hyun, Elif Ozkaya and Robert LaRose. 2014. "How does online social networking enhance life satisfaction? The relationships among online supportive interaction, affect, perceived social support, sense of community, and life satisfaction." *Computers in Human Behavior.* 30: 69–78. https://doi.org/10.1016/j.chb.2013.07.053.

76 **overuse can leave you lonely:** DesHarnais Bruce, Liana, Joshua S. Wu, Stuart L. Lustig, Daniel W. Russell and Douglas A. Nemecek. 2019. "Loneliness in the United States: A 2018 National Panel Survey of Demographic, Structural, Cognitive, and Behavioral Characteristics." *American Journal of Health Promotion.* 33(8): 1123–1133. https://doi.org/10.1177/0890117119856551. Primack, Brian A., Ariel Shensa, Jaime E. Sidani, Erin O. Whaite, Liu Yi Lin, Daniel Rosen, Jason B. Colditz, Ana Radovic and Elizabeth Miller. 2017. "Social Media Use and Perceived Social Isolation Among Young Adults in the U.S." *American Journal of Preventative Medicine.* 53(1): 1–8. https://doi.org /10.1016/j.amepre.2017.01.010.

76 **can better connect:** Hether, Heather J., Sheila T. Murphy and Thomas W. Valente. 2016. "A social network analysis of supportive interactions on prenatal sites." *Digital Health.* 2: 2055207616628700. https://doi.org/10.1177 /2055207616628700.

76 **comparing as the conduit:** Coyne, Sarah M., Brandon T. McDaniel and Laura A. Stockdale. 2017. "'Do you dare to compare?' Associations between maternal social comparisons on social networking sites and parenting, mental health, and romantic relationship outcomes." *Computers in Human Behavior.* 70: 335–340. https://doi.org/10.1016/j.chb.2016.12.081. Yang, Chia-chen. 2016. "Instagram Use, Loneliness, and Social Comparison Orientation: Interact and Browse on Social Media, But Don't Compare." *Cyberpsychology, Behavior, and Social Networking.* 19: 703–708. https://doi.org/10.1089 /cyber.2016.0201.

79 **filter out what doesn't change:** Hanson, Rick. 2013. *Hadwiring Happiness: The New Brain Science of Contentment, Calm, and Confidence.* 95. New York: Harmony.

79 **rush of dopamine:** Westbrook, Andrew, and Todd S. Braver. 2017. "Dopamine does double duty in motivating cognitive effort." *Neuron.* 89(4): 695–710. https://doi.org/10.1016/j.neuron.2015.12.029. Salamone, John D., and Mercè Correa. 2012. "The Mysterious Motivational Functions of Mesolimbic Dopamine." *Neuron.* 76(3): 470. https://doi.org/10.1016/j.neuron.2012.10.021.

79 **hit our positive-emotion buttons:** Berns, Gregory S., Samuel McClure, Giuseppe Pagnoni and Pendleton Read Montague. 2001. "Predictability Modulates Human Brain Response to Reward." *Journal of Neuroscience.* 21(8): 2793–8. https://doi.org/10.1523/JNEUROSCI.21-08-02793.2001.

79 **spontaneity is linked to:** Testoni, Ines, Michael Wieser, Alessandra Armenti, Lucia Ronconi, Maria Silvia Guglielmin, Paolo Cottone and Adriano Zamperini. 2016. "Spontaneity as predictive factor for well-being." In *Psychodrama. Empirical Research and Science 2.* Edited by Christia Stadler, Michael Wieser and Kate Kirk. Wiesbaden: Springer.

80 **nonsexual touch can boost mood:** Murphy, Michael L. M., Denise Janicki-Deverts, Sheldon Cohn and Nicholas D. Duran. 2018. "Receiving a hug is associated with the attenuation of negative mood that occurs on days with interpersonal conflict." *PloS One.* 13(10): e0203522. https://doi.org/10.1371/journal.pone.0203522. Gallace, Alberto, and Charles Spence. 2010. "The Science of Interpersonal Touch: An Overview." *Neuroscience Biobehavioral Reviews.* 34(2): 246–59. https://doi.org/10.1016/j.neubiorev.2008.10.004. Field, Tiffany. 2010. "Touch for socioemotional and physical well-being: A review." *Developmental Review.* 30(4): 367–383. https://doi.org/10.1016/j.dr.2011.01.001.

80 **NBA athletes gave:** Kraus, Michael W., Cassy Huang and Dacher Keltner. 2010. "Tactile Communication, Cooperation, and Performance: An Ethological Study of the NBA." *Emotion.* 10(5): 745–749. https://doi.org/10.1037/a0019382.

80 **touch from doctors:** Gunderman, Richard, and Brian LeLand. 2016. "Touch creates a healing bond in health care." *The Conversation.* May 23, 2016. https://theconversation.com/touch-creates-a-healing-bond-in-health-care-59637.

80 **student test performance:** Steward, A. Lee, and Michael Lupfer. 1987. "Touching as Teaching: The Effect of Touch on Students' Perceptions and Performance." *Journal of Applied Social Psychology.* 17(9): 800–809. https://doi.org/10.1111/j.1559-1816.1987.tb00340.x.

80 **release of oxytocin:** Ellingsen, Dan-Mikael, Siri Leknes, Guro Løseth, Johan Wessberg and Håkan Olausson. 2015. "The Neurobiology Shaping Affective Touch: Expectation, Motivation, and Meaning in the Multisensory Context." *Frontiers in* Psychology. 6: 1986. https://doi.org/10.3389/fpsyg.2015.01986.

80 **hormone that produces feelings of trust:** Olff, Miranda, Jessie L. Frijling, Laura D. Kubzansky, Bekh Bradley, Mark A. Ellenbogen, Christopher Cardoso, Jennifer A. Bartz, Jason R. Yee and Mirjam van Zuiden. 2013. "The role of oxytocin in social bonding, stress regulation and mental health: An update on the moderating effects of context and interindividual differences." *Psychneuroendocrinology*. 38(9): 1883–1894. https://doi.org/16 /j.psyneuen.2013.06.019.

81 **FOMO is linked to:** Milyavskaya, Marina, Mark Saffran, Nora Hope, and Richard Koestner. 2018. "Fear of missing out: prevalence, dynamics, and consequences of experiencing FOMO." *Motivation and Emotion*. 42: 725–737. https://doi.org/10.1007/s11031-018-9683-5.

81 **Another study found:** Rifkin, Jacqueline, Chan Cindy, and Barbara Kahn. 2015. "Fomo: How the Fear of Missing Out Leads to Missing Out." In *NA—Advances in Consumer Research*. Edited by Kristin Diehl and Carolyn Yoon. Association for Consumer Research. 43: 244–248. https://www .acrwebsite.org/volumes/1019794/volumes/v43/NA-43.

82 **we might bond better over negative:** Bosson, Jennifer, Amber B. Johnson, Kate Niederhoffer and William B. Swann Jr. 2006. "Interpersonal chemistry through negativity: Bonding by sharing negative attitudes about others." *Personal Relationships*. 13: 135–150. https://doi.org/10.1111/j.1475 -6811.2006.00109.x. Weaver, Jonathan R., and Jennifer K. Bosson. 2011. "I Feel Like I Know You: Sharing Negative Attitudes of Others Promotes Feelings of Familiarity." *Personality and Social Psychology Bulletin*. 37(4): 481–491. https://doi.org/10.1177/0146167211398364.

84 **secrets of Chitetsu Watanabe:** Williams, David. 2020. "The world's oldest living man is 112. His secret is to just keep smiling and never get angry." *CNN Health*. February 12. https://www.cnn.com/2020/02/12/health/oldest-living -man-guinness-wellness-trnd/index.html.

85 **for your health, energy:** Davison, Sonia Louise, Robin Jean Bell, Maria LaChina, Samantha Lee Holden and Susan Ruth Davis. 2009. "The Relationship Between Self-Reported Sexual Satisfaction and General Well-Being in Women." *Journal of Sexual Medicine*. 6(10): 2690–26907. https://doi .org/10.1111/j.1743-6109.2009.01406.x.

Chapter 4: The Work Charge

88 **two-way street between:** Bowling Nathan A., Kevin J. Eschleman and Qiang Wang. 2010. "A meta-analytic examination of the relationship between job satisfaction and subjective well-being." *Journal of Occupational and Organizational Psychology*. 83: 915–934. https://doi.org/10.1348/096317909 X478557. Unanue, Wenceslao, Marcos e. Gómez, Diego Cortex, Juan C. Oyanedel and Andrés Mendiburo-Seguel. 2017. "Revisiting the Link between Job Satisfaction and Life Satisfaction: The Role of Basic Psychological Needs." *Frontiers in* Psychology. 8: 680. https://doi.org/10.3389/fpsyg.2017.00680.

88   **shows that zestful people:** Peterson, Christopher, Nansook Park, Nicholas
      Hall and Martin Seligman. 2009. "Zest and Work." *Journal of Organizational
      Behavior.* 30: 161–172. https://doi.org/10.1002/job.584.
89   **research links it to better creativity:** Simon-Thomas, Emiliana R. 2018. "The
      Four Keys to Happiness at Work." *Greater Good.* Greater Good Science Center,
      University of California Berkeley. August 29. https://greatergood.berkeley
      .edu/article/item/the_four_keys_to_happiness_at_work.
89   **work often feels more like a drain:** Hellebuyck, Michele, Theresa Nguyen,
      Madeline Halphern, Danielle Fritze and Jessica Kennedy. 2017. "Mind the
      Workplace." Mental Health America. Sponsored by The Faas Foundation.
      https://www.mhanational.org/sites/default/files/Mind%20the%20Workplace
      %20-%20MHA%20Workplace%20Health%20Survey%202017%20FINAL
      .PDF. Harter, Jim. 2020. "4 Factors Driving Record-High Employee
      Engagement in U.S." Gallup. https://www.gallup.com/workplace/284180
      /factors-driving-record-high-employee-engagement.aspx.
90   **research is actually mixed:** Bowling, Nathan A. 2007. "Is the job satisfaction-
      job performance relationship spurious? A meta-analytic examination." *Journal
      of Vocational Behavior.* 71: 167–185. https://doi.org/10.1016/j.jvb.2007.04.007.
      Spicer, André, and Carl Cederström. 2015. "The Research We've Ignored About
      Happiness at Work." *Harvard Business Review.* July 21. https://hbr.org
      /2015/07/the-research-weve-ignored-about-happiness-at-work. Peiró, José,
      Malgorzata W. Kozusznik, Isabel Rodríguez-Molina and Núria Tordera. 2019.
      "The Happy-Productive Worker Model and Beyond: Patterns of Wellbeing and
      Performance at Work." *International Journal of Environmental Research and
      Public Health.* 16(3): 479. https://doi.org/10.3390/ijerph16030479.
90   **be the golden ticket:** Rosso, Brent D., Kathryn H. Dekas and Amy
      Wrzesniewski. 2010. "On the meaning of work: A theoretical integration and
      review." *Research in Organizational Behavior.* 30: 91–127. Allan, Blake A.,
      Cassondra Batz-Barbarich, Haley M. Sterline, Louis Tay. 2018. "Outcomes of
      Meaningful Work: A Meta-Analysis." *Journal of Management Studies.* 56(3):
      500–528. https://doi.org/10.1111/joms.12406. Martela, Frank, and Anne B.
      Pessi. 2018. "Significant Work Is About Self-Realization and Broader Purpose:
      Defining the Key Dimensions of Meaningful Work." *Frontiers in Psychology.* 9:
      363. https://doi.org/10.3389/fpsyg.2018.00363. Weir, Kirsten. 2013. "More than
      job satisfaction." *Monitor on Psychology.* 44(11). https://www.apa.org/monitor
      /2013/12/job-satisfaction. Baily, Catherine, Ruth Yeoman, Adrian Madden,
      Marc Thompson and Gary Kerridge. 2018. "A Review of the Empirical
      Literature on Meaningful Work: Progress and Research Agenda." *Human
      Resource Development Review.* 28(1): https://doi.org/10.1177/1534484318804653.
91   **happiness and increased job satisfaction:** Keles, Hatice, and Mine Fındıklı.
      2016. "The effect of the meaningfulness of work on job satisfaction, job stress
      and intention to leave." *Global Journal of Business, Economics and Management.*
      6: 61–69. https://doi.org/10.18844/gjbem.v6i2.1370.

91 **performance, motivation, engagement:** Van Wingerden, Jessica, and Joost Van der Stoep. 2018. "The motivational potential of meaningful work: Relationships with strengths use, work engagement, and performance." *PloS One.* 13(6): e0197599. https://doi.org/10.1371/journal.pone.0197599.

91 **and productivity:** Reece, Andrew, Gabriella Kellerman and Alexi Robichaux. 2018. "Meaning and Purpose At Work." Report, BetterUp. https://get.betterup .co/rs/600-WTC-654/images/betterup-meaning-purpose-at-work.pdf.

91 **positive employee experience:** Bolden-Barrett, Valerie. 2017. "Meaningful work is critical to worker happiness, study says." *HR Dive.* October 10. https://www.hrdive.com/news/meaningful-work-is-critical-to-worker -happiness-study-says/506877/.

91 **helps buffer stress:** Allan, Blake A., Richard P. Douglass, Ryan D. Duffy and Ryan McCarty. 2015. "Meaningful Work as a Moderator of the Relation Between Work Stress and Meaning in Life." *Journal of Career Assessment.* 24(3). https://doi.org/10.1177/1069072715599357.

91 **have better attitudes:** Allan, Blake. 2018. "Important, worthwhile and valuable employment." *Psychological Science Agenda.* American Psychological Association. July. https://www.apa.org/science/about/psa/2018/07/valuable -employment.

91 **value meaningful work:** Cascio, Wayne F. 2003. "Changes in Workers, Work and Organizations." In *Handbook of Psychology.* Edited by W. Borman, R. Klimoski and D. Ilgen. 401–422. Hoboken: John Wiley & Sons.

91 **single, simple definition:** Dik, Bryan J., Zinta S. Byrne and Michael F. Steger, editors. 2013. *Purpose and Meaning in the Workplace.* Washington, D.C.: American Psychological Association. Steger, Michael F. 2017. "Creating Meaning and Purpose at Work." In *The Wiley Blackwell Handbook of the Psychology of Positivity and Strengths-Based Approaches at Work.* Edited by Lindsay G. Oades, Michael F. Steger, Antonella Delle Fave and Jonathan Passmore. Hoboken: John Wiley & Sons. Rosso, Brent D., Kathryn H. Dekas and Amy Wrzesniewski. 2010. "On the meaning of work: A theoretical integration and review." *Research in Organizational Behavior.* 30: 91–127. https://doi.org/10.1016/j.riob.2010.09.001.

91 **"work becomes meaningful":** Steger, Michael F. 2019. "Does a Meaningful Job Need to Burn You Out?" *Greater Good.* Greater Good Science Center, University of California Berkeley. August 21. https://greatergood.berkeley .edu/article/item/does_a_meaningful_job_need_to_burn_you_out.

91 **In one study of doctors:** Shanafelt, Tait D., Colin P. West, Jeff A. Sloan, Paul J. Novotny, Greg A. Poland, Ron Menaker, Teresa A. Rummans and Lotte N. Dyrbye. 2009. "Career Fit and Burnout Among Academic Faculty." *JAMA Internal Medicine.* 10: 990–995. https://doi.org/10.1001 /archinternmed.2009.70.

91 **no simple answers:** Rosso, Brent D., Kathryn H. Dekas and Amy Wrzesniewski. 2010. "On the meaning of work: A theoretical integration and

review." *Research in Organizational Behavior.* 30: 91–127. https://doi.org
/10.1016/j.riob.2010.09.001.

92 **Purpose Beyond a Paycheck:** Allan, Blake A., Ryan D. Duffy and Brian
Collisson. 2018. "Helping Others Increases Meaningful Work: Evidence From
Three Experiments." *Journal of Counseling Psychology.* 65(2): 155–165. https://
doi.org/10.1037/cou0000228. Weir, Kirsten. 2013. "More than job
satisfaction." *Monitor on Psychology.* 44(11). https://www.apa.org/monitor/2013
/12/job-satisfaction.

92 **what made someone's work meaningful:** Allan, Blake A., Kelsey L. Autin
and Ryan D. Duffy. 2014. "Examining social class and work meaning within
the psychology of working framework." *Journal of Career Assessment.* 22(4):
543–561. https://doi.org/10.1177/1069072713514811.

92 **the more you can see and connect:** Grama, Blanca, and Ramona Todericiu.
2017. "What Makes Work Meaningful." *Studies in Business and Economics.*
12(2): 46–52. https://doi.org/10.1515/sbe-2017-0020.

92 **Positive Work Relationships:** Grama, Blanca, and Ramona Todericiu. 2017.
"What Makes Work Meaningful." *Studies in Business and Economics.* 12(2):
46–52. https://doi.org/10.1515/sbe-2017-0020. Mathieu, Michael, Kevin J.
Eschleman and Danqiao Cheng. 2019 "Meta-Analytic and Multiwave
Comparison of Emotional Support and Instrumental Support in the
Workplace." *Journal of Occupational Health Psychology.* 24(3): 387–409. https://
doi.org/10.1037/ocp0000135. Hansen, Morten, and Dacher Keltner. 2013.
"Eight Ways to Find More Meaning at Work." *Greater Good.* Greater Good
Science Center, University of California Berkeley. November 4. https://
greatergood.berkeley.edu/article/item/eight_ways_to_find_more
_meaning_work.

92 **can give our lives a sense of purpose:** Baily, Catherine, Ruth Yeoman, Adrian
Madden, Marc Thompson and Gary Kerridge. 2018. "A Review of the
Empirical Literature on Meaningful Work: Progress and Research Agenda."
Human Resource Development Review. 28(1). https://doi.org/10.1177
/1534484318804653.

92 **studies show it delivers:** Steger, Michael F. 2017. "Creating Meaning and
Purpose at Work." In *The Wiley Blackwell Handbook of the Psychology of
Positivity and Strengths-Based Approaches at Work.* Edited by Lindsay G. Oades,
Michael F. Steger, Antonella Delle Fave and Jonathan Passmore. Hoboken:
John Wiley & Sons.

92 **47 percent higher rating:** Achor, Shawn, Andrew Reece, Gabriella Rosen
Kellerman and Alexi Robichaux. 2018. "9 Out of 10 People Are Willing to
Earn Less Money to Do More-Meaningful Work." *Harvard Business Review.*
November 6. https://hbr.org/2018/11/9-out-of-10-people-are-willing-to
-earn-less-money-to-do-more-meaningful-work.

92 **showed that helping others:** Colbert, Amy E., Joyce E. Bono and Radostina
K. Purvanova. 2016. "Flourishing via Workplace Relationships: Moving

Beyond Instrumental Support." *Academy of Management Journal.* 59(4): 1199–1223. https://doi.org/10.5465/amj.2014.0506.

92 **thrive in other ways:** Colbert, Amy E., Joyce E. Bono and Radostina K. Purvanova. 2016. "Flourishing via Workplace Relationships: Moving Beyond Instrumental Support." *Academy of Management Journal.* 59(4): 1199–1223. https://doi.org/10.5465/amj.2014.0506. Ahmed, Umair, A. Majid, La`aleh Al-Aali and Soleman Mozammel. 2019. "Can meaningful work really moderate the relationship between supervisor support, coworker support and work Engagement?" *Management Science Letters.* 9: 229–242. https://doi.org /10.5267/j.msl.2018.11.016. Mastroianni, Karen, and Julia Storberg-Walker. 2014. "Do work relationships matter? Characteristics of workplace interactions that enhance or detract from employee perceptions of well-being and health behaviors." *Health Psychology and Behavioral Medicine.* 2(1): 798–819. https:// doi.org/10.1080/21642850.2014.933343.

92 **employee satisfaction by 50 percent:** Riordan, Christine M. 2013. "We All Need Friends at Work." *Harvard Business Review.* July 3. https://hbr.org /2013/07/we-all-need-friends-at-work.

92 **wrote the most touching goodbye:** Spencer, Susan (@susanspencer28). 2020. Instagram. February 29. https://www.instagram.com/p/B9JpLjenXcl/.

93 **Capability and Accomplishment:** Rosso, Brent D., Kathryn H. Dekas and Amy Wrzesniewski. 2010. "On the meaning of work: A theoretical integration and review." *Research in Organizational Behavior.* 30: 91–127. https://doi.org /10.1016/j.riob.2010.09.001. Grama, Blanca, and Ramona Todericiu. 2017. "What Makes Work Meaningful." *Studies in Business and Economics.* 12(2): 46–52. https://doi.org/10.1515/sbe-2017-0020.

93 **Using your strengths:** Steger, Michael F. 2017. "Creating Meaning and Purpose at Work." In *The Wiley Blackwell Handbook of the Psychology of Positivity and Strengths-Based Approaches at Work.* Edited by Lindsay G. Oades, Michael F. Steger, Antonella Delle Fave and Jonathan Passmore. Hoboken: John Wiley & Sons.

93 **grew from a sense of pride:** Bailey, Catherine, and Adrian Madden. 2016. "What Makes Work Meaningful—Or Meaningless." *MIT Sloan Management Review.* Summer. https://sloanreview.mit.edu/article/what-makes-work -meaningful-or-meaningless/.

93 **confidence in your abilities:** Rosso, Brent D., Kathryn H. Dekas and Amy Wrzesniewski. 2010. "On the meaning of work: A theoretical integration and review." *Research in Organizational Behavior.* 30: 91–127. https://doi.org /10.1016/j.riob.2010.09.001.

93 **having autonomy:** Martela, Frank, and Tapani J. J. Riekki. 2018. "Autonomy, Competence, Relatedness, and Beneficence: A Multicultural Comparison of the Four Pathways to Meaningful Work." *Frontiers in Psychology.* 9: 1157. https:// doi.org/10.3389/fpsyg.2018.01157.

93 **felt or captured in moments:** Bailey, Catherine, and Adrian Madden. 2016. "What Makes Work Meaningful—Or Meaningless." *MIT Sloan Management Review.* Summer. https://sloanreview.mit.edu/article/what-makes-work -meaningful-or-meaningless/.

94 **job crafting, a concept:** Wrzesniewski, Amy, and Jane Dutton. 2001. "Crafting a Job: Revisioning Employees as Active Crafters of Their Work." *Academy of Management Review.* 26: 179–201. https://doi.org/10.2307/259118. Berg, Justin M., Jane E. Dutton and May Wrzesniewski. 2013. "Job Crafting and Meaningful Work." In *Purpose and Meaning in the Workplace.* Edited by Bryan J. Dik, Zinta S. Byrne and Michael F. Steger. Washington, D.C.: American Psychological Association.

95 **corporate or employee volunteering:** Eva Boštjančič, Sandra Antolović, Vanja Frčulj. 2018. "Corporate Volunteering: Relationship to Job Resources and Work Engagement." *Frontiers in Psychology.* 9: 1884. https://doi.org/10.3389 /fpsyg.2018.01884.

95 **increase feelings of job meaningfulness:** Rodell, Jessica B. 2013. "Finding Meaning Through Volunteering: Why Do Employees Volunteer and What Does it Mean for their Jobs?" *Academy of Management Journal.* 56(5): 1274– 1294. https://doi.org/10.5465/amj.2012.0611.

95 **work engagement, especially:** Caligiuri, Paula, Ahsiya Mencin and Kaifeng Jiang. 2012. "Win–Win–Win: The Influence of Company-Sponsored Volunteerism Programs on Employees, NGOs, and Business Units." *Personnel Psychology.* 66(4): 825–860. https://doi.org/10.1111/peps.12019.

95 **job performance and builds skills:** Rodell, Jessica B., Heiko Breitsoh, Melanie Schroder and David J. Keating. 2015. "Volunteering: A Review and Framework for Future Research." *Journal of Management.* 42(1): 55–84. https:// doi.org/10.1177/0149206315614374.

97 **people don't feel valued:** Mastroianni, Karen, and Julia Storberg-Walker. 2014. "Do work relationships matter? Characteristics of workplace interactions that enhance or detract from employee perceptions of well-being and health behaviors." *Health Psychology and Behavioral Medicine.* 2(1): 798–819. https:// doi.org/10.1080/21642850.2014.933343.

97 **honor of learning from Chelsea C. Williams:** "Active Allyship and Courageous Conversations at Hearst." Seminar with Chelsea C. Williams, via Zoom. June 17, 2020.

98 **her time on Wall Street:** Chelsea C. Williams, telephone interview and email with the author. July 10, 2020.

99 **less energized at or about work:** Rothmann, Sebastiaan, and Candice Baumann. 2014. "Employee engagement: The effects of work-home/home-work interaction and psychological conditions." *South African Journal of Economic and Management Sciences.* 17(4): 1015-8812. https://doi.org/10.4102/sajems .v17i4.419.

100 **When we're recognized:** Montani, Francesco, Jean-Sébastien Boudrias and Marilyne Pigeon. 2020. "Employee recognition, meaningfulness and behavioural involvement: test of a moderated mediation model." *International Journal of Human Resource Management*. 31(3): 356–384. https://doi.org /10.1080/09585192.2017.1288153. Tessema, Mussie T., Kathryn J. Ready and Abel B. Embay. 2013. "The Effects of Employee Recognition, Pay, and Benefits on Job Satisfaction: Cross Country Evidence." *Journal of Business Economics*. 4(1): 1–12.

103 *thirty-four times* **more effective:** Roghanizad, M. Mahdi, and Vanessa Bohns. 2017. "Ask in person: You're less persuasive than you think over email." *Journal of Experimental Social Psychology*. 69: 223–226. https://doi.org/10.1016 /j.jesp.2016.10.002.

103 **Researchers like Steger:** Steger, Michael F. 2019. "Does a Meaningful Job Need to Burn You Out?" *Greater Good*. Greater Good Science Center University of California Berkeley. August 21. https://greatergood.berkeley.edu /article/item/does_a_meaningful_job_need_to_burn_you_out.

103 **including Jeff Bezos:** Berger, Sarah. 2018. "Jeff Bezos doesn't like the idea of 'work-life balance'—here's what he swears by instead." cnbc.com. August 9. https://www.cnbc.com/2018/08/09/what-jeff-bezos-does-instead-of-work-life -balance.html.

105 **moms spend more time:** Sani, Giulia M. Dotti, and Judith Treas. 2016. "Educational Gradients in Parents' Child-Care Time Across Countries, 1965–2012." *Journal of Marriage and Family*. 78(4): 1083–1096. https://doi.org /10.1111/jomf.12305.

105 **more stressed and less happy:** McDonnell, Cadhla, Nancy Luke and Susan E. Short. 2019. "Happy Moms, Happier Dads: Gendered Caregiving and Parents' Affect." *Journal of Family Issues*. 40(17): 2553–2581. https://doi.org/10.1177 /0192513X19860179.

105 **not the quantity of time:** Milkie, Melissa A., Kei M. Nomaguchi and Kathleen E. Denny. 2015. "Does the Amount of Time Mothers Spend With Children or Adolescents Matter?" *Journal of Marriage and Family*. 77(2): 355–372. https://doi.org/10.1111/jomf.12170.

106 **underestimate how willing people are:** Flynn, Francis J., and Vanessa Bohns. 2008. "If You Need Help, Just Ask: Underestimating Compliance With Direct Requests for Help." *Journal of Personality and Social Psychology*. 95(1): 128–143. https://doi.org/10.1037/0022-3514.95.1.128.

107 **Research on micromanaging:** Collins, Sandra K., and Kevin S. Collins. 2002. "Micromanagement—a costly management style." *Radiology Management*. 24(6): 32–35. https://pubmed.ncbi.nlm.nih.gov/12510608/. Wheatley, Daniel. 2017. "Autonomy in Paid Work and Employee Subjective Well-Being." *Work and Occupations*. 44(3): 296–328. https://doi.org/10.1177 /0730888417697232. Martela, Frank, and Tapani J. J. Riekki. 2018. "Autonomy, Competence, Relatedness, and Beneficence: A Multicultural

Comparison of the Four Pathways to Meaningful Work." *Frontiers in Psychology.* 9: 1157. https://doi.org/10.3389/fpsyg.2018.01157. Gonzalez-Mulé, Erik, and Bethany Cockburn. 2016. "Worked to Death: The Relationships of Job Demands and Job Control with Mortality." *Personnel Psychology.* 70(1): 73–112. https://doi.org/10.1111/peps.12206.

111 **brain does not function best:** Schwartz, Tony. 2010. "For Real Productivity, Less is Truly More." *Harvard Business Review.* May 17. https://hbr.org /2010/05/for-real-productivity-less-is. Jabr, Ferris. 2013. "Why Your Brain Needs More Downtime." *Scientific American.* October 15. https://www .scientificamerican.com/article/mental-downtime/. Thompson, Derek. 2014. "A Formula for Perfect Productivity: Work for 52 Minutes, Break for 17." *The Atlantic.* September 17. https://www.theatlantic.com/business/archive /2014/09/science-tells-you-how-many-minutes-should-you-take-a-break-for -work-17/380369/. MIT Executive Education Blog. 2017. "Want to be more productive in 2018? Take more breaks." December 3. https://executive .mit.edu/blog/want-to-be-more-productive-in-2018-take-more-breaks. Epstein, Daniel A., Daniel Avrahami and Jacob T. Biehl. 2016. "Taking 5: Work-Breaks, Productivity, and Opportunities for Personal Informatics for Knowledge Workers." CHI '16: Proceedings of the 2016 CHI Conference on Human Factors in Computing Systems. May: 673–684. https://doi.org /10.1145/2858036.2858066.

111 **used to process information:** Immordino-Yang, Mary Helen, Joanna A. Christodoulou and Vanessa Singh. 2012. "Rest Is Not Idleness: Implications of the Brain's Default Mode for Human Development and Education." *Perspectives on Psychological Science.* 7(4): 352–364. https://doi.org/10.1177 /1745691612447308.

111 **potential to blow your fuse:** Steger, Michael F. 2019. "Does a Meaningful Job Need to Burn You Out?" *Greater Good.* Greater Good Science Center, University of California Berkeley. August 21. https://greatergood.berkeley.edu /article/item/does_a_meaningful_job_need_to_burn_you_out.

111 **That's burnout:** Koutsimani, Panagiota, Anthony Montgomery and Katerina Georganta. 2019. "The Relationship Between Burnout, Depression, and Anxiety: A Systematic Review and Meta-Analysis." *Frontiers in Psychology.* 10: 284. https://doi.org/10.3389/fpsyg.2019.00284.

112 **Half of Americans don't use:** U.S. Travel Association. 2019. "Study: A Record 768 Million U.S. Vacation Days Went Unused in '18, Opportunity Cost in the Billions." Press Release. August 16. https://www.ustravel.org/press /study-record-768-million-us-vacation-days-went-unused-18-opportunity-cost -billions.

112 **vacations are essential:** Achor, Shawn, and Michelle Gielan. 2016. "The Data-Driven Case for Vacation." *Harvard Business Review.* July 13. https:// hbr.org/2016/07/the-data-driven-case-for-vacation. Westman, Mina, and Dalia Etzion. 2001. "The impact of vacation and job stress on burnout and

absenteeism." *Psychology & Health.* 16(5): 595–606. https://doi.org/10.1080 /08870440108405529. Seppala, Emma. 2017. "Why You Should Take More Time Off from Work." *Greater Good.* Greater Good Science Center, University of California Berkeley. August 10. https://greatergood .berkeley.edu/article/item/why_you_should_take_more_time_off_from _work.

112 **productivity drops significantly:** Pencavel, John. 2014. "The Productivity of Working Hours." Discussion Paper Series. IZA: Institute for the Study of Labor. April. http://ftp.iza.org/dp8129.pdf.

112 **offset the demands on your brain:** Eschleman, Kevin J., Michael Mathieu and Jehangir Cooper. 2017. "Creating a Recovery Filled Weekend: The Moderating Effect of Occupation Type on the Relationship between Non-work Creative Activity and State of Feeling Recovered at Work." *Creativity Research Journal.* 29(2): 97–107. https://doi.org/10.1080/10400419.2017.1302756.

112 **"a high-end, haute couture":** Gilbert, Elizabeth. 2016. *Big Magic.* New York: Riverhead Books.

112 **energy cost is high:** Limburg, Karina, Hunna J. Watson, Martin S. Hagger, Sarah J. Egan. 2016. "The Relationship Between Perfectionism and Psychopathology: A Meta-Analysis." *Journal of Clinical Psychology.* 73(10): 1301–1326. https://doi.org/10.1002/jclp.22435.

113 **suggests they hurt productivity:** Housman, Michael, and Dylan Minor. 2015. "Toxic Workers." Working Paper. Harvard Business School. November. https://www.hbs.edu/faculty/Publication%20Files/16-057_d45c0b4f-fa19 -49de-8f1b-4b12fe054fea.pdf. Fisher-Blando, Jennifer. 2010. "Workplace Bullying: Aggressive Behavior and Its Effect on Job Satisfaction and Productivity." Saarbrücken, Germany: Lambert Academic Publishing.

114 **being unprovokeable:** Terri Cole, interview by Meaghan Murphy, Heidi Kristoffer, Jamie Hess and Christine Bibbo Herr. *Off the Gram,* podcast audio. January 27, 2020. https://podcasts.apple.com/us/podcast/terri-cole-friendship -breakups/id1494608415?i=1000463793680.

115 **work environment impacts:** Sander, Libby. 2019. "The Case for Finally Cleaning Your Desk." March 25. https://hbr.org/2019/03/the-case-for-finally -cleaning-your-desk.

Chapter 5: The Health Charge

119 **to come out about COVID-19:** University of Virginia Health Systems. 2020. "COVID-19: Exercise May Help Prevent Deadly Complication." Newsroom. April 15. https://newsroom.uvahealth.com/2020/04/15/covid-19-exercise-may -help-prevent-deadly-complication/.

120 **more or as effective:** Baptista, Liliana C., Aristides M. Machado-Rodrigues and Raul A. Martins. 2018. "Back to basics with active lifestyles: exercise is more effective than metformin to reduce cardiovascular risk in older adults with type 2 diabetes." *Biology of Sport.* 35(4): 363–372. https://doi.org/10.5114

/biolsport.2018.78057. Naci, Huseyin, Maximilian Salcher-Konrad, Sofia Dias, Manuel R Blum, Samali Anova Sahoo, David Nunan, John P A Ioannidis. 2019. "How does exercise treatment compare with antihypertensive medications? A network meta-analysis of 391 randomised controlled trials assessing exercise and medication effects on systolic blood pressure." *British Journal of Sports Medicine* 53: 859–869. https://doi.org/10.1136/bjsports-2018 -099921. Harvard Health Publishing. 2014. "Help for your cholesterol when the statins won't do." *Harvard Men's Health Watch*. March 2014. https://www .health.harvard.edu/newsletter_article/help-for-your-cholesterol-when-the -statins-wont-do. Netz, Yael. 2017. "Is the Comparison between Exercise and Pharmacologic Treatment of Depression in the Clinical Practice Guideline of the American College of Physicians Evidence-Based?" *Frontiers in Pharmacology*. 8: 257. https://doi.org/10.3389/fphar.2017.00257.

120 **thirteen types of cancer:** Cristol, Hope. 2016. "Exercise Linked with Lower Risk of 13 Types of Cancer." American Cancer Society. May 17. https://www .cancer.org/latest-news/exercise-linked-with-lower-risk-of-13-types-of-cancer .html.

121 **release of growth factors:** Echave, Pedro, Gisela Machado-da-Silva, Rebecca S. Arkell, Michael R. Duchen, Jake Jacobson, Richard Mitter and Alison C. Lloyd. 2009. "Extracellular growth factors and mitogens cooperate to drive mitochondrial biogenesis." *Journal of Cell Science*. 122: 4516–4525. https://doi .org/10.1242/jcs.049734.

121 **It's mitochondria that manufacture:** Menshikova, Elizabeth V., Vladimir B. Ritov, Liane Fairfull, Robert E. Ferrell, David E. Kelley and Bret H. Goodpaster. 2006. "Effects of Exercise on Mitochondrial Content and Function in Aging Human Skeletal Muscle." *The Journals of Gerontology. Series A, Biological Sciences and Medical Sciences*. 61(6): 534–540. https://doi.org /10.1093/gerona/61.6.534.

121 **controls your stress response:** Childs, Emma, and Harriet de Wit. 2014. "Regular exercise is associated with emotional resilience to acute stress in healthy adults." *Frontiers in Physiology*. 5: 161. https://doi.org/10.3389 /fphys.2014.00161.

121 **release of endorphins:** Heijnen, Saskia, Bernhard Hommel, Armin Kibele and Lorenza S. Colzato. 2016. "Neuromodulation of Aerobic Exercise—A Review." *Frontiers in Psychology*. 6: 1890. https://doi.org/10.3389/fpsyg.2015.01890. Maddock, Richard J., Gretchen A. Casazza, Dione H. Fernandez and Michael I. Maddock. 2016. "Acute Modulation of Cortical Glutamate and GABA Content by Physical Activity." *Journal of Neuroscience*. 36 (8): 2449. https://doi .org/10.1523/JNEUROSCI.3455-15.2016.

121 **A study that measured people's activity:** Ries Merikangas, Kathleen, Joel Swendsen, Ian B. Hickie, Lihong Cui, Haochang Shou, Alison K. Merikangas, Jihui Zhang, Femke Lamers, Ciprian Crainiceanu, Nora D. Volkow and Vadim Zipunnikov. 2018. "Real-time Mobile Monitoring of the Dynamic Associations

Among Motor Activity, Energy, Mood, and Sleep in Adults with Bipolar Disorder." *JAMA Psychiatry.* 76(2):190–198. https://doi.org/10.1001 /jamapsychiatry.2018.3546.

121 **adults with unexplained fatigue:** Puetz, Timothy W., Sara S. Flowers and Patrick J. O'Connor. 2008. "A Randomized Controlled Trial of the Effect of Aerobic Exercise Training on Feelings of Energy and Fatigue in Sedentary Young Adults with Persistent Fatigue." *Psychotherapy and Psychosomatics.* 77(3): 167–74. https://doi.org/10.1159/000116610.

121 **worked out at their office:** Coulson, J. C., Jim McKenna and M. Field. 2008. "Exercising at Work and Self-Reported Work Performance." *International Journal of Workplace Health Management.* 1:176–197. https://doi.org/10.1108 /17538350810926534.

122 **Piles of research show:** Craft, Lynette L., and Frank M. Perna. 2004. "The Benefits of Exercise for the Clinically Depressed." *Primary Care Companion to the Journal of Clinical Psychiatry.* 6(3): 104–111. https://doi.org/10.4088/pcc .v06n0301. Wipfli, Bradley M., Chad D. Rethorst and Daniel M. Landers. 2008. "The Anxiolytic Effects of Exercise: A Meta-Analysis of Randomized Trials and Dose–Response Analysis." *Journal of Sport and Exercise Psychology.* 30(4):392-410. https://doi.org/10.1123/jsep.30.4.392.

122 **well-being as a $25,000 per year:** Chekroud, Sammi R., Ralitza Gueorguieva, Amanda B. Zheutlin, Martin Paulus, Harlan M. Krumholz, John H. Krystal, Adam M. Chekroud. 2018. "Association between physical exercise and mental health in 1·2 million individuals in the USA between 2011 and 2015: a cross-sectional study." *The Lancet Psychiatry.* 5(9): 739–746.

122 **how little exercise you actually need:** Zhang, Zhanjia, and Weiyun Chen. 2019. "A Systematic Review of the Relationship Between Physical Activity and Happiness." *Journal of Happiness Studies.* 20: 1305–1322. https://doi.org /10.1007/s10902-018-9976-0.

122 **collapsing from exhaustion:** Katz, Emily Tess. 2014. "Arianna Huffington Reveals How Fainting Changed Her Whole Life." March 25. https://www .huffpost.com/entry/arianna-huffington-fainting_n_5030365.

123 **irritable and stressed:** Saghir, Zahid, Javeria N. Syeda, Adnan S. Muhammad and Tareg H. Balla Abdalla. 2018. "The Amygdala, Sleep Debt, Sleep Deprivation, and the Emotion of Anger: A Possible Connection?" *Cureus.* 10(7): e2912. https://doi.org/10.7759/cureus.2912.

123 **increases risk of depression:** National Sleep Foundation. "The Complex Relationship Between Sleep, Depression & Anxiety." Accessed on May 18, 2020. https://www.sleepfoundation.org/excessive-sleepiness/health-impact /complex-relationship-between-sleep-depression-anxiety.

123 **burnout:** Söderström, Marie, Kerstin Jeding, Mirjam Ekstedt, Aleksander Perski and Torbjörn Akerstedt. 2012. "Insufficient Sleep Predicts Clinical Burnout." *Journal of Occupational Health Psychology.* 17(2): 175–83. https://doi .org/10.1037/a0027518.

123 **messes with your immune system:** Watson, N. F., D. Buchwald, J. J. Delrow, W. A. Altemeier, M. V. Vitiello, A. I. Pack, M. Bamshad, C. Noonan, S. A. Gharib. 2017. "Transcriptional Signatures of Sleep Duration Discordance in Monozygotic Twins." *Sleep.* 40(1): zsw019. https://doi.org/10.1093/sleep /zsw019. Olson, Eric J. 2018. "Lack of sleep: Can it make you sick?" Mayo Clinic. November 28. https://www.mayoclinic.org/diseases-conditions /insomnia/expert-answers/lack-of-sleep/faq-20057757.

123 **ATP (what your cells use for energy) may flood:** Dworak, Markus, Robert W. McCarley, Tae Kim, Anna V. Kalinchuk and Radhika Basheer. 2010. "Sleep and Brain Energy Levels: ATP Changes during Sleep." *Journal of Neuroscience.* 30(26): 9007–9016. https://doi.org/10.1523/JNEUROSCI.1423-10.2010.

123 **seven to nine hours a night:** Hirshkowitz, Max, et al. 2015. "National Sleep Foundation's sleep time duration recommendations: methodology and results summary." *Sleep Health: Journal of the National Sleep Foundation.* 1(1): 40–43. https://doi.org/10.1016/j.sleh.2014.12.010.

123 **reporters at the BBC:** BBC News. 2013. "How much can an extra hour's sleep change you?" *BBC Magazine.* October 9. https://www.bbc.com/news/magazine -24444634.

123 **put a price tag on an extra hour:** Gibson, Matthew, and Jeffrey Shrader. 2014. "Time Use and Productivity: The Wage Returns to Sleep." Working Paper, Williams College, Department of Economics. July 10. http://online.wsj .com/public/resources/documents/091814sleep.pdf.

123 **improve athletic performance:** American Academy of Sleep Medicine. "Sleep extension improves response time, reduces fatigue in professional baseball players: Short-term sleep loading can improve sports performance." *ScienceDaily.* Accessed May 18, 2020. www.sciencedaily.com/releases/2017/06 /170605085329.htm.

123 **dangerous calcium deposits:** King, Christopher Ryan, Kristen L. Knutson, Paul J. Rathouz, Steve Sidney, Kiang Liu and Diane S. Lauderdale. 2008. "Short sleep duration and incident coronary artery calcification." *JAMA.* 300(24): 2859–2866. https://doi.org/10.1001/jama.2008.867.

124 **A study published in *Sleep*:** Manber, Rachel, Richard R. Bootzin, Christine Acebo and Mary A. Carskadon. 1996. "The Effects of Regularizing Sleep-Wake Schedules on Daytime Sleepiness." *Sleep.* 19(5): 432-441. https://doi.org /10.1093/sleep/19.5.432. Okano, Kana, Jakub R. Kaczmarzyk, Neha Dave, John D. E. Gabrieli and Jeffrey C. Grossman. 2019. "Sleep quality, duration, and consistency are associated with better academic performance in college students." *NPJ Science of Learning.* 4: 16. https://doi.org/10.1177 /074873099129000894.

125 **sets your circadian rhythm:** Kang, Jiunn-Horng, and Shih-Ching Chen. 2009. "Effects of an irregular bedtime schedule on sleep quality, daytime sleepiness, and fatigue among university students in Taiwan." *BMC Public Health.* 9: 248. https://doi.org/10.1186/1471-2458-9-248.

126 **Other sources claim:** Popova, Maria. 2014. "How Long It Takes to Form a New Habit." *Brain Pickings.* January 2. Accessed on May 19, 2020. https://www.brainpickings.org/2014/01/02/how-long-it-takes-to-form-a-new-habit/.

126 **average of sixty-six days:** Lally, Phillippa, Cornelia H. M. van Jaarsveld, Henry W. W. Potts and Jane Wardle. 2009. "How are habits formed: Modelling habit formation in the real world." *European Journal of Social Psychology.* 40(6): 998–1009. https://doi.org/10.1002/ejsp.674.

127 **It suppresses melatonin:** Change, Anne-Marie, Daniel Aeschbach, Jeanne F. Duffy and Charles A. Czeisler. 2015. "Evening use of light-emitting eReaders negatively affects sleep, circadian timing, and next-morning alertness." *PNAS.* 112 (4): 1232–1237. https://doi.org/10.1073/pnas.1418490112.

127 **everything your phone feeds:** National Sleep Foundation. "Three ways gadgets are keeping you awake." Sleep.org. Accessed on May 18, 2020. https://www.sleep.org/articles/ways-technology-affects-sleep/.

127 **wake up feeling more groggy:** Chinoy, Evan D., Jeanne F. Duffy and Charles A. Czeisler. 2018. "Unrestricted evening use of light-emitting tablet computers delays self-selected bedtime and disrupts circadian timing and alertness." *Psychological Reports.* 6(10): e13692. https://doi.org/10.14814/phy2.13692.

127 **Caffeine blocks adenosine:** Ribeiro, Joaquim, and Ana M. Sebastião. 2010. "Caffeine and Adenosine." *Journal of Alzheimer's Disease.* 20 Suppl 1:S3–15. https://doi.org/10.3233/JAD-2010-1379.

127 **Sixty-five degrees:** National Sleep Foundation. "What Temperature Should Your Bedroom Be?" Accessed on May 18, 2020. https://www.sleepfoundation.org/bedroom-environment/touch/what-temperature-should-your-bedroom-be.

128 **block receptors in the brain:** López, Victor, Birgitte Nielsen, Maite Solas, Maria J. Ramírez and Anna K. Jager. 2017. "Exploring Pharmacological Mechanisms of Lavender (*Lavandula angustifolia*) Essential Oil on Central Nervous System Targets." *Frontiers in Pharmacology.* 8: 280. https://doi.org/10.3389/fphar.2017.00280. Harada, Hiroki, Hideki Kashiwadani, Yuichi Kanmura and Tomoyuki Kuwaki. 2018. "Linalool Odor-Induced Anxiolytic Effects in Mice." *Frontiers in Behavioral Neuroscience.* 12: 241. https://doi.org/10.3389/fnbeh.2018.00241.

128 **helped some sleep better:** Smith Lillehei, Angela, Linda L. Halcón, Kay Savik and Reilly Reis. 2015. "Effect of Inhaled Lavender and Sleep Hygiene on Self-Reported Sleep Issues: A Randomized Controlled Trial." *Journal of Alternative and Complementary Medicine.* 21(7): 430–438. https://doi.org/10.1089/acm.2014.0327.

128 **people with insomnia said:** Ackerley, Rochelle, Gaby Badre and Håkan Olausson. 2015. "Positive effects of a weighted blanket on insomnia." *Journal of Sleep Medicine and Disorders.* 2(3): 1022.

129 **Watching TV for a few hours:** Exelmans, Liese, and Jan Van den Bulck. 2017. "Binge Viewing, Sleep, and the Role of Pre-Sleep Arousal." *Journal of Clinical Sleep Medicine.* 13(8). https://doi.org/10.5664/jcsm.6704.

130 **"decision fatigue":** Tierney, John. 2011. "Do you suffer from decision fatigue." *New York Times.* August 17. Accessed on May 19, 2020. https://www.nytimes.com/2011/08/21/magazine/do-you-suffer-from-decision-fatigue.html.

130 **walked forty-five minutes in the morning:** Wheeler, Michael J., et al. 2019. "Distinct effects of acute exercise and breaks in sitting on working memory and executive function in older adults: a three-arm, randomised cross-over trial to evaluate the effects of exercise with and without breaks in sitting on cognition." *British Journal of Sports Medicine.* Published online April 29. https://doi.org/10.1136/bjsports-2018-100168.

130 **boost a growth factor:** Baker Heart and Diabetes Institute. 2019. "Morning exercise can improve decision-making across the day in older adults." Media release. April 30. https://baker.edu.au/news/media-releases/exercise-decision-making.

130 **reduce levels of melatonin:** Carlson, Lara A., Kaylee M. Pobocik, Michael A. Lawrence, Daniel A. Brazeau and Alexander J. Koch. 2019. "Influence of Exercise Time of Day on Salivary Melatonin Responses." *International Journal of Sports Physiology and Performance.* 14(3): 351–353. https://doi.org/10.1123/ijspp.2018-0073.

131 **stick with it:** Sniehotta, Falko F., Urte Scholz, Ralf Schwarzer. 2006. "Action Plans and Coping Plans for Physical Exercise: A Longitudinal Intervention Study in Cardiac Rehabilitation." *British Journal of Health Psychology.* 11(Pt 1):23-37. https://doi.org/10.1348/135910705X43804. Orbell, Sheina, Sarah Hodgkins and Paschal Sheeran. 1997. "Implementation Intentions and the Theory of Planned Behavior." 23(9):945-954. https://doi.org/10.1177/0146167297239004.

131 **those who took group workout classes:** Yorks, Dayna M., Christopher A. Frothingham and Mark D. Schuenke. 2017. Effects of Group Fitness Classes on Stress and Quality of Life of Medical Students." *Journal of the American Osteopathic Association.* 117(11): e17–e25. https://doi.org/10.7556/jaoa.2017.140.

131 **rowers' pain thresholds:** Cohen, Emma E. A., Robin Ejsmond-Frey, Nicola Knight and R. I. M. Dunbar. 2010. "Rowers' High: Behavioural Synchrony Is Correlated With Elevated Pain Thresholds." *Biology Letters.* 6(1): 106–8. https://doi.org/10.1098/rsbl.2009.0670.

135 **the term "enclothed cognition":** Hajo, Adam, and Adam D. Galinsky. 2012. "Enclothed cognition." *Journal of Experimental Social Psychology.* 48(4): 918–925. https://doi.org/10.1016/j.jesp.2012.02.008.

136 **more active sleep better:** Dolezal, Brett A., Eric V. Neufeld, David M. Boland, Jennifer L. Martin and Christopher B. Cooper. 2017. "Interrelationship

between Sleep and Exercise: A Systematic Review." *Advances in Preventative Medicine.* 1364387. https://doi.org/10.1155/2017/1364387.

136 **make healthier food choices:** Jaehyun Joo, Sinead A. Williamson, Ana I. Vazquez, Jose R. Fernandez and Molly S. Bray. 2019. "The influence of 15-week exercise training on dietary patterns among young adults." *International Journal of Obesity.* 43: 1681–1690. https://doi.org/10.1038/s41366-018-0299-3.

136 **get enough sleep eat healthier:** Zuraikat, Faris M., Nour Makarem, Ming Liao, Marie-Pierre St.-Onge and Brooke Aggarwal. 2020. "Measures of Poor Sleep Quality Are Associated With Higher Energy Intake and Poor Diet Quality in a Diverse Sample of Women From the Go Red for Women Strategically Focused Research Network." *Journal of the American Heart Association.* 9(4). https://doi.org/10.1161/JAHA.119.014587.

136 **modest improvements to your diet:** Firth, Joseph, et al. 2019. "The Effects of Dietary Improvement on Symptoms of Depression and Anxiety: A Meta-Analysis of Randomized Controlled Trials." *Psychosomatic Medicine.* 81(3): 265–280. https://doi.org/10.1097/PSY.0000000000000673. Rahe, Corinna, Michael Unrath and Klaus Berger. 2014. "Dietary Patterns and the Risk of Depression in Adults: A Systematic Review of Observational Studies." *European Journal of Nutrition.* 53(4): 997–1013. https://doi.org/10.1007/s00394-014 -0652-9. Mujcic, Redzo, and Andrew J. Oswald. 2016. "Evolution of Well-Being and Happiness After Increases in Consumption of Fruit and Vegetables." *American Journal of Public Health.* 106(8): 1504–1510. https://doi.org/10.2105 /AJPH.2016.303260.

137 **similar and scary health problems:** Levine, James A. 2015. "Sick of sitting." *Diabetologia.* 58(8): 1751–1758. https://doi.org/10.1007/s00125-015-3624-6. Biswas, Aviroop, Paul I. Oh, Guy E. Faulkner, Ravi R. Bajaj, Michael A. Silver, Marc S. Mitchell and David A. Alter. 2015. "Sedentary Time and Its Association With Risk for Disease Incidence, Mortality, and Hospitalization in Adults: A Systematic Review and Meta-Analysis." *Annals of Internal Medicine.* 162(2): 123–32. https://doi.org/10.7326/M14-1651.

137 **more time people spend sitting:** Rebar, Amanda L., Corneel Vandelanotte, Jannique van Uffelen, Camille Short and Mitch J. Duncan. 2014. "Associations of overall sitting time and sitting time in different contexts with depression, anxiety, and stress symptoms." *Mental Health and Physical Activity.* 7(2): 105–110. https://doi.org/10.1016/j.mhpa .2014.02.004.

137 **given adjustable desks:** Garrett, Gregory, Mark Benden, Ranjana Mehta, Adam Pickens, Camille Peres and Hongwei Zhao. 2016. "Call Center Productivity Over 6 Months Following a Standing Desk Intervention." *IIE Transactions on Occupational Ergonomics and Human Factors.* 4(2-3): 188 95. https://doi.org/10.1080/21577323.2016.1183534.

138 **the results were amazing:** Bergouignan, Audrey, et al. 2016. "Effect of frequent interruptions of prolonged sitting on self-perceived levels of energy,

mood, food cravings and cognitive function." *International Journal of Behavioral Nutrition and Physical Activity.* 13(1): 113. https://doi.org/10.1186 /s12966-016-0437-z.

Chapter 6: The Extra Charge

144 **when women wore makeup:** Palumbo, Rocco, Beth Fairfield, Nicola Mammarella and Alberto Di Domenico. 2017. "Does make-up make you feel smarter? The 'lipstick effect' extended to academic achievement." *Cogent Psychology.* 4(1): 1327635. https://doi.org/10.1080/23311908 .2017.1327635.

144 **report being happy in life:** Happiness Research Institute. 2019. "In Celebration of Happy Homes." June 28. https://www.happiness researchinstitute.com/news3. Happiness Research Institute. 2019. "Happy Home Report." Prepared for King Fisher. https://docs.wixstatic.com /ugd/928487_eb2adab5e0a140baa345eab483fcae83.pdf.

144 **visual art can reduce stress:** Nanda, Upali, Cheryl Chanaud, Michael Nelson, Robyn Bajema and Ben H. Jansen. 2012. "Impact of Visual Art on Patient Behavior in the Emergency Department Waiting Room." *Journal of Emergency Medicine.* 43(1): 172–181. https://doi.org/10.1016/j.jemermed.2011.06.138.

144 **clutter may spike it:** Roster, Catherine A., Joseph R. Ferrari and M. Peter Jurkat. 2016. "The dark side of home: Assessing possession 'clutter' on subjective well-being." *Journal of Environmental Psychology.* 46: 32–41. https:// doi.org/10.1016/j.jenvp.2016.03.003.

144 **a nice view:** Ulrich, Roger S. 1984. "View through a window may influence recovery from surgery." *Science.* 27:224(4647): 420–1. https://doi.org/10.1126 /science.6143402.

145 **leading with how you want to feel:** Fetell Lee, Ingrid. 2020. "One question that can help you create more joy at home—and in life." *The Aesthetics of Joy.* January 18. https://www.aestheticsofjoy.com/2020/01/one-question-that -can-help-you-create-more-joy-at-home-and-in-life/.

147 **Part of his reasoning:** McRaven, William H. 2017. *Make Your Bed: Little Things That Can Change Your Life . . . and Maybe the World.* New York: Grand Central Publishing.

147 **one survey found:** Monroy, Lauren. 2020. "Can Making the Bed in the Morning Make You Happier?" April 17, 2020. https://bestmattress-brand.org /making-the-bed/.

147 **habits . . . made the biggest difference:** Rubin, Gretchen. 2009. "Make Your Bed." *Gretchen Rubin.* August 28. https://gretchenrubin.com/2009/08 /make-your-bed/

147 **I sleep better:** The National Sleep Foundation. 2011. "Americans' Bedrooms Are Key to Better Sleep According to New National Sleep Foundation Poll." January 25. https://www.sleepfoundation.org/press-release/americans -bedrooms-are-key-better-sleep-according-new-national-sleep-foundation-pol

147 **Bed-makers report:** Monroy, Lauren. 2020. "Can Making the Bed in the Morning Make You Happier?" April 17. https://bestmattress-brand.org /making-the-bed/.

148 **actually rings true:** Kaya, Naz, and Helen H. Epps. 2004. "Relationship between color and emotion: A study of college students." *College Student Journal.* 38(3): 396–405. https://pdfs.semanticscholar.org/e227 /372d80f0d1853894d5eb452c74c8f78a95c2.pdf.

148 **Color, period, especially bright:** Meadows, Chris M. 2013. *A Psychological Perspective on Joy and Emotional Fulfillment.* London: Routledge.

148 **that vivid shades:** Fetell Lee, Ingrid. 2018. "Scared of too much color in your life? Learn to let go of your fear—and find more joy." TED. September 4. https://ideas.ted.com/scared-of-too-much-color-in-your-life-learn-to-let-go-of -your-fear-and-find-more-joy/. Happiness Research Institute. 2019. "In Celebration of Happy Homes." June 28. https://www.happinessresearch institute.com/news3.

149 **linked to procrastination:** Ferrari, Joseph R., and Catherine A. Roster. 2018. "Delaying Disposing: Examining the Relationship between Procrastination and Clutter across Generations." *Current Psychology.* 37: 426–431. https://doi.org /10.1007/s12144-017-9679-4.

149 **stress hormones in working moms:** Saxbe, Darby, and Rene L. Repetti. "For better or worse? Coregulation of couples' cortisol levels and mood states." *Journal of Personality and Social Psychology.* 98(1): 92–103. https://doi.org /10.1037/a0016959.

149 **may encourage overeating:** Vartanian, Lenny, Kristin Kernan and Brian Wansink. 2017. "Clutter, Chaos, and Overconsumption: The Role of Mind-Set in Stressful and Chaotic Food Environments." *Environment and Behavior.* 49(2): 215–223. https://doi.org/10.1177/0013916516628178.

149 **Neuroscientists discovered through:** McMains, Stephanie, and Sabine Kastner. "Interactions of Top-Down and Bottom-Up Mechanisms in Human Visual Cortex." 2011. *Journal of Neuroscience.* 31(2): 587–597. https://doi .org/10.1523/JNEUROSCI.3766-10.2011.

149 **ding your memory:** Gaspar, John M., Gregory J. Christie, David J. Prime, Pierre Jolicœur and John J. McDonald. 2016. "Inability to suppress salient distractors predicts low visual working memory capacity." *PNAS.* 113(13): 201523471. https://doi.org/10.1073/pnas.1523471113.

149 **trigger anxiety and:** Clark, Matthew. 2018. "How decluttering your space could make you healthier and happier." Mayo Clinic. April 5. https://www .mayoclinic.org/healthy-lifestyle/stress-management/in-depth/how -decluttering-your-space-could-make-you-healthier-and-happier/art-20390064.

150 **Kids given only four toys:** Dauch, Carly, Michelle Imwalle, Brooke Ocasio and Alexia E. Metz. 2018. "The influence of the number of toys in the environment on toddlers' play." *Infant Development and Behavior.* 50: 78–87. https://doi.org/10.1016/j.infbeh.2017.11.005.

153 **Harvard researcher Nancy Etcoff:** Etcoff, Nancy, Lauren Haley and Zachary Warren. 2014. "Increasing Positive Affect: A Test of the Biophilia Hypothesis." https://www.semanticscholar.org/paper/Increasing-Positive-Affect%3A-A-Test-of -the-Biophilia-Etcoff-Haley/78c6e7c71ad6485500ed4c89344813efcc4e4936. Goldsmith, William. 2006. "A Bouquet a Day . . ." *The Harvard Crimson.* October 26. https://www.thecrimson.com/article/2006/10/26/a-bouquet-a-day-a-new/.

153 **Rutgers researchers found:** Haviland-Jones, Jeannette, Holly Hale Rosario, Patricia Wilson, Terry R. McGuire. 2005. *Evolutionary Psychology.* https://doi .org/10.1177/147470490500300109.

153 **Studies show certain outfits:** Slepian, Michael L., Simon N. Ferber, Joshua M. Gold and Abraham M. Rutchick. 2015. "The Cognitive Consequences of Formal Clothing." *Social Psychological and Personality Science.* 6(6): 661–668. https://doi.org/10.1177/1948550615579462. Hajo, Adam, and Adam G. Galinsky. 2012. "Enclothed cognition." *Journal of Experimental Social Psychology.* 48(4): 918–925. https://doi.org/10.1016/j.jesp.2012.02.008. Bellezza, Silvia, Francesca Gino and Anat Keinan. 2014. "The red sneakers effect: Inferring status and competence from signals of nonconformity." Journal of Consumer Research. 41(1): 35–54. https://doi.org/10.1086/674870. https:// www.psychologicalscience.org/news/minds-business/dressing-for-success-from -lucky-socks-to-the-red-sneaker-effect.html.

154 **good vibes stick to clothes:** Frith, Hannah, and Kate Gleeson. 2008. "Dressing the Body: The Role of Clothing in Sustaining Body Pride and Managing Body Distress." *Qualitative Research in Psychology.* 5(4): 249–264. https://doi.org /10.1080/14780880701752950.

154 **"crop top on any block":** Turini, Shiona (@shionat). Instagram. September 30, 2018. https://www.instagram.com/p/BoXMC2HgJ4Y/.

156 **acne is linked to lower:** Gorelick, Joe, Selena R. Daniels, Ariane K. Kawata, Arnold Degboe, Teresa K. Wilcox, Caroline T. Burk and Tracee Douse-Dean. 2015. "Acne-Related Quality of Life Among Female Adults of Different Races/ Ethnicities." *Journal of the Dermatology Nurses' Association.* 7(3): 154–162. https://doi.org/10.1097/JDN.0000000000000129. Lasek, Rebecca Jane, and Mary-Margaret Chren. 1998. "Acne Vulgaris and the Quality of Life of Adult Dermatology Patients." *Archives of Dermatology.* 134(4):454-458. https://doi .org/10.1001/archderm.134.4.454.

159 **feelings of gratitude:** Lambert, Nathaniel M., Frank D. Fincham, Tyler F. Stillman and Lukas R. Dean. 2009. "More gratitude, less materialism: The mediating role of life satisfaction." *Journal of Positive Psychology.* 4(1): 32–42. https://doi.org/10.1080/17439760802216311. Breines, Juliana. 2013. "Five Ways to Ease Your Envy." *Greater Good.* Greater Good Science Center, University of California Berkeley. August 1. https://greatergood.berkeley.edu /article/item/five_ways_to_ease_your_envy.

160 **can buffer stress:** Speer, Megan E., and Mauricio R. Delgado. 2017. "Reminiscing about positive memories buffers acute stress responses." *Nature*

Human Behaviour. 1(5).Article: 0093. https://doi.org/10.1038/s41562-017 -0093.

Chapter 7: The Recharge

163 **officially defined as:** American Psychological Association. 2020. "Building your resilience." Accessed on May 18, 2020. https://www.apa.org/topics/resilience.

163 **closely linked to:** Southwick, Steven M., Meena Vythilingam and Dennis S. Charney. 2005. "The psychobiology of depression and resilience to stress: implications for prevention and treatment." *Annual Review of Clinical Psychology.* 1: 255–91. https://doi.org/10.1146/annurev .clinpsy.1.102803.143948. Zautra, Alex, John Hall and Kate Murray. 2010. "Resilience: A new definition of health for people and communities." In *Handbook of Adult Resilience.* Edited by J. R. Reich, Alex J. Zautra and John S. Hall. 3–30. New York: Guilford.

163 **corporate executives with high:** Kermott, Cindy A., Ruth E. Johnson, Richa Sood, Sarah M. Jenkins and Amit Sood. 2019. "Is higher resilience predictive of lower stress and better mental health among corporate executives?" *PloS One.* 14 (6): e0218092. https://doi.org/10.1371/journal.pone.0218092.

163 **keeps you physically healthier:** Van Schrojenstein Lantman, Marith, Marlou Mackus, Leila S. Otten, Debora de Kruijff, Aurora JAE van de Loo, Aletta D. Kraneveld, Johan Garssen and Joris C. Verster. 2017. "Mental resilience, perceived immune functioning, and health." *Journal of Multidisciplinary Healthcare.* 10: 107–112. https://doi.org/10.2147/JMDH.S130432.

164 **older adults who scored:** Ezeamama, Amara E., Jennifer Elkins, Simpson Cherie, Shaniqua L. Smith, Joseph C. Allegra and Toni P. Miles. 2016. "Indicators of resilience and healthcare outcomes: findings from the 2010 health and retirement survey." *Quality of Life Research.* 25: 1007–1015. https:// doi.org/10.1007/s11136-015-1144-y.

164 **analyzed data with greater nuance:** Infurna, Frank J., and Suniya S. Luthar. 2016. "Resilience to major life stressors is not as common as thought." *Perspectives in Psychological Science.* 11(2): 175–194. https://doi.org/10.1177 /1745691615621271.

164 **level of resilience:** Niitsu, Kosuke, Michael J. Rice, Julia F. Houfek, Scott F. Stoltenberg, Kevin A. Kuzyk and Cecilia R. Barron. 2019. "A Systematic Review of Genetic Influence on Psychological Resilience." *Biological Research for Nursing.* 21(1): 61–71. https://doi.org/10.1177/1099800418800396.

164 **according to psychiatrists:** Southwick, Steven M., and Dennis S. Charney. 2018. *Resilience: The Science of Mastering Life's Greatest Challenges* 2nd Edition. Cambridge University Press.

164 **"Prescription for Resilience":** Charney, Dennis S. 2018. "Ten-Step Prescription for Resilience." Icahn School of Medicine at Mount Sinai. https://icahn.mssm .edu/files/ISMMS/Assets/About%20the%20School/Leadership/CRTV-3841 -ICAHN_Charney_10StepPrescription_Resilience_Infographic_Nov_20.pdf.

165 **take moments to notice the good:** Cohn, Michael A., Barbara L. Fredrickson, Stephanie L. Brown, Joseph A. Mikels and Anne M. Conway. 2009. "Happiness Unpacked: Positive Emotions Increase Life Satisfaction by Building Resilience." *Emotion*. June; 9(3): 361–368. https://doi.org/10.1037 /a0015952.

166 **good to be found:** Iacoviello, Brian, and Dennis S. Charney. 2014. "Psychosocial facets of resilience: implications for preventing posttrauma psychopathology, treating trauma survivors, and enhancing community resilience." *European Journal of Psychotraumatology*. 5. https://doi.org/10.3402 /ejpt.v5.23970.

167 **former prisoners of war:** Segovia, Francine, Jeffrey L. Moore, Steven E. Linnville, Robert E. Hoyt and Robert E. Hain. 2012. "Optimism predicts resilience in repatriated prisoners of war: a 37-year longitudinal study." *Journal of Traumatic Stress*. 25(3): 330–6. https://doi.org/10.1002/jts.21691.

167 **Optimism also helps predict:** Panchal, Sandeep, Swati Mukherjee and Updesh Kumar. 2016. "Optimism in Relation to Well-Being, Resilience and Perceived Stress." *International Journal of Education and Psychological Research*. 5(2): 1–6. http://ijepr.org/panels/admin/papers/256ij1.pdf.

167 **the most resilient people:** Southwick, Steven M., and Dennis S. Charney. 2018. *Resilience: The Science of Mastering Life's Greatest Challenges* 2nd Edition. Cambridge University Press.

167 **consistently associated with the ability:** Wu, Gang, Adriana Feder, Hagit Cohen, Joanna J. Kim, Solara Calderon, Dennis S. Charney and Aleksander A. Mathé. 2013. "Understanding Resilience." *Frontiers in Behavioral Neuroscience*. 7: 10. https://doi.org/10.3389/fnbeh.2013.00010.

167 **wrote that resilient individuals:** Iacoviello, Brian, and Dennis S. Charney. 2014. "Psychosocial facets of resilience: implications for preventing posttrauma psychopathology, treating trauma survivors, and enhancing community resilience." *European Journal of Psychotraumatology*. 5. https://doi.org/10.3402 /ejpt.v5.23970.

169 **Mindfulness and acceptance:** Ford, Brett Q., Phoebe Lam, Oliver P. John and Iris B. Mauss. 2018. "The Psychological Health Benefits of Accepting Negative Emotions and Thoughts: Laboratory, Diary, and Longitudinal Evidence." *Journal of Personality and Social Psychology*. 115(6): 1075–1092. https://doi.org /10.1037/pspp0000157.

169 **and accompanying article:** Hone, Lucy. 2019. "Sorrow and tragedy will happen to us all—here are 3 strategies to help you cope." TED. November 13. https://ideas.ted.com/sorrow-and-tragedy-will-happen-to-us-all-here-are-3 -strategies-to-help-you-cope/.

171 **Vitality. Researchers use:** Ryan, Richard M., Netta Weinstein, Jessey Bernstein, Kirk Warren Brown, Louis Mistretta and Marylène Gagne. 2010. "Vitalizing effects of being outdoors and in nature." *Journal of Environmental Psychology*. 30(2): 159–168. https://doi.org/10.1016/j.jenvp.2009.10.009.

171 **Healthier thoughts:** Bratman, Gregory N., Gretchen C. Daily, Benjamin J. Levy and James J. Gross. 2015. "The benefits of nature experience: Improved affect and cognition." *Landscape and Urban Planning.* 138: 41–50. https://doi .org/10.1016/j.landurbplan.2015.02.005.

171 **brain scans showed:** Bratman, Gregory N., J. Paul Hamilton, Kevin S. Hahn, Gretchen C. Daily and James J. Gross. 2015. "Nature experience reduces rumination and subgenual prefrontal cortex activation." *PNAS.* 112(28): 8567–8572. https://doi.org/10.1073/pnas.1510459112.

171 **more satisfied with life:** Anderson, Craig L., Maura Monroy and Dacher Keltner. 2018. "Awe in nature heals: Evidence from military veterans, at-risk youth, and college students." *Emotion.* 18(8): 1195–1202. https://doi.org /10.1037/emo0000442.

171 **significant boost in psychological well-being:** White, Matthew P., Ian Alcock, James Grellier, Benedict W. Wheeler, Terry Hartig, Sara L. Warber, Angie Bone Michael H. Depledge and Lora E. Fleming. "Spending at least 120 minutes a week in nature is associated with good health and wellbeing." *Scientific Reports.* 9: 7730. https://doi.org/10.1038/s41598-019-44097-3.

171 **Less stress, more positive emotions:** Suttie, Jill. 2016. "How Nature Can Make You Kinder, Happier, and More Creative." *Greater Good.* Greater Good Science Center, University of California Berkeley. March 2. https:// greatergood.berkeley.edu/article/item/how_nature_makes_you_kinder _happier_more_creative.

171 **reset or restore attention:** Clay, Rebecca A. 2001. "Green is Good for You." *Monitor on Psychology.* American Psychological Association. 32(4): 40. https:// www.apa.org/monitor/apr01/greengood.

171 **Lower PTSD-related symptoms:** Varning Poulsen, Dorthe, Ulrika K. Stigsdotter, Dorthe Djernis and Ulrik Sidenius. 2016. "'Everything just seems much more right in nature': How veterans with post-traumatic stress disorder experience nature-based activities in a forest therapy garden." *Health Psychology Open.* 3(1): 1-14. https://doi.org/10.1177/2055102916637090.

172 **Emotional, mental and physical healing:** Chang, Kaowen Grace, and Hungju Chien. 2017. "The Influences of Landscape Features on Visitation of Hospital Green Spaces—A Choice Experiment Approach." *International Journal of Environmental Research and Public Health.* 14(7). pii: E724. https:// doi.org/10.3390/ijerph14070724. Franklin, Deborah. 2012. "How Hospital Gardens Help Patients Heal." *Scientific American.* March 1. https://www .scientificamerican.com/article/nature-that-nurtures/.

172 **crying-as-catharsis theory:** Gračanin, Asmir, Lauran M. Bylsma and Ad J. J. M Vingerhoets. 2014. "Is Crying a Self-Soothing Behavior?" *Frontiers in Psychology.* 5: 502. https://doi.org/10.3389/fpsyg.2014.00502.

173 **it's subjective:** Sharman, Leah. 2018. "No, crying doesn't release toxins, though it might make you feel better . . . if that's what you believe." *The Conversation.* November 22. https://theconversation.com/no-crying

-doesnt-release-toxins-though-it-might-make-you-feel-better-if-thats-what
-you-believe-106860.

174 **people who are able to reframe:** Wu, Gang, Adriana Feder, Hagit Cohen,
Joanna J. Kim, Solara Calderon, Dennis S. Charney and Aleksander A. Mathé.
2013. "Understanding Resilience." *Frontiers in Behavioral Neuroscience.* 7: 10.
https://doi.org/10.3389/fnbeh.2013.00010.

174 **develop more abstract, long-term goals:** Fredrickson, Barbara L. 2000.
"Cultivating Positive Emotions to Optimize Health and Well-Being."
Prevention & Treatment. 3(1a). https://doi.org/10.1037/1522-3736.3.1.31a.

176 **reading in the *New York Times*:** Khullar, Dhruv. 2018. "Finding Purpose for
a Good Life. But Also a Healthy One." *New York Times.* January 1. https://
www.nytimes.com/2018/01/01/upshot/finding-purpose-for-a-good-life
-but-also-a-healthy-one.html.

177 **The research on having purpose:** Alimujiant, Aliya, Ashley Wiensch,
Jonathan Boss, Nancy L. Fleischer, Alison M. Mondul, Karen McLean,
Bhramar Mukherjee and Celeste Leigh Pearce. 2019. "Association Between Life
Purpose and Mortality Among US Adults Older Than 50 Years." *JAMA
Network Open.* 2(5): e194270. https://doi.org/10.1001
/jamanetworkopen.2019.4270. Cohen, Randy, Chirag Bavishi, Alan Rozanski.
2016. "Purpose in Life and Its Relationship to All-Cause Mortality and
Cardiovascular Events: A Meta-Analysis." *Psychosomatic Medicine.* 78(2):122-
33. https://doi.org/10.1097/PSY.0000000000000274

177 **linked to increased resilience:** Isaacs, Kayla, Natalie P. Mota, Jack Tsai, Ilan
Harpaz-Rotem, Joan M. Cook, Paul D. Kirwin, John H. Krystal, Steven M.
Southwick and Robert H. Pietrzak. 2017. "Psychological resilience in U.S.
military veterans: A 2-year, nationally representative prospective cohort study."
Journal of Psychiatric Research. 84: 301–309. https://doi.org/10.1016
/j.jpsychires.2016.10.017. Schaefer, Stacey M., Jennifer Morozink Boylan, Carien
M. van Reekum, Regina C. Lapate, Catherin J. Norris, Carol D. Ryff and
Richard J. Davidson. 2013. "Purpose in Life Predicts Better Emotional Recovery
from Negative Stimuli." *PloS One.* 8(11): e80329. https://doi.org/10.1371
/journal.pone.0080329. Lewis, Nathan A., Nicholas A. Turiano, Brennan R.
Payne, and Patrick L. Hill. 2017. "Purpose in life and cognitive functioning in
adulthood." *Aging, Neuropsychology, and Cogntion.* 24(6): 662-671. https://doi
.org/10.1080/13825585.2016.1251549. Li, Fei, Jieyu Chen, Lin Yu, Yuan Jing,
Pingping Jiang, Xiuqiong Fu, Shengwei Wu, Xiaomin Sun, Ren luo, Hiuyee
Kwan, Xiaoshan Zhao, Yanyan Liu. 2016. "The Role of Stress Management in
the Relationship between Purpose in Life and Self-Rated Health in Teachers: A
Mediation Analysis." *International Journal of Environmental Research and Public
Health.* 13(7), 719. https://doi.org/10.3390/ijerph13070719.

177 **Even hamsters, finches:** Brooks, Helen, Kelly Rushton, Sandra Walker, Karina
Lovell and Anne Rogers. 2016. "Ontological security and connectivity provided
by pets: a study in the self-management of the everyday lives of people

diagnosed with a long term mental health condition." *BMC Psychiatry.* 16: 409. https://doi.org/10.1186/s12888-016-1111-3.

177 **shows animals reduce:** Altschuler, Eric L. 2018. "Animal-Assisted Therapy for Post-traumatic Stress Disorder: Lessons from 'Case Reports' in Media Stories." *Military Medicine.* 183(1-2): 11–13. https://doi.org/10.1093/milmed/usx073. Wells, Deborah L. 2010. "Domestic dogs and human health: An overview." *British Journal of Health Psychology.* 12(1): 145–156. https://doi.org/10.1348 /135910706X103284. Wells, Deborah L. 2019. "The State of Research on Human–Animal Relations: Implications for Human Health." *Anthrozoös.* 32(2): 169–181. https://doi.org/10.1080/08927936.2019.1569902.

177 **increase sense of purpose:** Hamblin, James. 2015. "The Physiological Power of Altruism." *The Atlantic.* December 30. https://www.theatlantic.com/health /archive/2015/12/altruism-for-a-better-body/422280/.

177 **especially significant impact:** Matthieu, Monica M., Karen A. Lawrence and Emma Robertson-Blackmore. 2017. "The impact of a civic service program on biopsychosocial outcomes of post 9/11 U.S. military veterans." *Psychiatry Research.* 248: 111. https://doi.org/10.1016/j.psychres.2016.12.028. McCaslin, Shannon E., Damian Bramlett, Katherine Juhasz, Margaret Mackintosh and Shauna Springer. 2020. "Veterans and Disaster Response Work: The Role of Continued Service in Meaning Making and Recovery." In *Positive Psychological Approaches to Disaster.* Edited by Stefan Schulenberg. Springer Nature Switzerland. https://doi.org/10.1007/978-3-030-32007-2.

178 **are strongly linked to:** Hopper, Elizabeth. 2016. "Can Helping Others Help You Find Meaning in Life?" *Greater Good.* Greater Good Science Center, University of California Berkeley. February 16. https://greatergood.berkeley .edu/article/item/can_helping_others_help_you_find_meaning_in _life.

178 **even make us more empathetic:** Irani, Anna S. 2018. "Positive Altruism: Helping that Benefits Both the Recipient and Giver." Master of Applied Positive Psychology (MAPP) Capstone Projects. University of Pennsylvania. 152. https://repository.upenn.edu/mapp_capstone/152.

178 **good deeds are worth double:** Hayhurst, Jill G., John A. Hunter and Ted Ruffman. 2019. "Encouraging flourishing following tragedy: The role of civic engagement in well-being and resilience." *New Zealand Journal of Psychology.* 48(1): 71–79. https://www.researchgate.net/publication/332769082 _Encouraging_flourishing_following_tragedy_The_role_of_civic_engagement _in_well-being_and_resilience.

178 **sending a thank-you note:** Toepfer, Steven M., Kelly Cichy, and Patti Peters. 2012. "Letters of Gratitude: Further Evidence for Author Benefits." *Journal of Happiness Studies: An Interdisciplinary Forum on Subjective Well-Being.* 13(1), 187–201. https://doi.org/10.1007/s10902-011-9257-7.

179 **spikes dopamine:** The Harvard Mahoney Neuroscience Institute. 2010. "Humor, Laughter, and Those Aha Moments." *On the Brain.* 16(2). Edited by

Ann Marie Menting. https://hms.harvard.edu/sites/default/files/HMS_OTB _Spring10_Vol16_No2.pdf.

179 **engage in the reappraisal:** Southwick, Steven M., and Dennis S. Charney. 2018. *Resilience: The Science of Mastering Life's Greatest Challenges* 2nd Edition. Cambridge University Press.

179 **lower anxiety and catastrophizing:** Pérez-Aranda, Adrián, Jennifer Hofmann, Albert Feliu-Soler, Carmen Ramírez-Maestre, Laura Andrés-Rodríguez, Willibald Ruch and Juan V. Luciano. 2019. "Laughing away the pain: A narrative review of humour, sense of humour and pain." *European Journal of Pain.* 23(2): 220–233. https://doi.org/10.1002/ejp.1309.

179 **don't lose our appreciation:** Braniecka, Anna, Malgorzata Hanc, Iwona Wolkowicz, Agnieszka Chrzczonowicz-Stepien, Agnieszka Mikolajonek and Monika Lipiec. 2019. "Is it worth turning a trigger into a joke? Humor as an emotion regulation strategy in remitted depression." *Brain and Behavior.* 9(2): e01213. https://doi.org/10.1002/brb3.1213.

180 **better cope and adapt:** Iacoviello, Brian, and Dennis S. Charney. 2014. "Psychosocial facets of resilience: implications for preventing posttrauma psychopathology, treating trauma survivors, and enhancing community resilience." *European Journal of Psychotraumatology.* 5. https://doi.org/10.3402 /ejpt.v5.23970.

180 **Research has shown again:** Wu, Gang, Adriana Feder, Hagit Cohen, Joanna J. Kim, Solara Calderon, Dennis S. Charney and Aleksander A. Mathé. 2013. "Understanding Resilience." *Frontiers in Behavioral Neuroscience.* 7: 10. https:// doi.org/10.3389/fnbeh.2013.00010.

180 **either talk, write or think:** Lyubomirsky, Sonja, Lorie Sousa and Rene Dickerhoff. 2006. "The Costs and Benefits of Writing, Talking, and Thinking About Life's Triumphs and Defeats." *Journal of Personality and Social Psychology.* 90(4): 692–708. https://doi.org/0.1037/0022-3514.90.4.692.

183 **help build resilience:** Iacoviello, Brian, and Dennis S. Charney. 2014. "Psychosocial facets of resilience: implications for preventing posttrauma psychopathology, treating trauma survivors, and enhancing community resilience." *European Journal of Psychotraumatology.* 5. https://doi.org/10.3402 /ejpt.v5.23970.

About the Author

Meaghan B Murphy (no period after the B!) is a Fully Charged mama of three, the editor-in-chief of *Woman's Day* magazine and veteran editor with twenty-plus years' experience, a cohost of the *Off the Gram* podcast and a life hacker who pops up on morning TV and other shows.